Alt COMIC BOOK

APPROACHING ARCHITECTURE

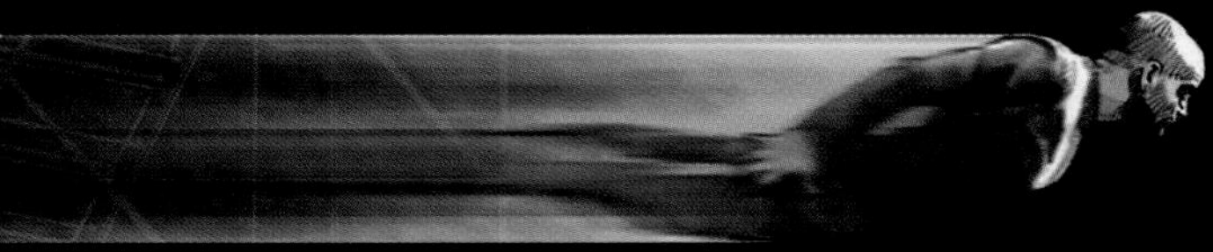

WRITER, PENCILLER, INKER AND COLORIST

ÁNGEL LUIS TENDERO MARTÍN

SPECIAL COLABORATION

BERNARDO CUMMINS NOGUEIRA

Dedicated to my parents because everything I am I owe to them. My brothers Dulce and Jose for their unconditional support and because they always trusted me.

And Yasmin because I forget everything when I see her smile ...

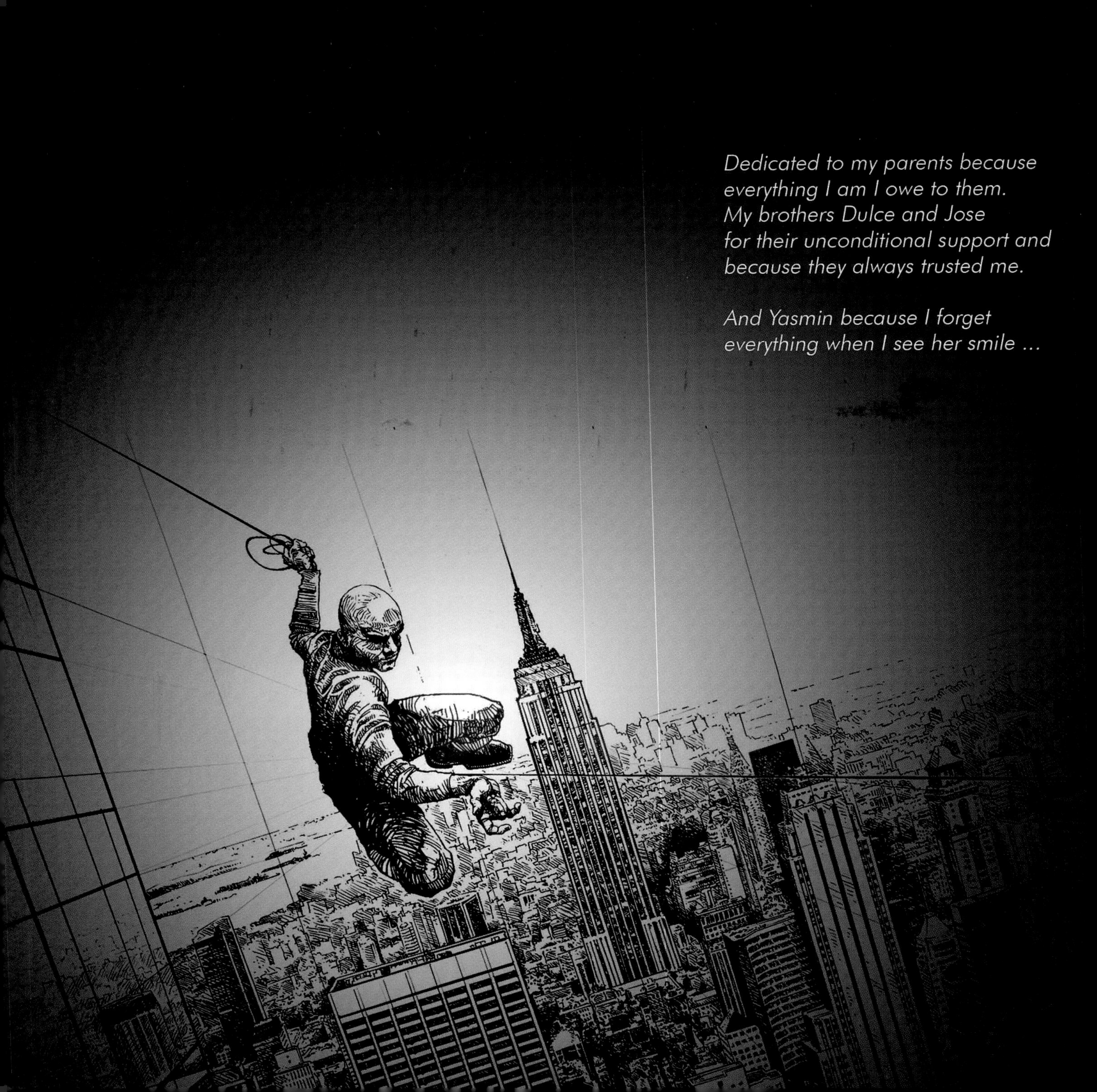

Alt Comic Book
Copyright @ 2014 By Architect Publications s.l.

Publisher:
Marti Berrio

Script, drawing and color:
Ángel Luís Tendero

Collaboration:
Bernardo Cummins

Publishing project:
By Architect Publications s.l.
Pla dels Avellaners, 6, Nave 3
08210 Barberà del Valles, Barcelona
Info@by-architect.com
www.by-architect.com

ISBN: 978-84-941915-2-7
D.L.: B-13781-2014

Printing in Spain

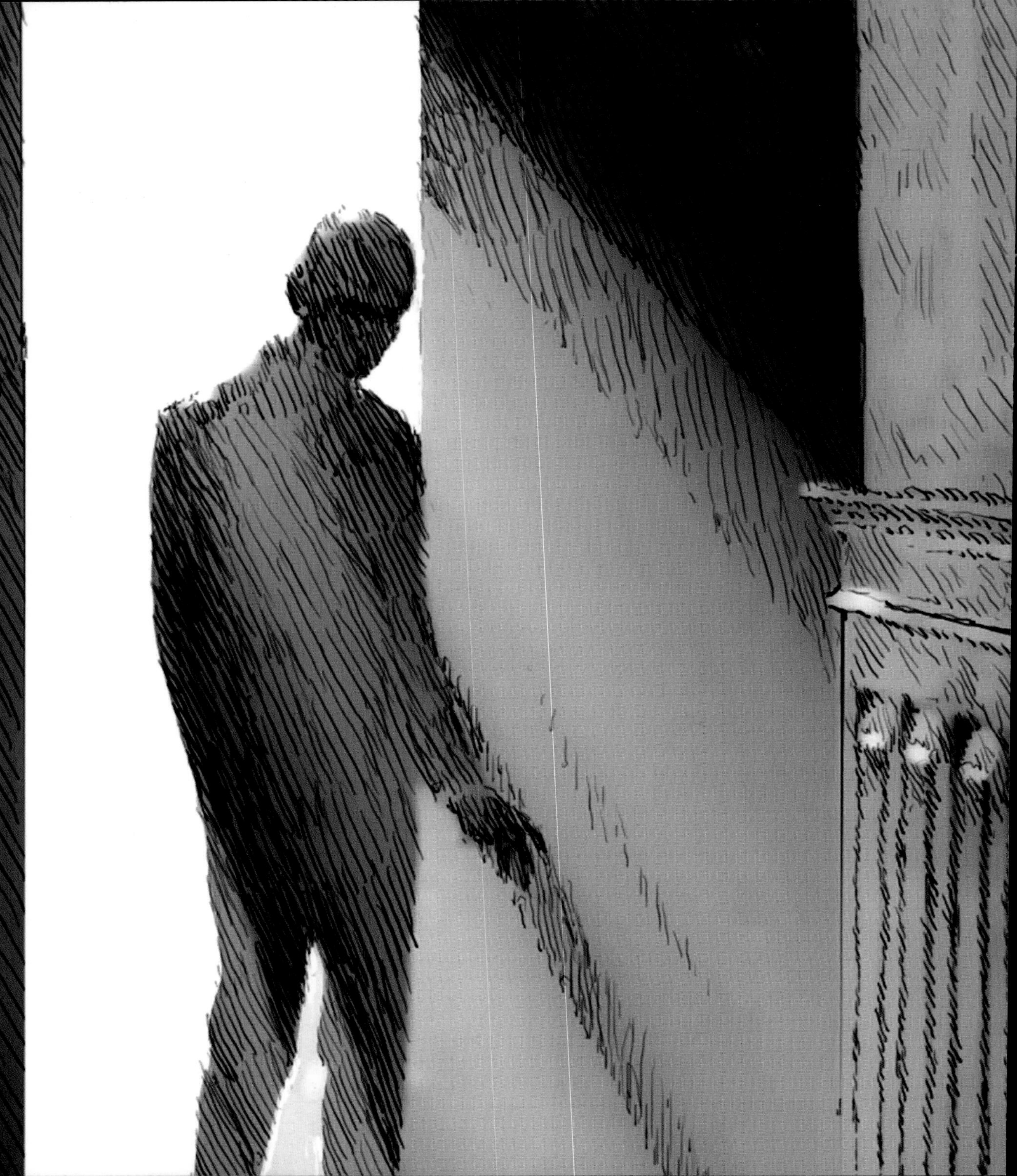

Alt comic book

APPROACHING ARCHITECTURE

Why a comic?.

Those who know little about ALT architecture, locate us as a media phenomenon with a surprising mass of people following our work on facebook.
In fact we are the world´s most followed architecture office, with more than one million followers by early 2014. Not bad at all...

The great majority of society has very little knowledge of the issues related to our profession.
This means that architects have no impact on decisions affecting conservation, restructuration or the growth of our cities. Politicians take advantage of this ignorance to do and undo at will, thinking only in the short term during their mandates, often resulting catastrophic results.

This ignorance is also reflected in a fear of society towards architects, which in most cases are forced to perform work without architectural value, filling our cities with bad copies of architectures of the past.

So ... What can we do?

We decided to undertake an educational work from our facebook page, which so far has been very successful, demonstrating that people are very receptive when contents are clear, attractive and exposed with a simple vocabulary.

This is where the drawing appears as an essential tool to attract attention. Nothing is as educational and easy to understand as a drawing, and we thought we should use this tool as a way of dissemination.

We wanted to tell our vision of architecture and use the drawing as a medium.
Texts mixed with drawings ... a comic.

ALT arquitectura

The work you are about to see is a journey, in which I try to analize, using the drawing with a simple and accessible language, issues like space and form. And how we can extract from the observation of the environment important tools to understand the architecture ... or create it.

It is a personal reflection where I present my thoughts, without further claim that introduce topics giving rise to the interest of the reader, and encouraging him to subsequently deepen them on their own.

I have deliberately omitted any reference topic to modern or contemporary architecture. Finding values of architecture in the environment that surrounds us, is the first essential step to appreciate architecture.
And those values are there, in front of our eyes, at every step.

I want to show the gradual transformation of space, from the vertical, artificial and technological, that could be a big city like New York, towards the more horizontal, natural and devoid of human action, exemplified here in the Salar of Uyuni, in Bolivia.

With some moments of fantasy, in which I reflect on the scale of the universe, traveling through the stars or approaching the minimum unit of matter, the atom.

To make the journey more fluid and enjoyable, the main character moves in the environment with unrestricted movements, whether spatial or temporal. Thus he will be able to travel around the city balancing between buildings like spiderman, flying to the stars or flirting with Lauren Bacall, for example.

I won´t digress more and I invite you to come with me in this trip, that basically is only a personal declaration of love to the world around us.

If I can get you to reflect an instant on what I'm trying to convey, the effort will be worth.

A big hug.

Angel Luis Tendero (ALT)

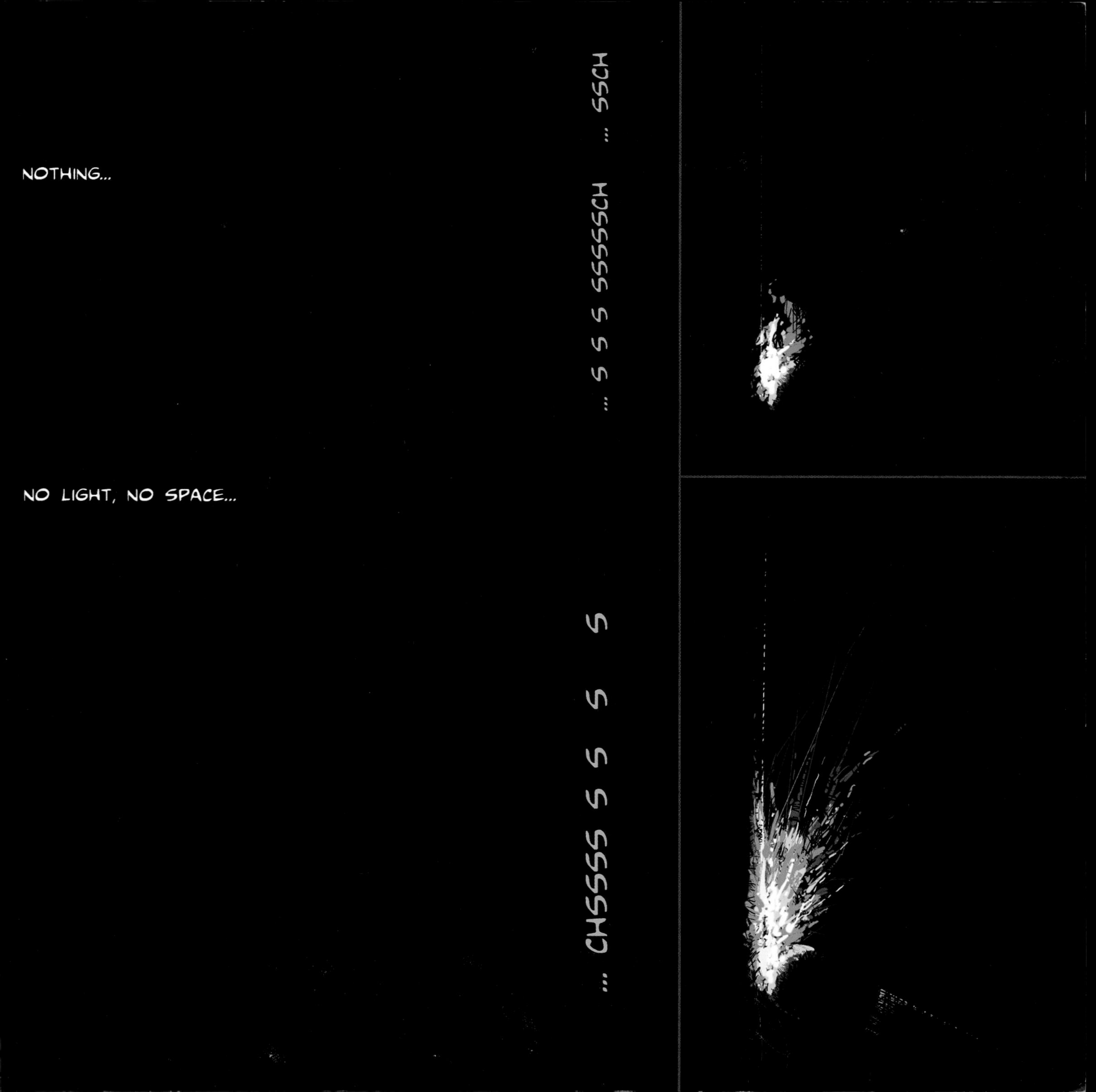
NOTHING...
NO LIGHT, NO SPACE...
... S S S SSSSSCH ... SSCH
... CHSSSSS S S S S

NOW WE HAVE SPACE.

SPACE: (LATIN SPATIUM)
MEANS EVERYTHING AROUND

CONTAINED IN OUR HANDS,
DEFINED BY A SMALL LIGHT.

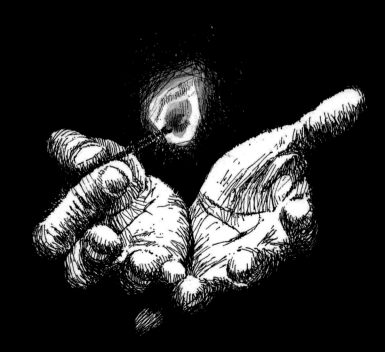

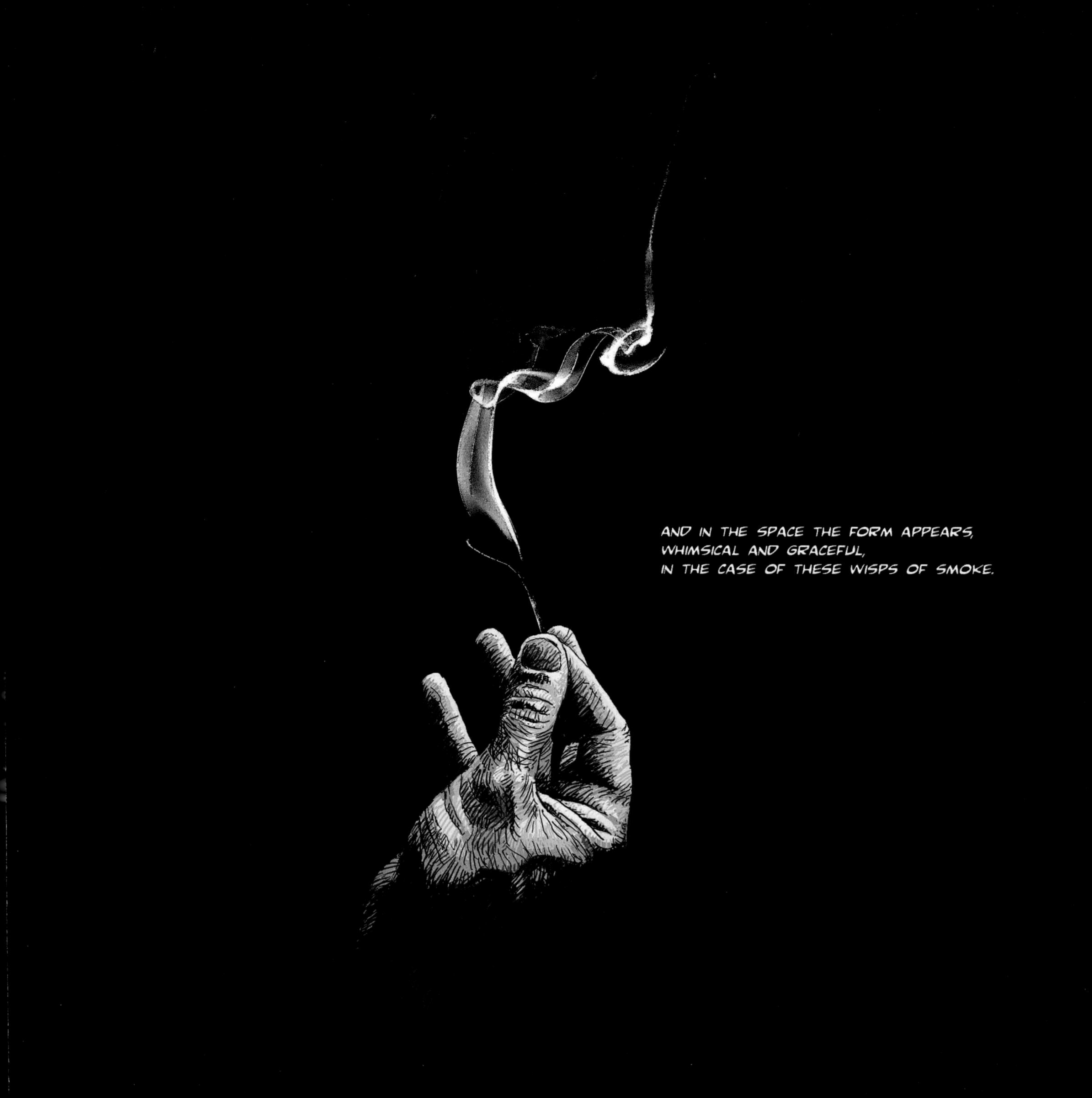
AND IN THE SPACE THE FORM APPEARS,
WHIMSICAL AND GRACEFUL,
IN THE CASE OF THESE WISPS OF SMOKE.

THE FORM...

...IS THE DESCRIPTION OF THE PART OF THE SPACE OCCUPIED BY THE OBJECT.

AND IT´S DEFINED ONLY BY ITS OUTER LIMIT.

IRRESPECTIVE OF ITS LOCATION AND ORIENTATION IN SPACE, OR SIZE, NEITHER OTHER PROPERTIES SUCH AS COLOR, CONTENT OR MATERIAL COMPOSITION.

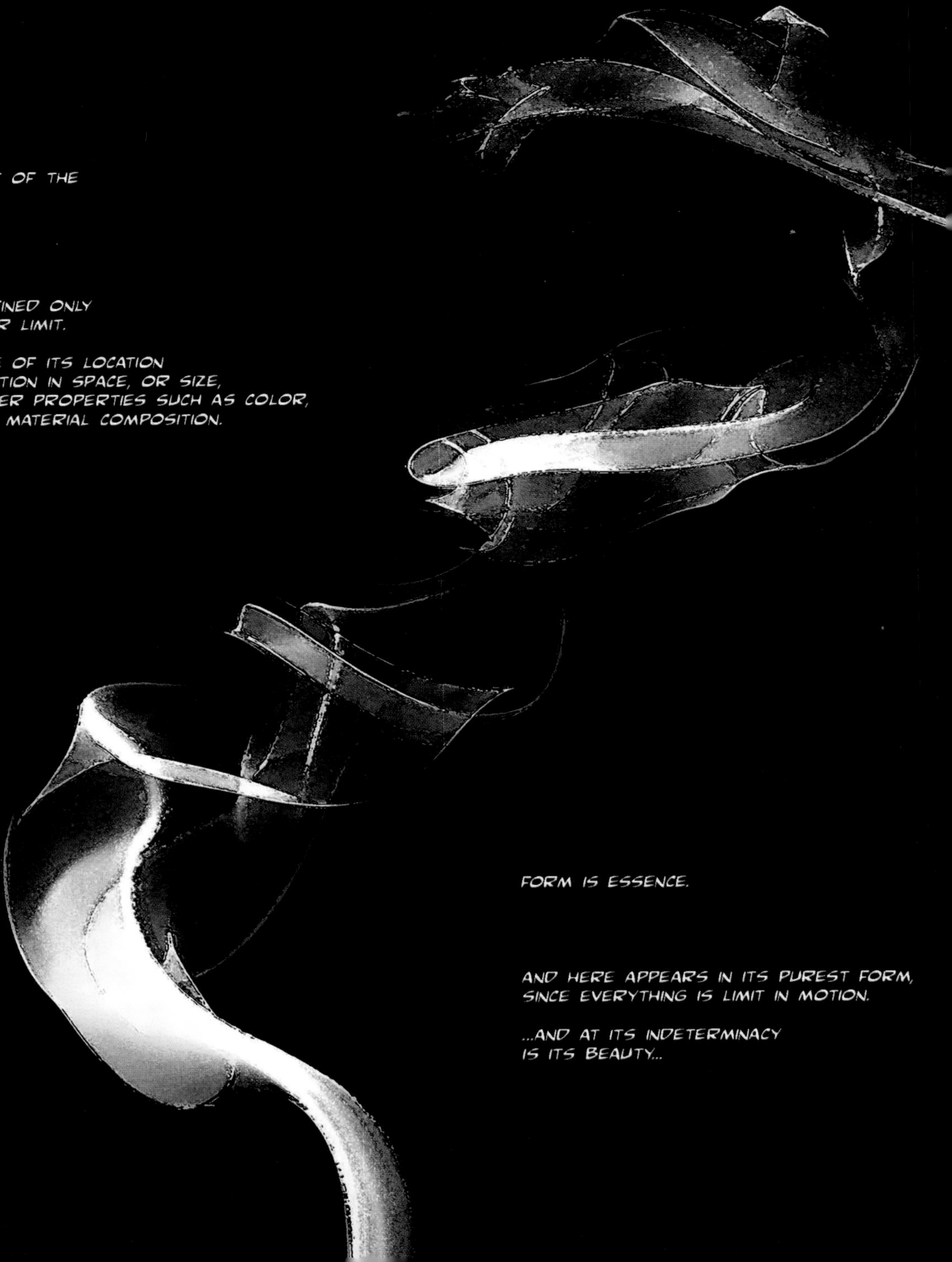

FORM IS ESSENCE.

AND HERE APPEARS IN ITS PUREST FORM, SINCE EVERYTHING IS LIMIT IN MOTION.

...AND AT ITS INDETERMINACY IS ITS BEAUTY...

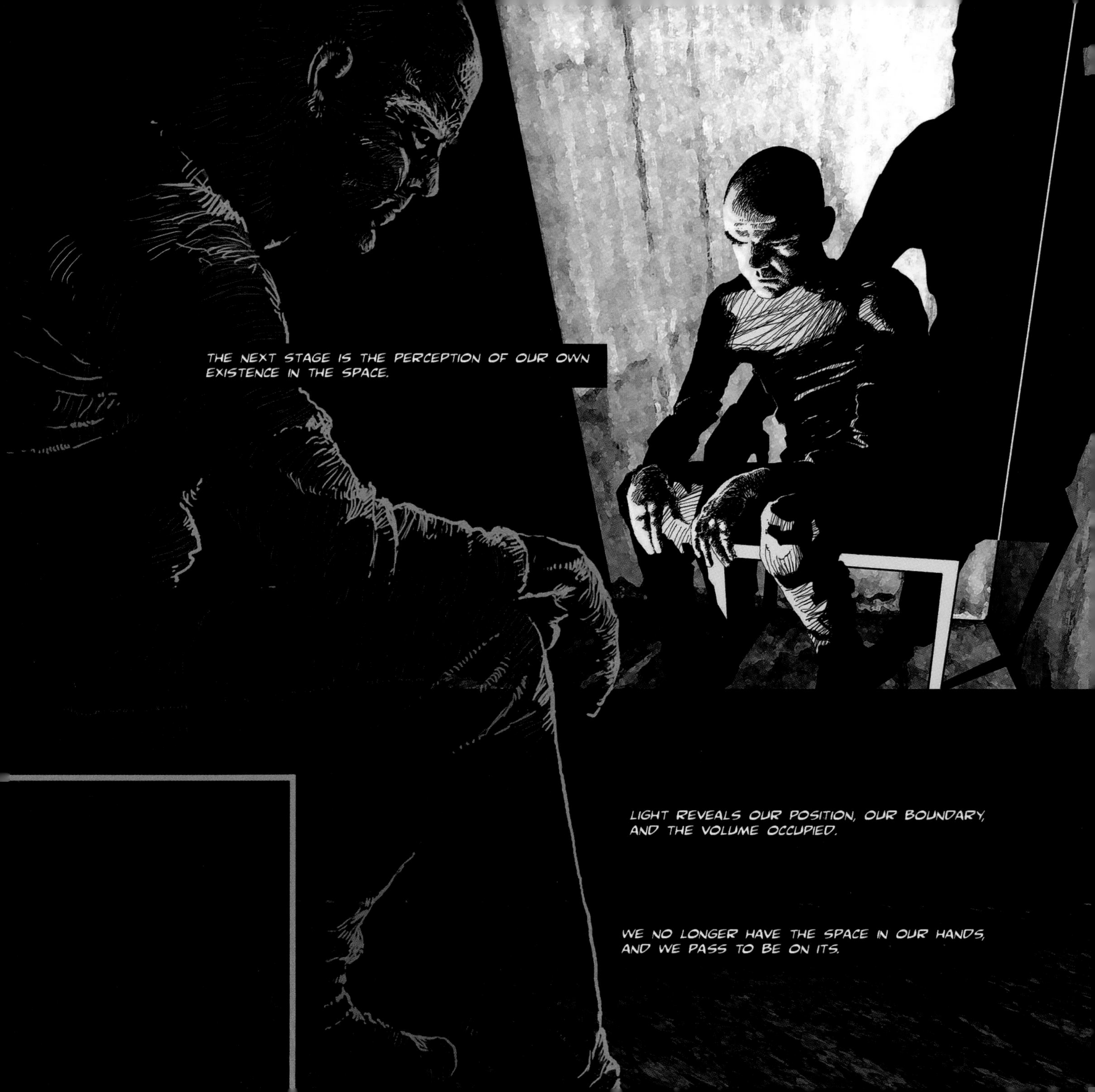
THE NEXT STAGE IS THE PERCEPTION OF OUR OWN EXISTENCE IN THE SPACE.
LIGHT REVEALS OUR POSITION, OUR BOUNDARY, AND THE VOLUME OCCUPIED.
WE NO LONGER HAVE THE SPACE IN OUR HANDS, AND WE PASS TO BE ON ITS.

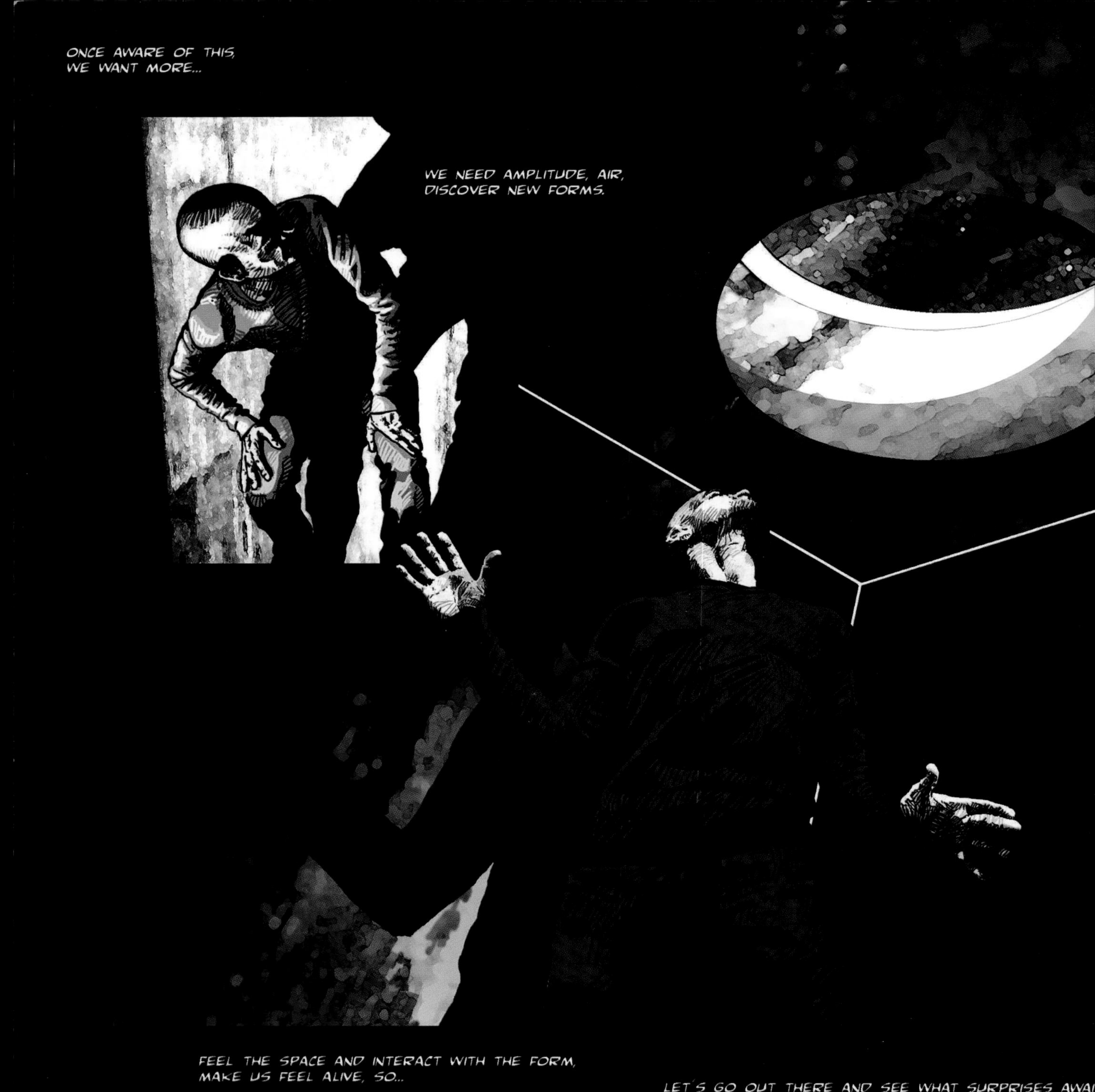
ONCE AWARE OF THIS, WE WANT MORE...
WE NEED AMPLITUDE, AIR, DISCOVER NEW FORMS.
FEEL THE SPACE AND INTERACT WITH THE FORM, MAKE US FEEL ALIVE, SO...
LET'S GO OUT THERE AND SEE WHAT SURPRISES

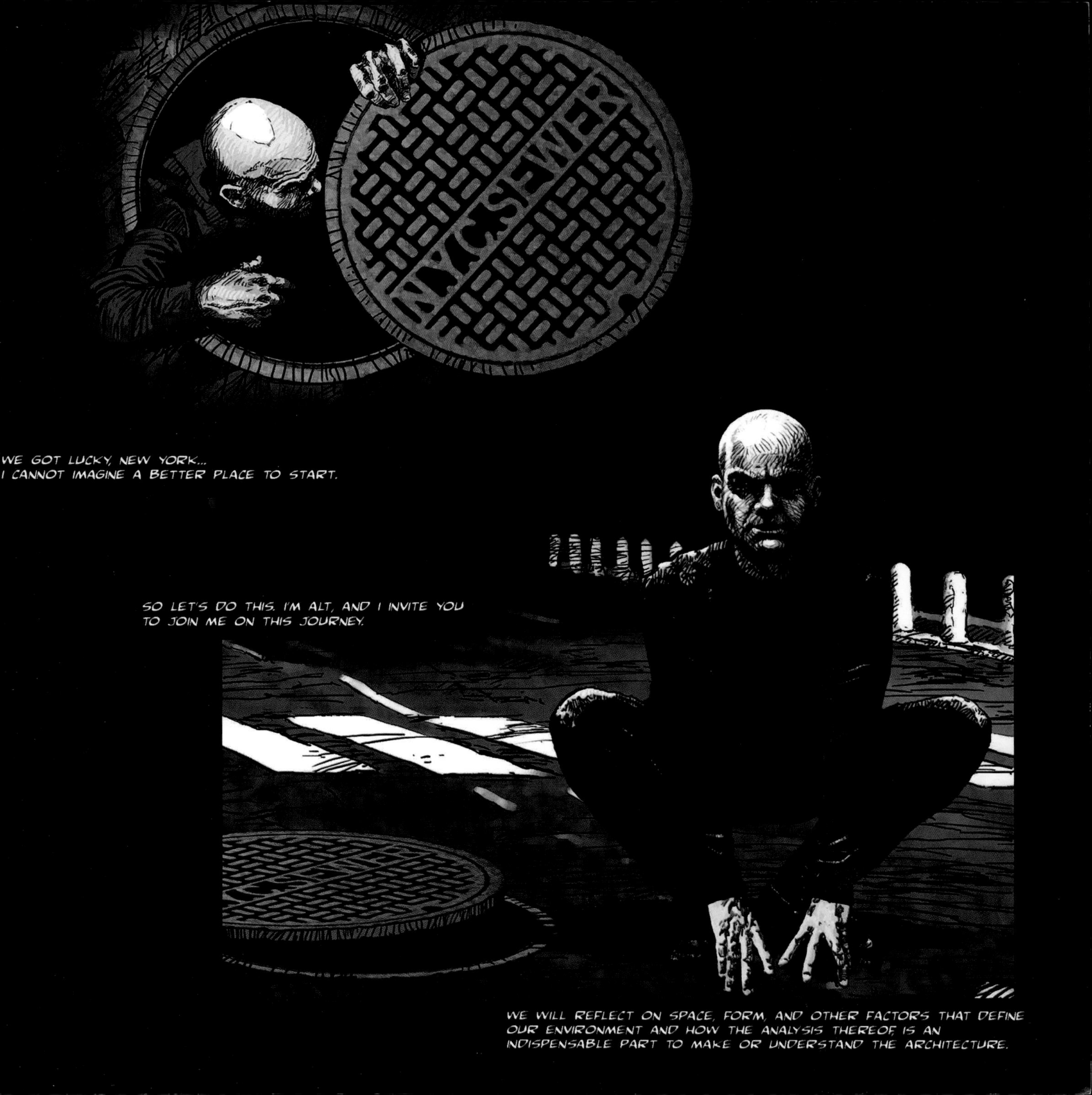
NYC SEWER
WE GOT LUCKY, NEW YORK...
I CANNOT IMAGINE A BETTER PLACE TO START.
SO LET'S DO THIS. I'M ALT, AND I INVITE YOU TO JOIN ME ON THIS JOURNEY.
WE WILL REFLECT ON SPACE, FORM, AND OTHER FACTORS THAT DEFINE OUR ENVIRONMENT AND HOW THE ANALYSIS THEREOF IS AN INDISPENSABLE PART TO MAKE OR UNDERSTAND THE ARCHITECTURE.

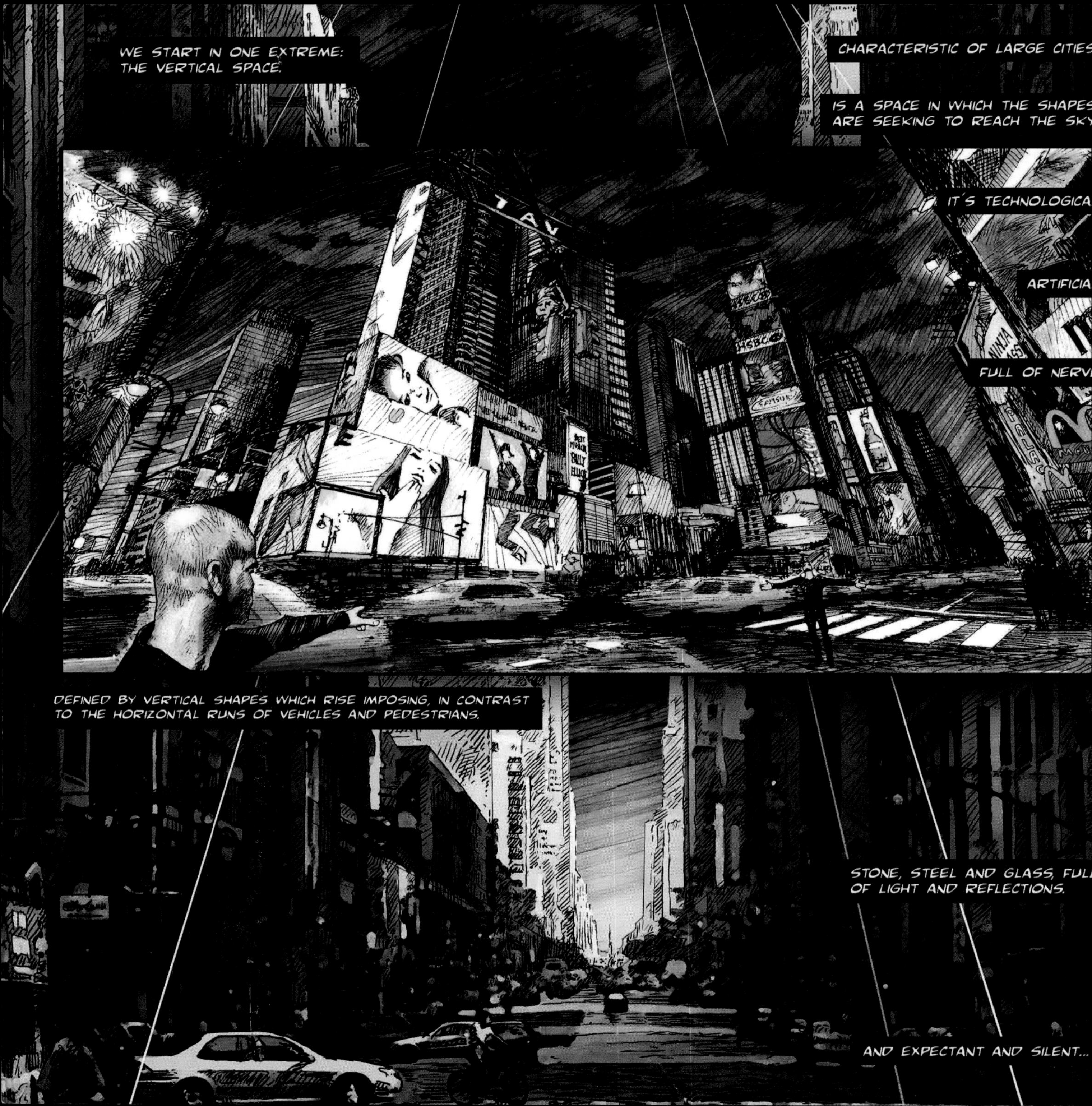

WE START IN ONE EXTREME:
THE VERTICAL SPACE.
CHARACTERISTIC OF LARGE CITIES
IS A SPACE IN WHICH THE SHAPES
ARE SEEKING TO REACH THE SK
IT'S TECHNOLOGICA
ARTIFICIA
FULL OF NERV
DEFINED BY VERTICAL SHAPES WHICH RISE IMPOSING, IN CONTRAST
TO THE HORIZONTAL RUNS OF VEHICLES AND PEDESTRIANS.
STONE, STEEL AND GLASS, FUL
OF LIGHT AND REFLECTIONS.
AND EXPECTANT AND SILENT...

...THE SKY.

SHOWN IN A SMALL WAY, BUT SURELY.

FILLING VOIDS...

DOMINATING, BECAUSE THE LINES THAT DEFINE THE VERTICAL
FORMS ARE DIRECTED TOWARD HIM.
AND IN IT LIES THE POINT OF LEAKAGE, VIGILANT, FOLLOWING
US FROM ABOVE, AT INFINITY, AND CONTROLS EVERY MOVE
WE MAKE.

CRYSTAL VOLUMES APPEAR, ALMOST VIRTUAL,
CATCHING PORTIONS OF SKY BY REFLECTIONS,
CREATING A MYSTERIOUS ENVIRONMENT, MAGICAL...

THE SHAPE DERIVES FROM SIMPLE GEOMETRY, THE EUCLIDEAN,
THE STRAIGHT LINE APPEARS AS THE PREDOMINANT ELEMENT,
GENERATING ORTHOGONAL PLANES AND VOLUMES.

CREATING AN ENVELOPING SPACE THAT ISOLATES US FROM NATURE,
BEING THE REFLECTION OF THE SKY IN THE WALLS THE ONLY APPEARANCE OF HER.

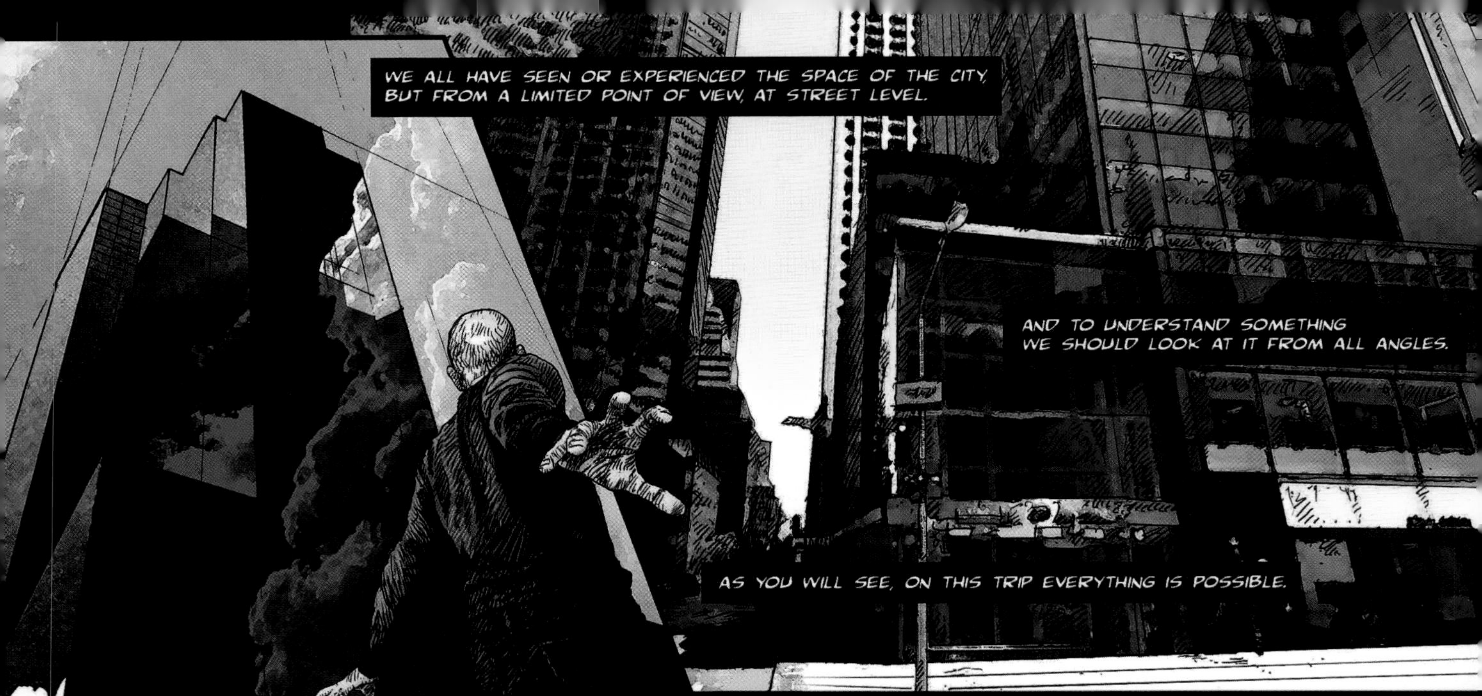
WE ALL HAVE SEEN OR EXPERIENCED THE SPACE OF THE CITY, BUT FROM A LIMITED POINT OF VIEW, AT STREET LEVEL.
AND TO UNDERSTAND SOMETHING WE SHOULD LOOK AT IT FROM ALL ANGLES.
AS YOU WILL SEE, ON THIS TRIP EVERYTHING IS POSSIBLE.

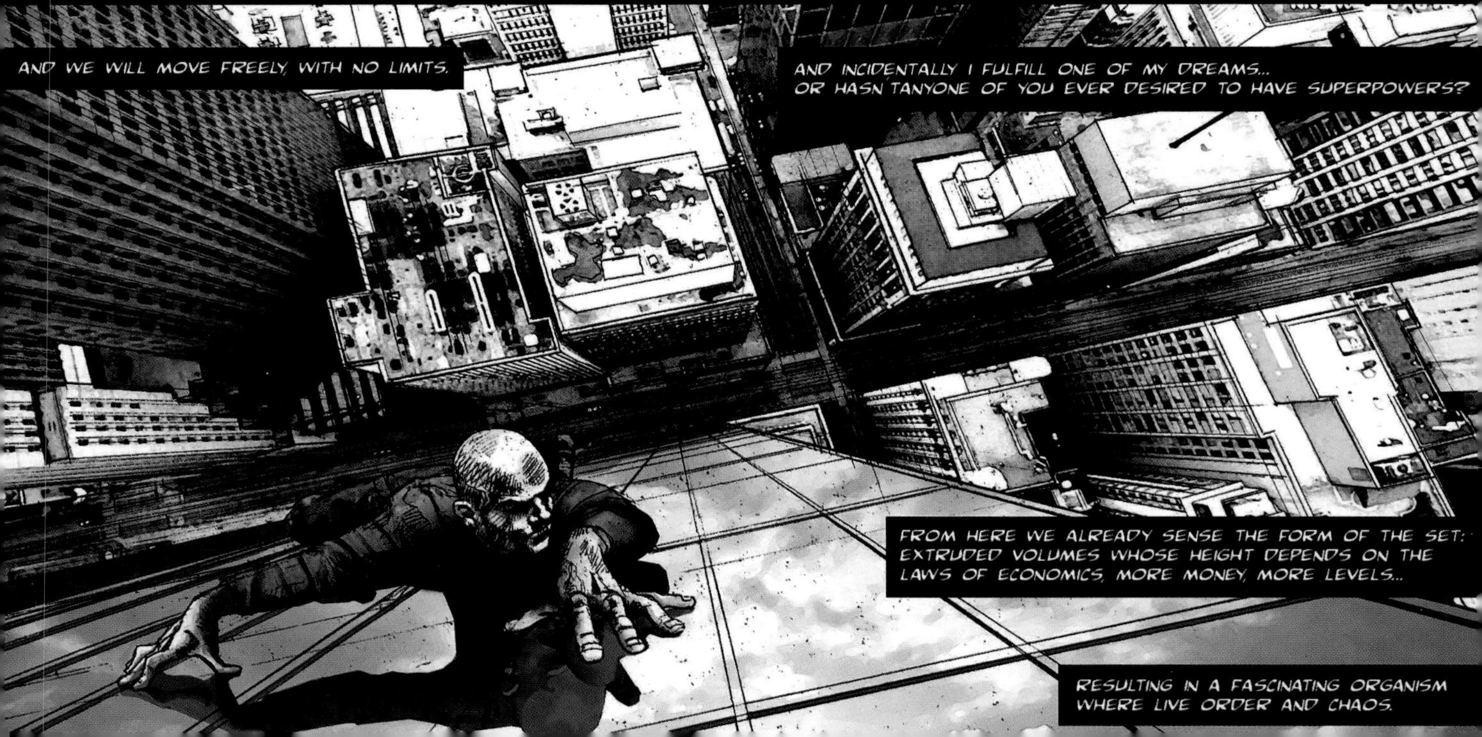
AND WE WILL MOVE FREELY, WITH NO LIMITS.
AND INCIDENTALLY I FULFILL ONE OF MY DREAMS... OR HASN'TANYONE OF YOU EVER DESIRED TO HAVE SUPERPOWERS?
FROM HERE WE ALREADY SENSE THE FORM OF THE SET: EXTRUDED VOLUMES WHOSE HEIGHT DEPENDS ON THE LAWS OF ECONOMICS, MORE MONEY, MORE LEVELS...
RESULTING IN A FASCINATING ORGANISM WHERE LIVE ORDER AND CHAOS.

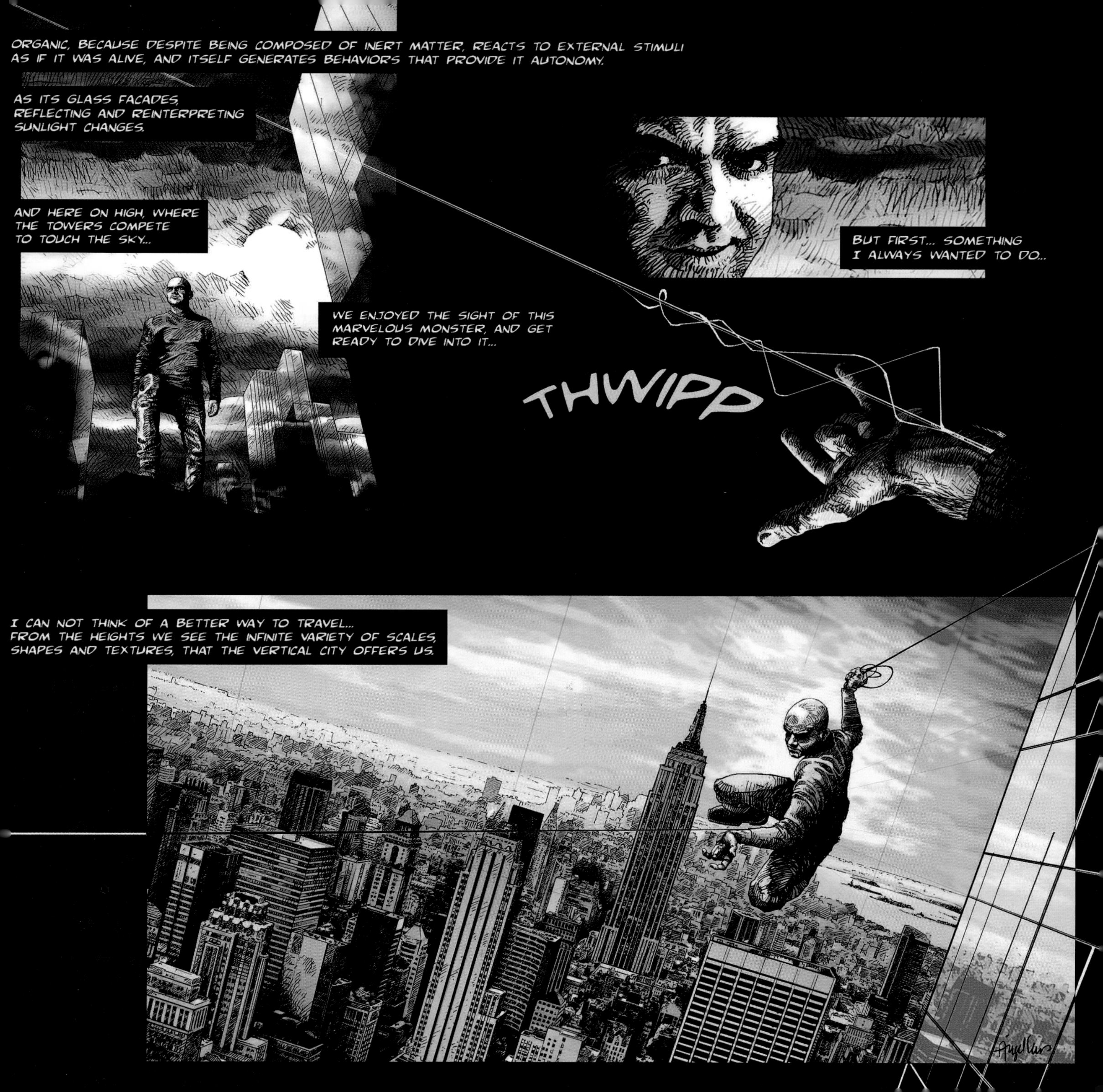
ORGANIC, BECAUSE DESPITE BEING COMPOSED OF INERT MATTER, REACTS TO EXTERNAL STIMULI AS IF IT WAS ALIVE, AND ITSELF GENERATES BEHAVIORS THAT PROVIDE IT AUTONOMY.
AS ITS GLASS FACADES, REFLECTING AND REINTERPRETING SUNLIGHT CHANGES.
AND HERE ON HIGH, WHERE THE TOWERS COMPETE TO TOUCH THE SKY...
WE ENJOYED THE SIGHT OF THIS MARVELOUS MONSTER, AND GET READY TO DIVE INTO IT...
BUT FIRST... SOMETHING I ALWAYS WANTED TO DO...
THWIPP
I CAN NOT THINK OF A BETTER WAY TO TRAVEL... FROM THE HEIGHTS WE SEE THE INFINITE VARIETY OF SCALES, SHAPES AND TEXTURES, THAT THE VERTICAL CITY OFFERS US.

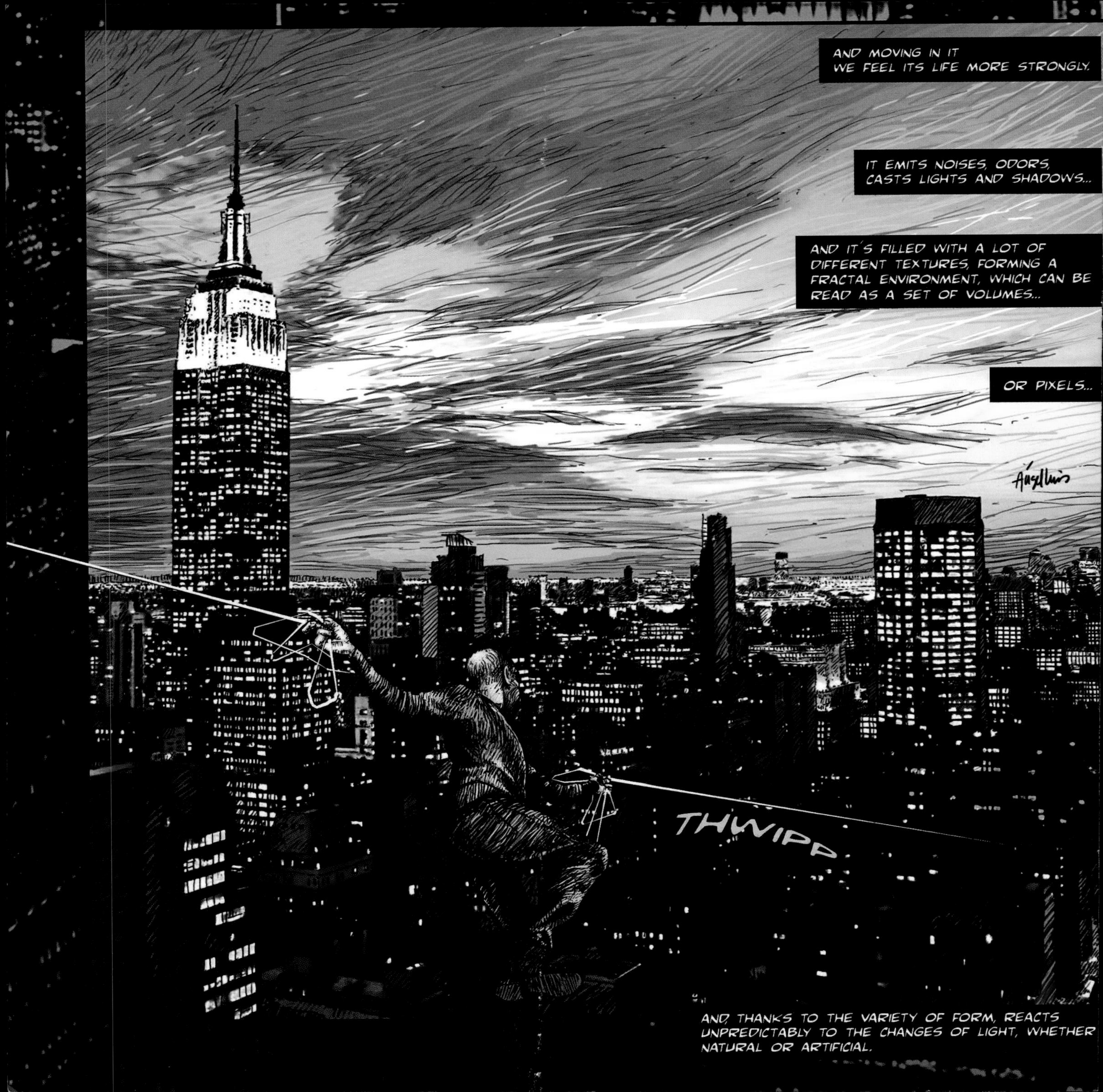
AND MOVING IN IT WE FEEL ITS LIFE MORE STRONGLY.
IT EMITS NOISES, ODORS, CASTS LIGHTS AND SHADOWS...
AND IT'S FILLED WITH A LOT OF DIFFERENT TEXTURES, FORMING A FRACTAL ENVIRONMENT, WHICH CAN BE READ AS A SET OF VOLUMES...
OR PIXELS...
THWIPP
AND, THANKS TO THE VARIETY OF FORM, REACTS UNPREDICTABLY TO THE CHANGES OF LIGHT, WHETHER NATURAL OR ARTIFICIAL.

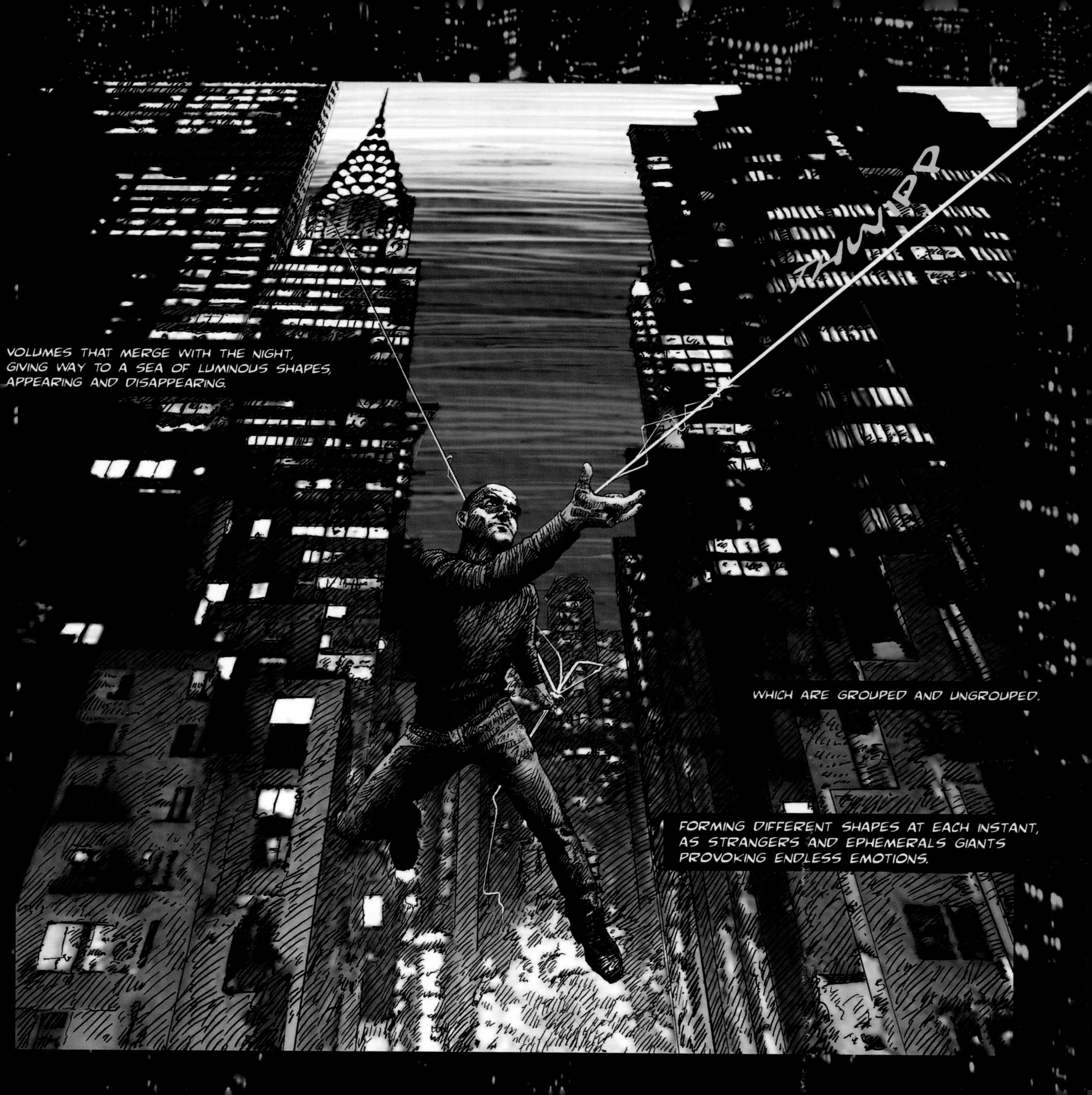
VOLUMES THAT MERGE WITH THE NIGHT, GIVING WAY TO A SEA OF LUMINOUS SHAPES, APPEARING AND DISAPPEARING.
WHICH ARE GROUPED AND UNGROUPED.
FORMING DIFFERENT SHAPES AT EACH INSTANT, AS STRANGERS AND EPHEMERALS GIANTS PROVOKING ENDLESS EMOTIONS.

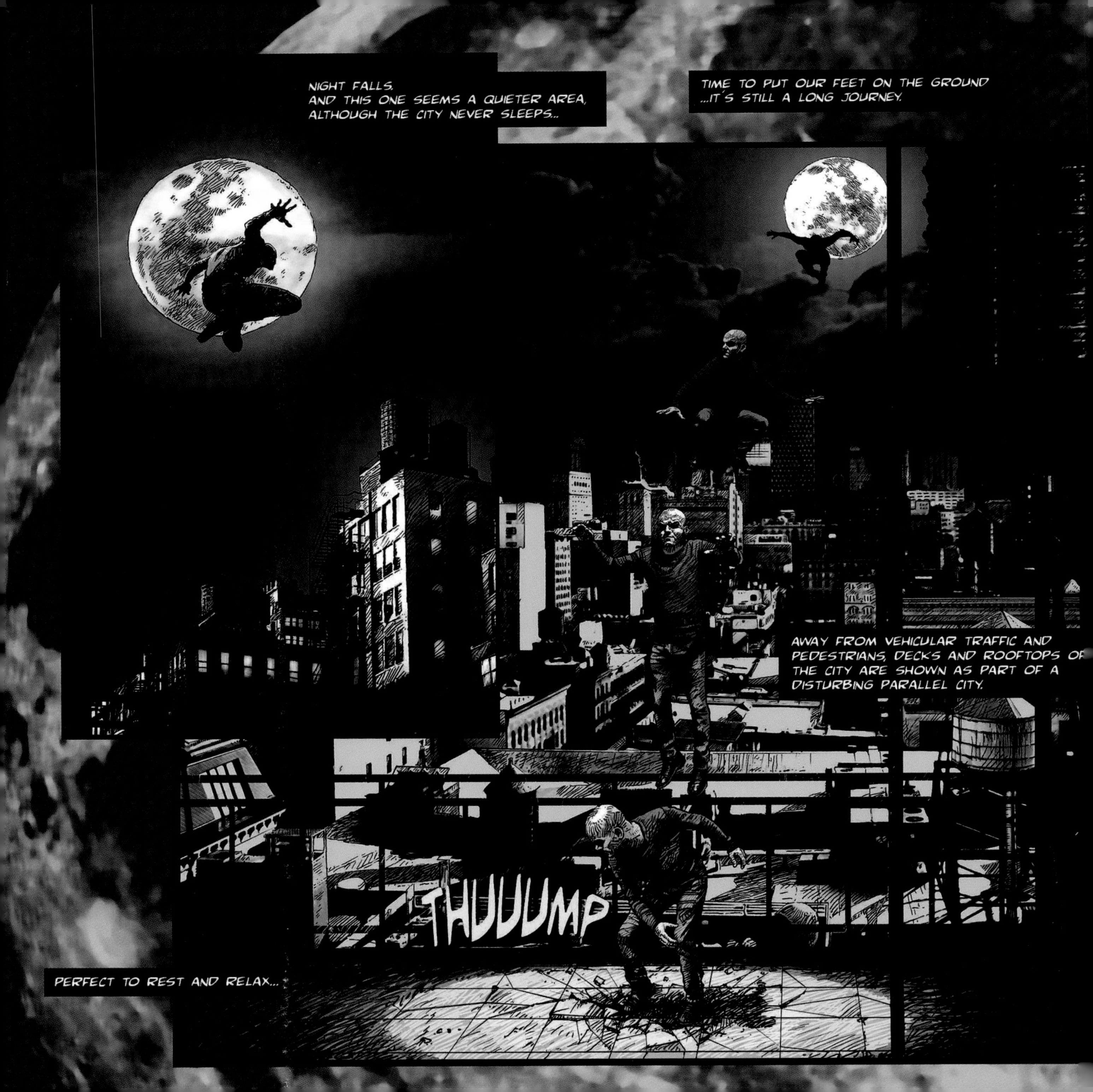
NIGHT FALLS.
AND THIS ONE SEEMS A QUIETER AREA, ALTHOUGH THE CITY NEVER SLEEPS...
TIME TO PUT OUR FEET ON THE GROUND ...IT´S STILL A LONG JOURNEY.
AWAY FROM VEHICULAR TRAFFIC AND PEDESTRIANS, DECKS AND ROOFTOPS OF THE CITY ARE SHOWN AS PART OF A DISTURBING PARALLEL CITY.
THUUUMP
PERFECT TO REST AND RELAX...

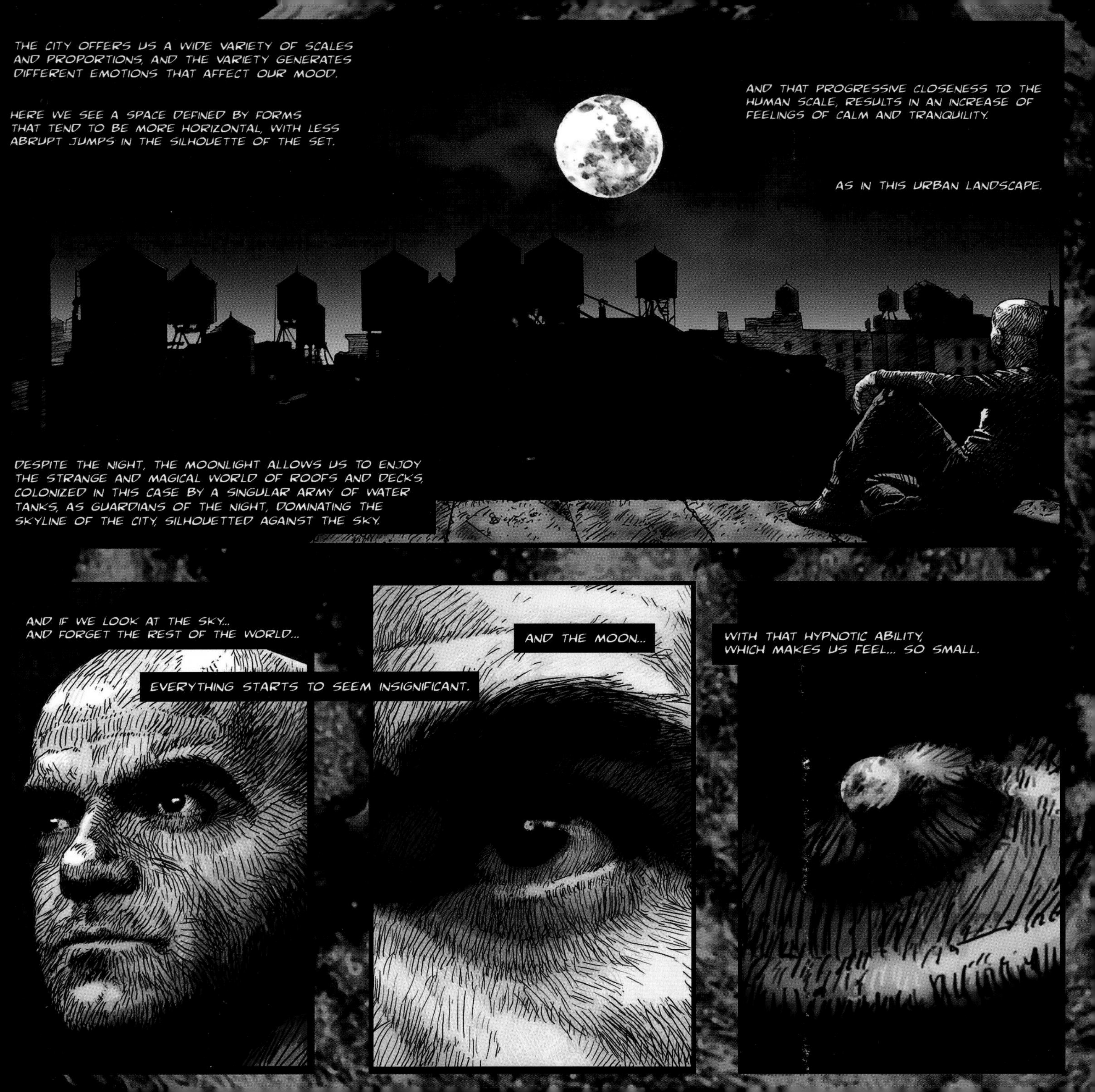
THE CITY OFFERS US A WIDE VARIETY OF SCALES AND PROPORTIONS, AND THE VARIETY GENERATES DIFFERENT EMOTIONS THAT AFFECT OUR MOOD.
HERE WE SEE A SPACE DEFINED BY FORMS THAT TEND TO BE MORE HORIZONTAL, WITH LESS ABRUPT JUMPS IN THE SILHOUETTE OF THE SET.
AND THAT PROGRESSIVE CLOSENESS TO THE HUMAN SCALE, RESULTS IN AN INCREASE OF FEELINGS OF CALM AND TRANQUILITY.
AS IN THIS URBAN LANDSCAPE.
DESPITE THE NIGHT, THE MOONLIGHT ALLOWS US TO ENJOY THE STRANGE AND MAGICAL WORLD OF ROOFS AND DECKS, COLONIZED IN THIS CASE BY A SINGULAR ARMY OF WATER TANKS, AS GUARDIANS OF THE NIGHT, DOMINATING THE SKYLINE OF THE CITY, SILHOUETTED AGAINST THE SKY.
AND IF WE LOOK AT THE SKY... AND FORGET THE REST OF THE WORLD...
EVERYTHING STARTS TO SEEM INSIGNIFICANT.
AND THE MOON...
WITH THAT HYPNOTIC ABILITY, WHICH MAKES US FEEL... SO SMALL.

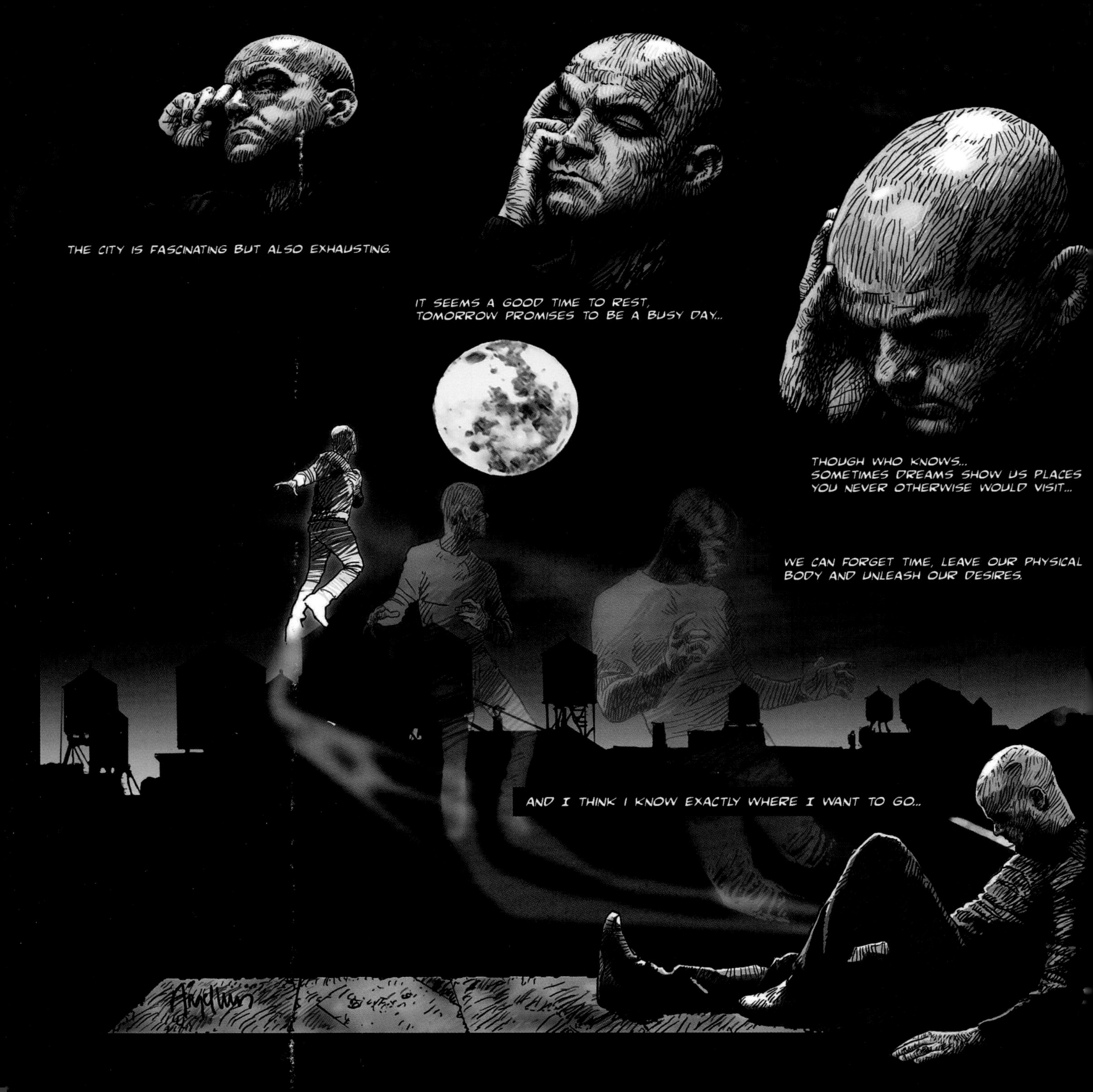
THE CITY IS FASCINATING BUT ALSO EXHAUSTING.
IT SEEMS A GOOD TIME TO REST, TOMORROW PROMISES TO BE A BUSY DAY...
THOUGH WHO KNOWS... SOMETIMES DREAMS SHOW US PLACES YOU NEVER OTHERWISE WOULD VISIT...
WE CAN FORGET TIME, LEAVE OUR PHYSICAL BODY AND UNLEASH OUR DESIRES.
AND I THINK I KNOW EXACTLY WHERE I WANT TO GO...

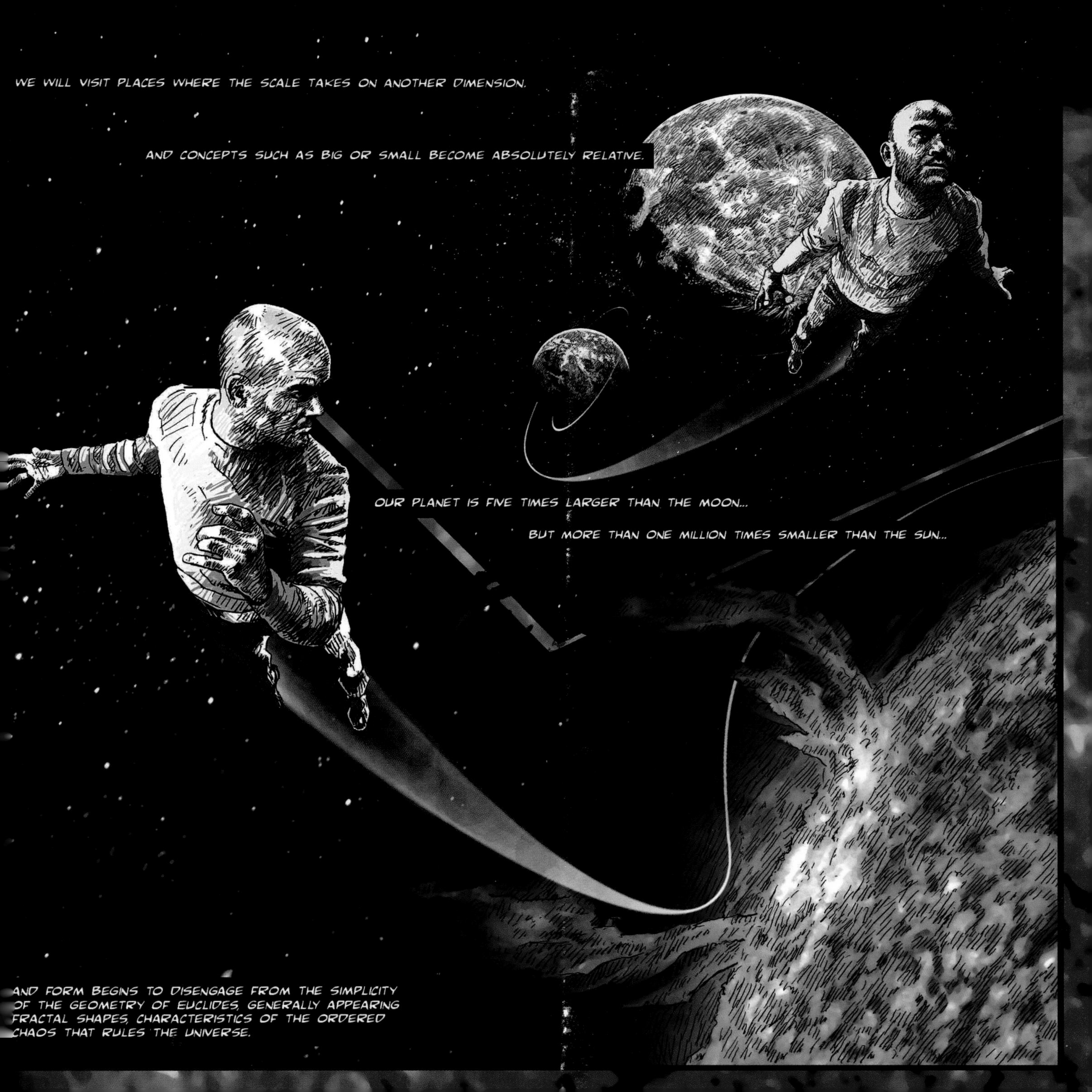
WE WILL VISIT PLACES WHERE THE SCALE TAKES ON ANOTHER DIMENSION.
AND CONCEPTS SUCH AS BIG OR SMALL BECOME ABSOLUTELY RELATIVE.
OUR PLANET IS FIVE TIMES LARGER THAN THE MOON...
BUT MORE THAN ONE MILLION TIMES SMALLER THAN THE SUN...
AND FORM BEGINS TO DISENGAGE FROM THE SIMPLICITY OF THE GEOMETRY OF EUCLIDES, GENERALLY APPEARING FRACTAL SHAPES, CHARACTERISTICS OF THE ORDERED CHAOS THAT RULES THE UNIVERSE.

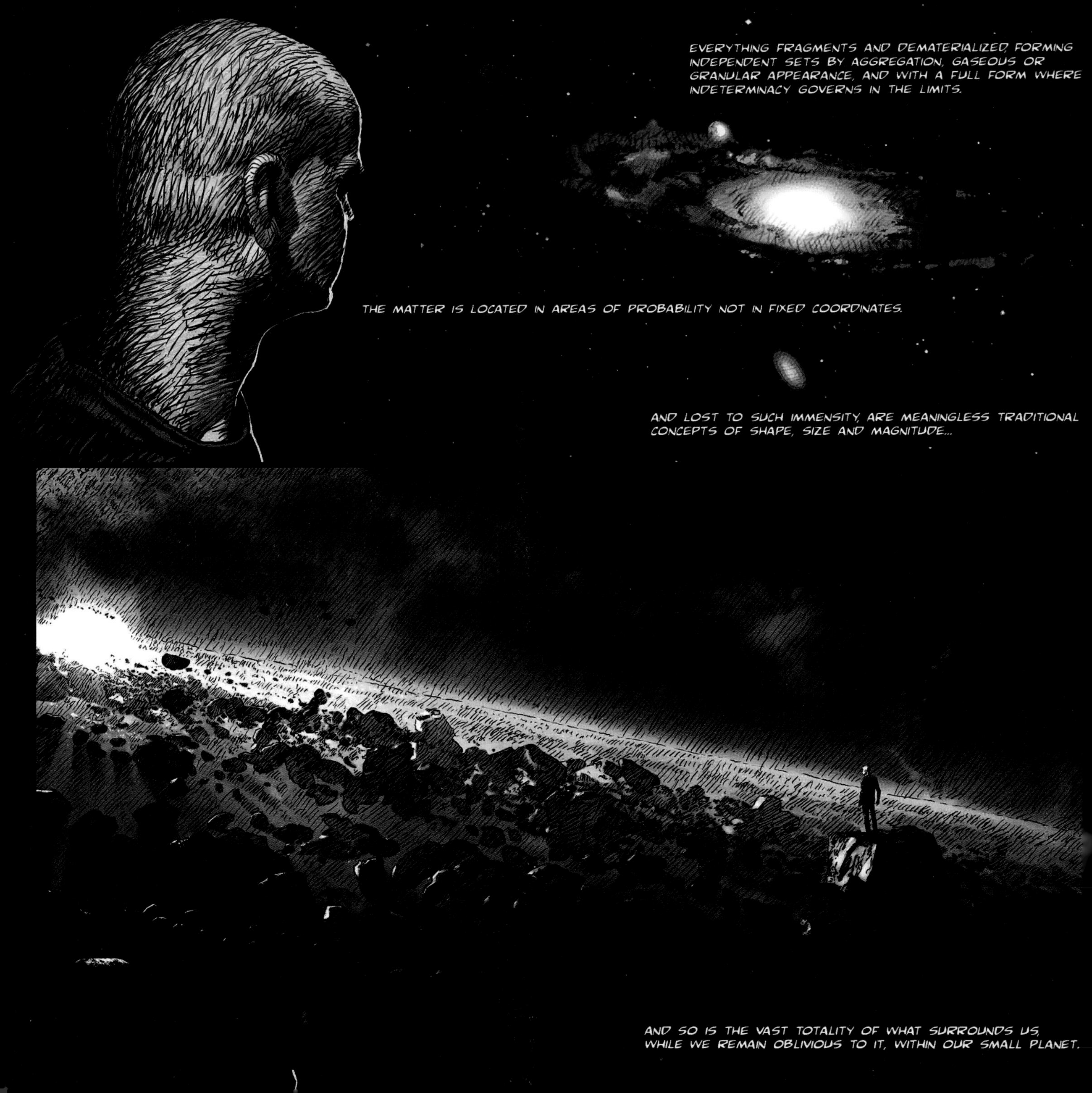
EVERYTHING FRAGMENTS AND DEMATERIALIZED, FORMING INDEPENDENT SETS BY AGGREGATION, GASEOUS OR GRANULAR APPEARANCE, AND WITH A FULL FORM WHERE INDETERMINACY GOVERNS IN THE LIMITS.
THE MATTER IS LOCATED IN AREAS OF PROBABILITY NOT IN FIXED COORDINATES.
AND LOST TO SUCH IMMENSITY, ARE MEANINGLESS TRADITIONAL CONCEPTS OF SHAPE, SIZE AND MAGNITUDE...
AND SO IS THE VAST TOTALITY OF WHAT SURROUNDS US, WHILE WE REMAIN OBLIVIOUS TO IT, WITHIN OUR SMALL PLANET.

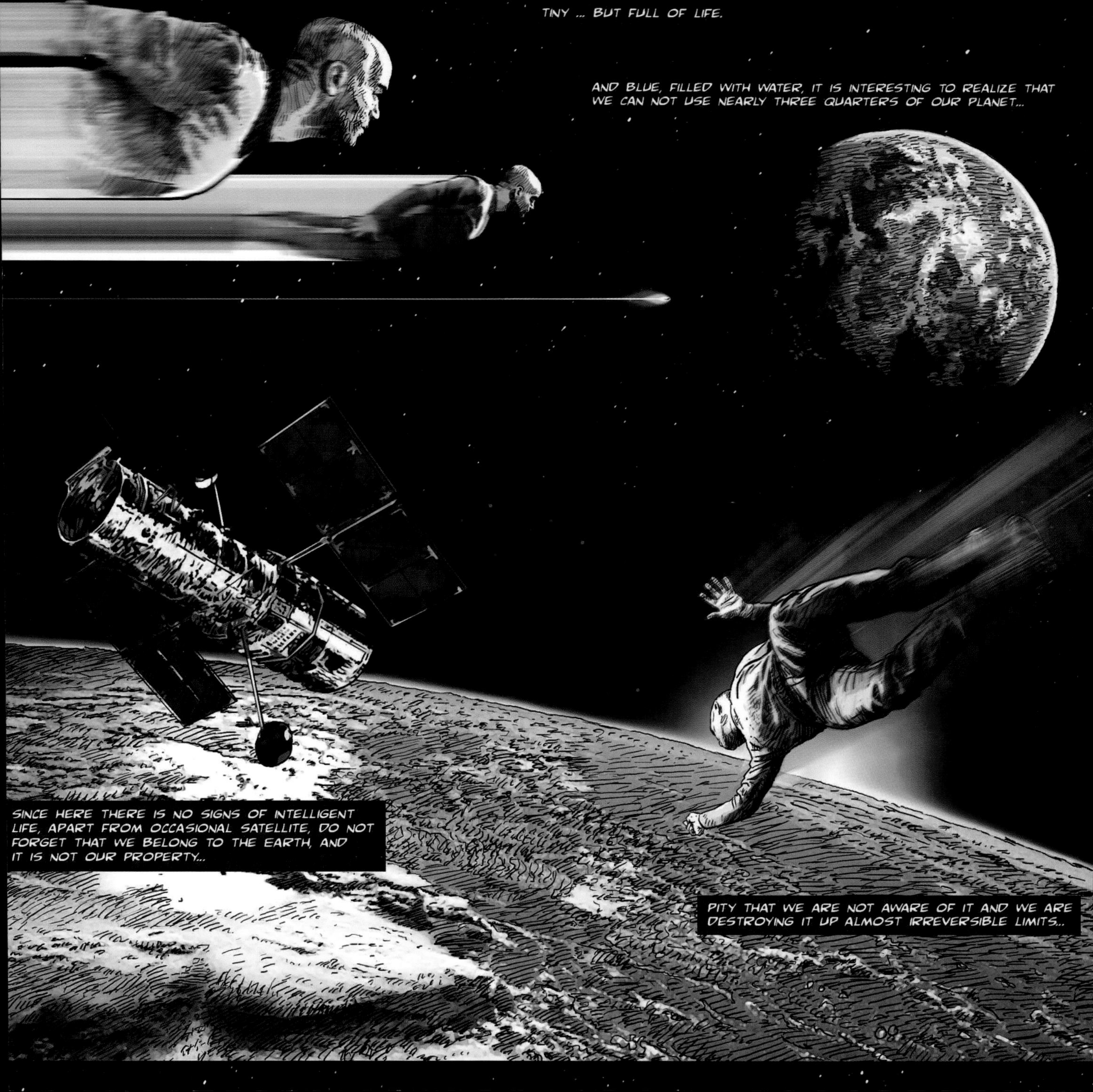
TINY ... BUT FULL OF LIFE.
AND BLUE, FILLED WITH WATER, IT IS INTERESTING TO REALIZE THAT WE CAN NOT USE NEARLY THREE QUARTERS OF OUR PLANET...
SINCE HERE THERE IS NO SIGNS OF INTELLIGENT LIFE, APART FROM OCCASIONAL SATELLITE, DO NOT FORGET THAT WE BELONG TO THE EARTH, AND IT IS NOT OUR PROPERTY...
PITY THAT WE ARE NOT AWARE OF IT AND WE ARE DESTROYING IT UP ALMOST IRREVERSIBLE LIMITS...

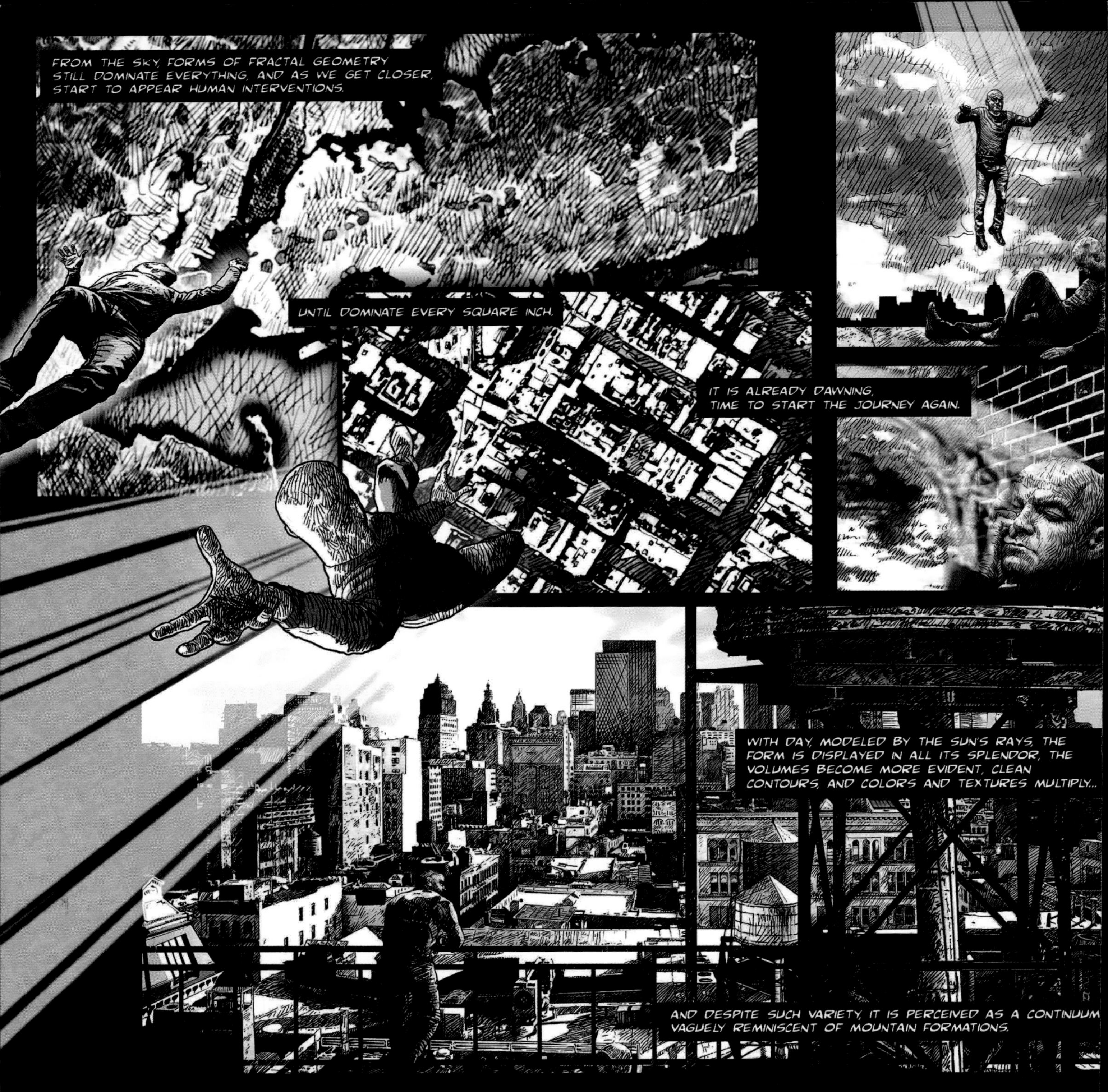
FROM THE SKY, FORMS OF FRACTAL GEOMETRY STILL DOMINATE EVERYTHING, AND AS WE GET CLOSER, START TO APPEAR HUMAN INTERVENTIONS.
UNTIL DOMINATE EVERY SQUARE INCH.
IT IS ALREADY DAWNING, TIME TO START THE JOURNEY AGAIN.
WITH DAY, MODELED BY THE SUN'S RAYS, THE FORM IS DISPLAYED IN ALL ITS SPLENDOR, THE VOLUMES BECOME MORE EVIDENT, CLEAN CONTOURS, AND COLORS AND TEXTURES MULTIPLY...
AND DESPITE SUCH VARIETY, IT IS PERCEIVED AS A CONTINUUM VAGUELY REMINISCENT OF MOUNTAIN FORMATIONS.

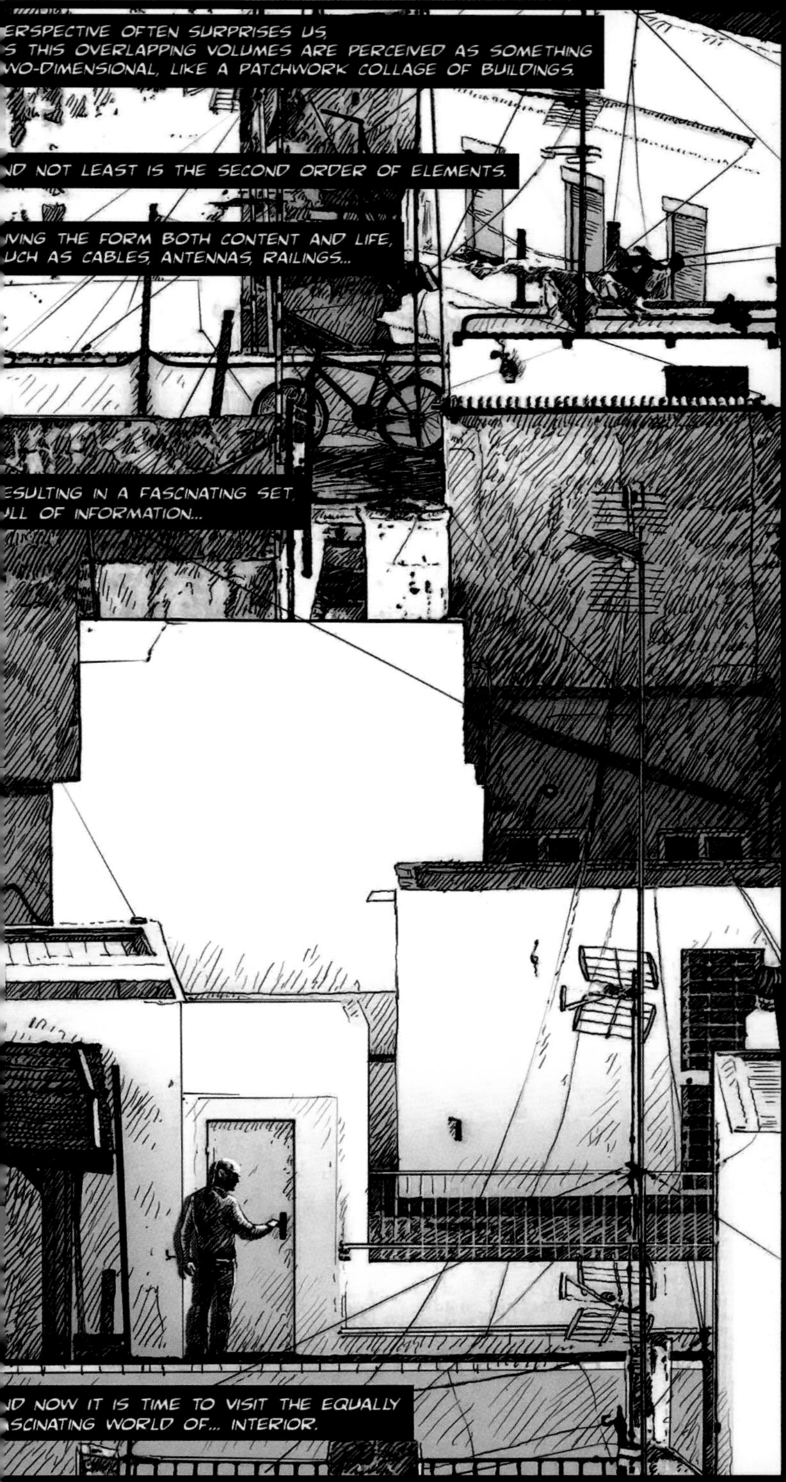

ERSPECTIVE OFTEN SURPRISES US,
S THIS OVERLAPPING VOLUMES ARE PERCEIVED AS SOMETHING
WO-DIMENSIONAL, LIKE A PATCHWORK COLLAGE OF BUILDINGS.
ND NOT LEAST IS THE SECOND ORDER OF ELEMENTS.
IVING THE FORM BOTH CONTENT AND LIFE,
UCH AS CABLES, ANTENNAS, RAILINGS...
ESULTING IN A FASCINATING SET,
LL OF INFORMATION...
ND NOW IT IS TIME TO VISIT THE EQUALLY
SCINATING WORLD OF... INTERIOR.

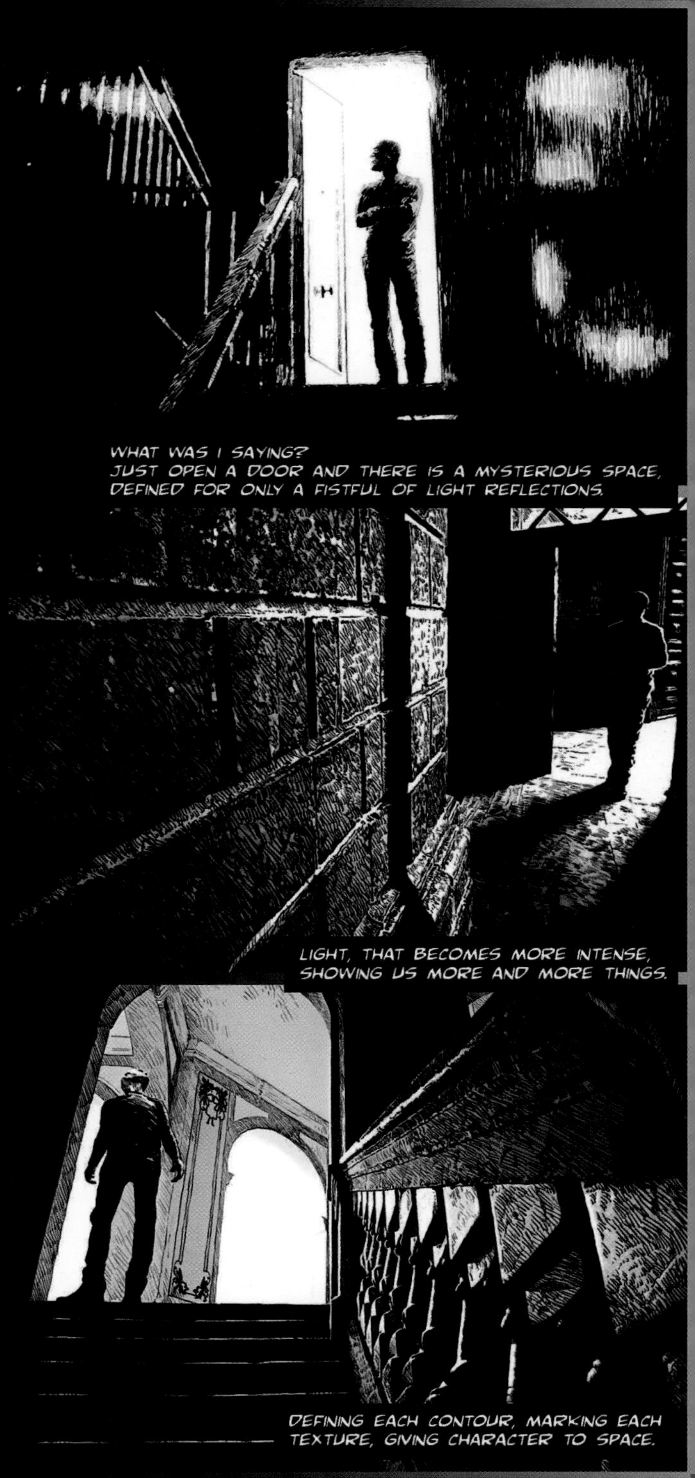

WHAT WAS I SAYING?
JUST OPEN A DOOR AND THERE IS A MYSTERIOUS SPACE,
DEFINED FOR ONLY A FISTFUL OF LIGHT REFLECTIONS.
LIGHT, THAT BECOMES MORE INTENSE,
SHOWING US MORE AND MORE THINGS.
DEFINING EACH CONTOUR, MARKING EACH
TEXTURE, GIVING CHARACTER TO SPACE.

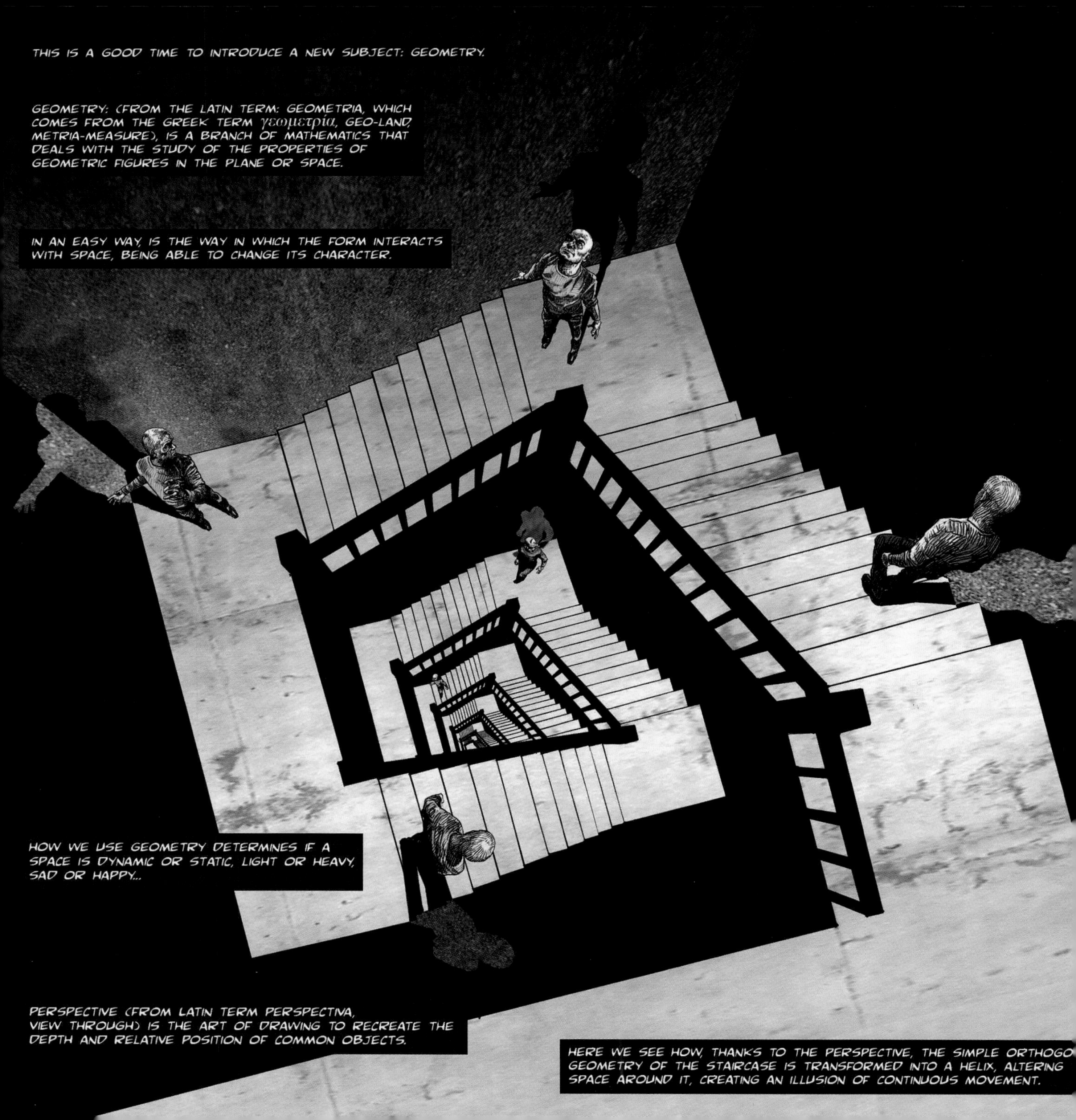
THIS IS A GOOD TIME TO INTRODUCE A NEW SUBJECT: GEOMETRY.
GEOMETRY: (FROM THE LATIN TERM: GEOMETRIA, WHICH COMES FROM THE GREEK TERM γεωμετρία, GEO-LAND, METRIA-MEASURE), IS A BRANCH OF MATHEMATICS THAT DEALS WITH THE STUDY OF THE PROPERTIES OF GEOMETRIC FIGURES IN THE PLANE OR SPACE.
IN AN EASY WAY, IS THE WAY IN WHICH THE FORM INTERACTS WITH SPACE, BEING ABLE TO CHANGE ITS CHARACTER.
HOW WE USE GEOMETRY DETERMINES IF A SPACE IS DYNAMIC OR STATIC, LIGHT OR HEAVY, SAD OR HAPPY...
PERSPECTIVE (FROM LATIN TERM PERSPECTIVA, VIEW THROUGH) IS THE ART OF DRAWING TO RECREATE THE DEPTH AND RELATIVE POSITION OF COMMON OBJECTS.
HERE WE SEE HOW, THANKS TO THE PERSPECTIVE, THE SIMPLE ORTHOGO GEOMETRY OF THE STAIRCASE IS TRANSFORMED INTO A HELIX, ALTERING SPACE AROUND IT, CREATING AN ILLUSION OF CONTINUOUS MOVEMENT.

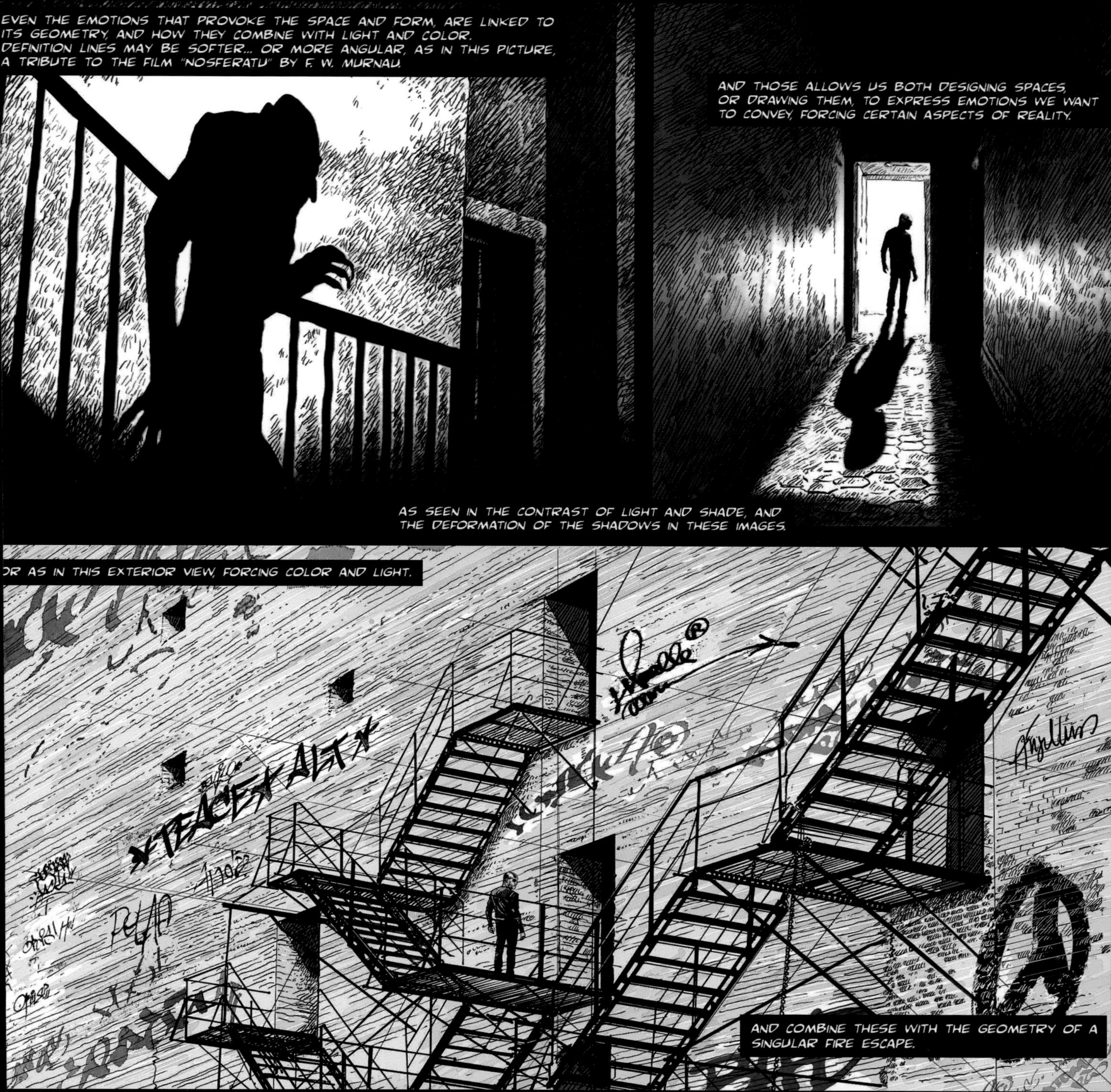
EVEN THE EMOTIONS THAT PROVOKE THE SPACE AND FORM, ARE LINKED TO ITS GEOMETRY, AND HOW THEY COMBINE WITH LIGHT AND COLOR. DEFINITION LINES MAY BE SOFTER... OR MORE ANGULAR, AS IN THIS PICTURE, A TRIBUTE TO THE FILM "NOSFERATU" BY F. W. MURNAU.
AND THOSE ALLOWS US BOTH DESIGNING SPACES, OR DRAWING THEM, TO EXPRESS EMOTIONS WE WANT TO CONVEY, FORCING CERTAIN ASPECTS OF REALITY.
AS SEEN IN THE CONTRAST OF LIGHT AND SHADE, AND THE DEFORMATION OF THE SHADOWS IN THESE IMAGES.
OR AS IN THIS EXTERIOR VIEW, FORCING COLOR AND LIGHT.
AND COMBINE THESE WITH THE GEOMETRY OF A SINGULAR FIRE ESCAPE.

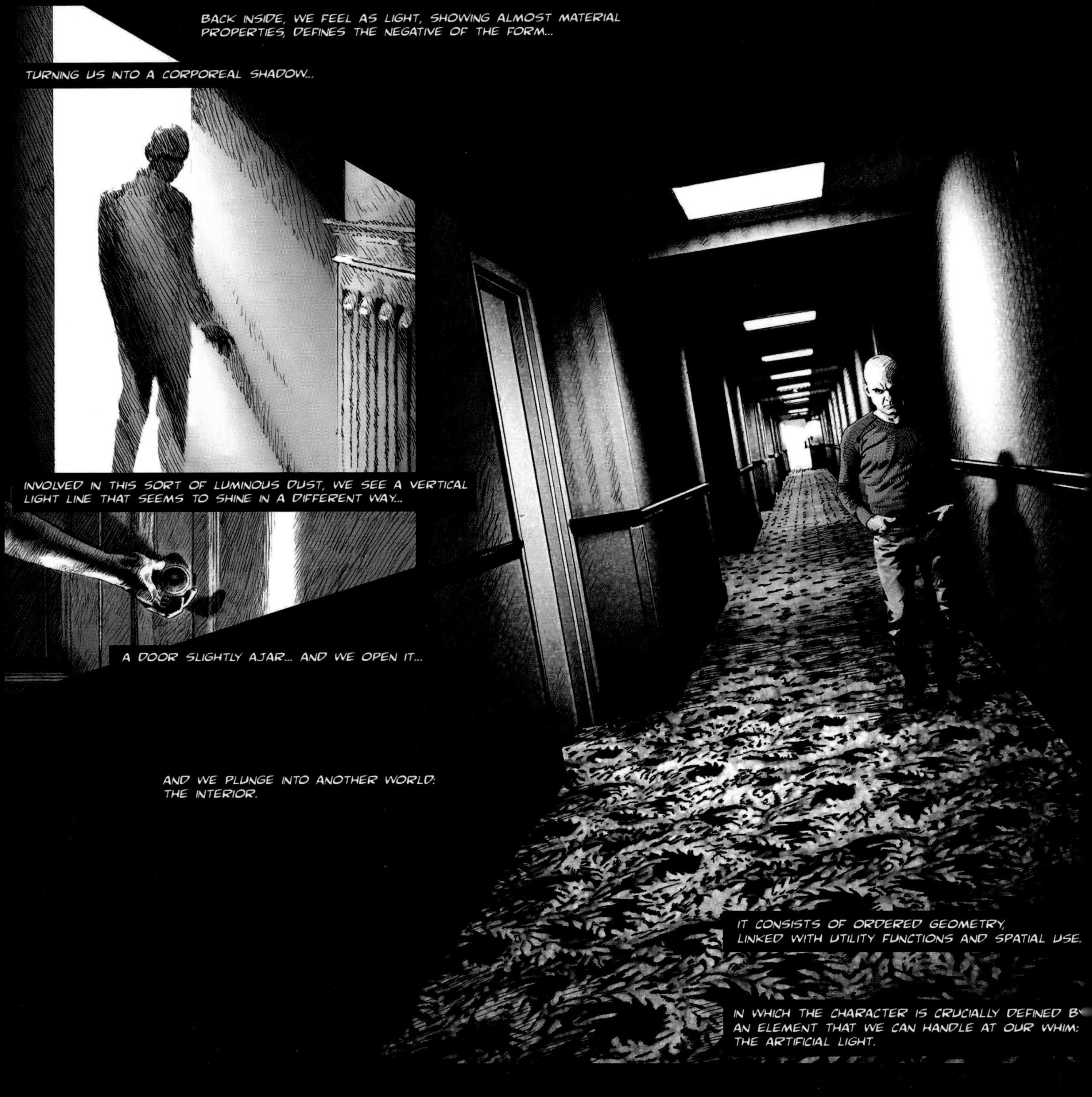
BACK INSIDE, WE FEEL AS LIGHT, SHOWING ALMOST MATERIAL PROPERTIES, DEFINES THE NEGATIVE OF THE FORM...
TURNING US INTO A CORPOREAL SHADOW...
INVOLVED IN THIS SORT OF LUMINOUS DUST, WE SEE A VERTICAL LIGHT LINE THAT SEEMS TO SHINE IN A DIFFERENT WAY...
A DOOR SLIGHTLY AJAR... AND WE OPEN IT...
AND WE PLUNGE INTO ANOTHER WORLD: THE INTERIOR.
IT CONSISTS OF ORDERED GEOMETRY, LINKED WITH UTILITY FUNCTIONS AND SPATIAL USE.
IN WHICH THE CHARACTER IS CRUCIALLY DEFINED BY AN ELEMENT THAT WE CAN HANDLE AT OUR WHIM: THE ARTIFICIAL LIGHT.

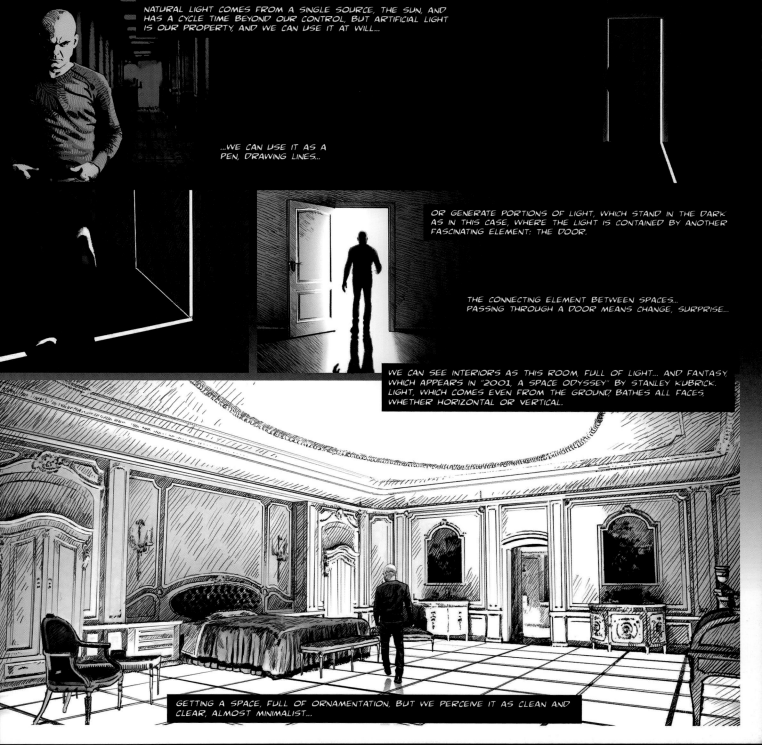

NATURAL LIGHT COMES FROM A SINGLE SOURCE, THE SUN, AND HAS A CYCLE TIME BEYOND OUR CONTROL, BUT ARTIFICIAL LIGHT IS OUR PROPERTY, AND WE CAN USE IT AT WILL...

...WE CAN USE IT AS A PEN, DRAWING LINES...

OR GENERATE PORTIONS OF LIGHT, WHICH STAND IN THE DARK AS IN THIS CASE, WHERE THE LIGHT IS CONTAINED BY ANOTHER FASCINATING ELEMENT: THE DOOR.

THE CONNECTING ELEMENT BETWEEN SPACES... PASSING THROUGH A DOOR MEANS CHANGE, SURPRISE...

WE CAN SEE INTERIORS AS THIS ROOM, FULL OF LIGHT... AND FANTASY, WHICH APPEARS IN "2001, A SPACE ODYSSEY" BY STANLEY KUBRICK. LIGHT, WHICH COMES EVEN FROM THE GROUND, BATHES ALL FACES, WHETHER HORIZONTAL OR VERTICAL.

GETTING A SPACE, FULL OF ORNAMENTATION, BUT WE PERCEIVE IT AS CLEAN AND CLEAR, ALMOST MINIMALIST...

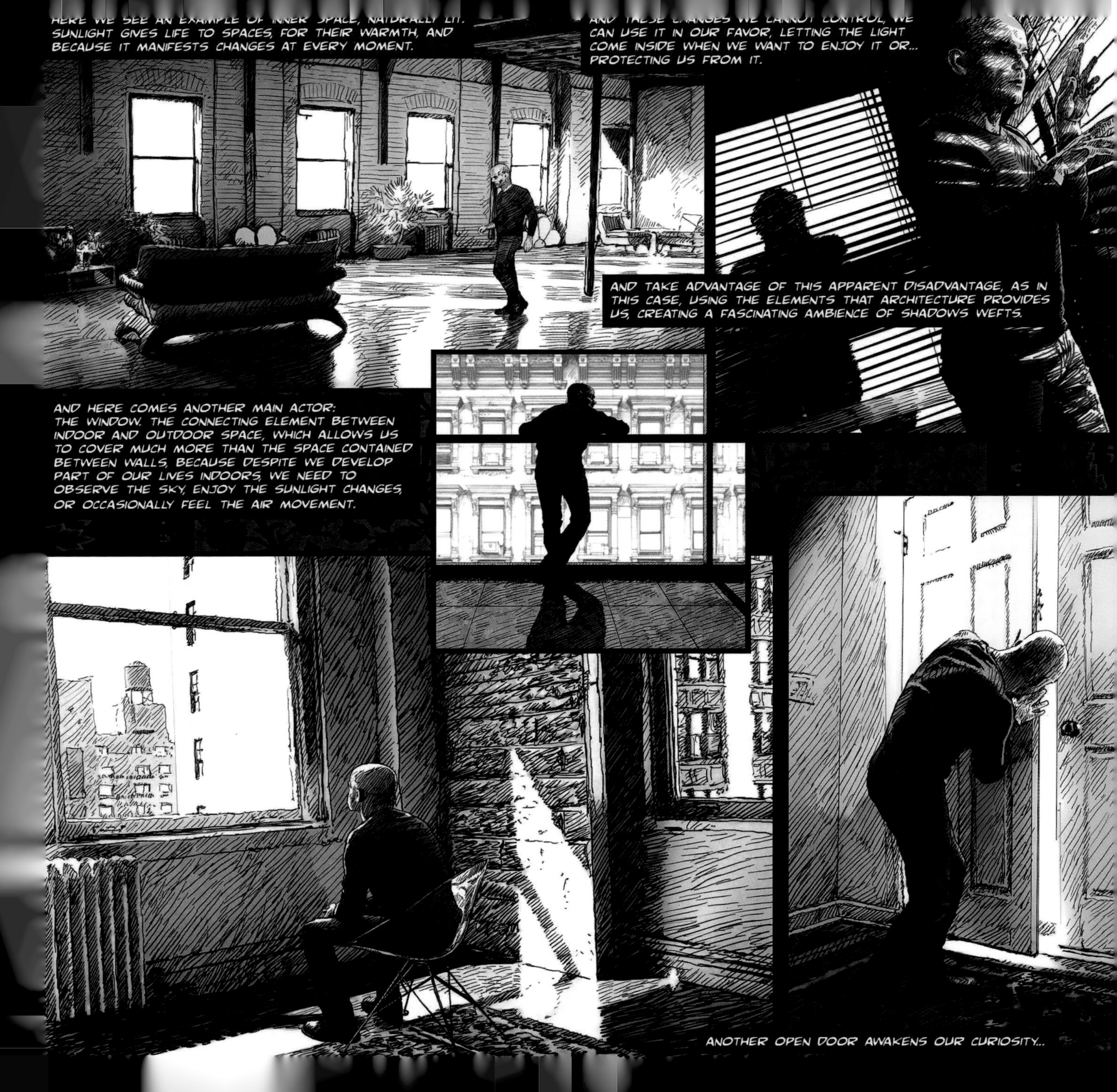
HERE WE SEE AN EXAMPLE OF INNER SPACE, NATURALLY LIT. SUNLIGHT GIVES LIFE TO SPACES, FOR THEIR WARMTH, AND BECAUSE IT MANIFESTS CHANGES AT EVERY MOMENT.
AND THESE CHANGES WE CANNOT CONTROL, WE CAN USE IT IN OUR FAVOR, LETTING THE LIGHT COME INSIDE WHEN WE WANT TO ENJOY IT OR... PROTECTING US FROM IT.
AND TAKE ADVANTAGE OF THIS APPARENT DISADVANTAGE, AS IN THIS CASE, USING THE ELEMENTS THAT ARCHITECTURE PROVIDES US, CREATING A FASCINATING AMBIENCE OF SHADOWS WEFTS.
AND HERE COMES ANOTHER MAIN ACTOR: THE WINDOW. THE CONNECTING ELEMENT BETWEEN INDOOR AND OUTDOOR SPACE, WHICH ALLOWS US TO COVER MUCH MORE THAN THE SPACE CONTAINED BETWEEN WALLS, BECAUSE DESPITE WE DEVELOP PART OF OUR LIVES INDOORS, WE NEED TO OBSERVE THE SKY, ENJOY THE SUNLIGHT CHANGES, OR OCCASIONALLY FEEL THE AIR MOVEMENT.
ANOTHER OPEN DOOR AWAKENS OUR CURIOSITY...

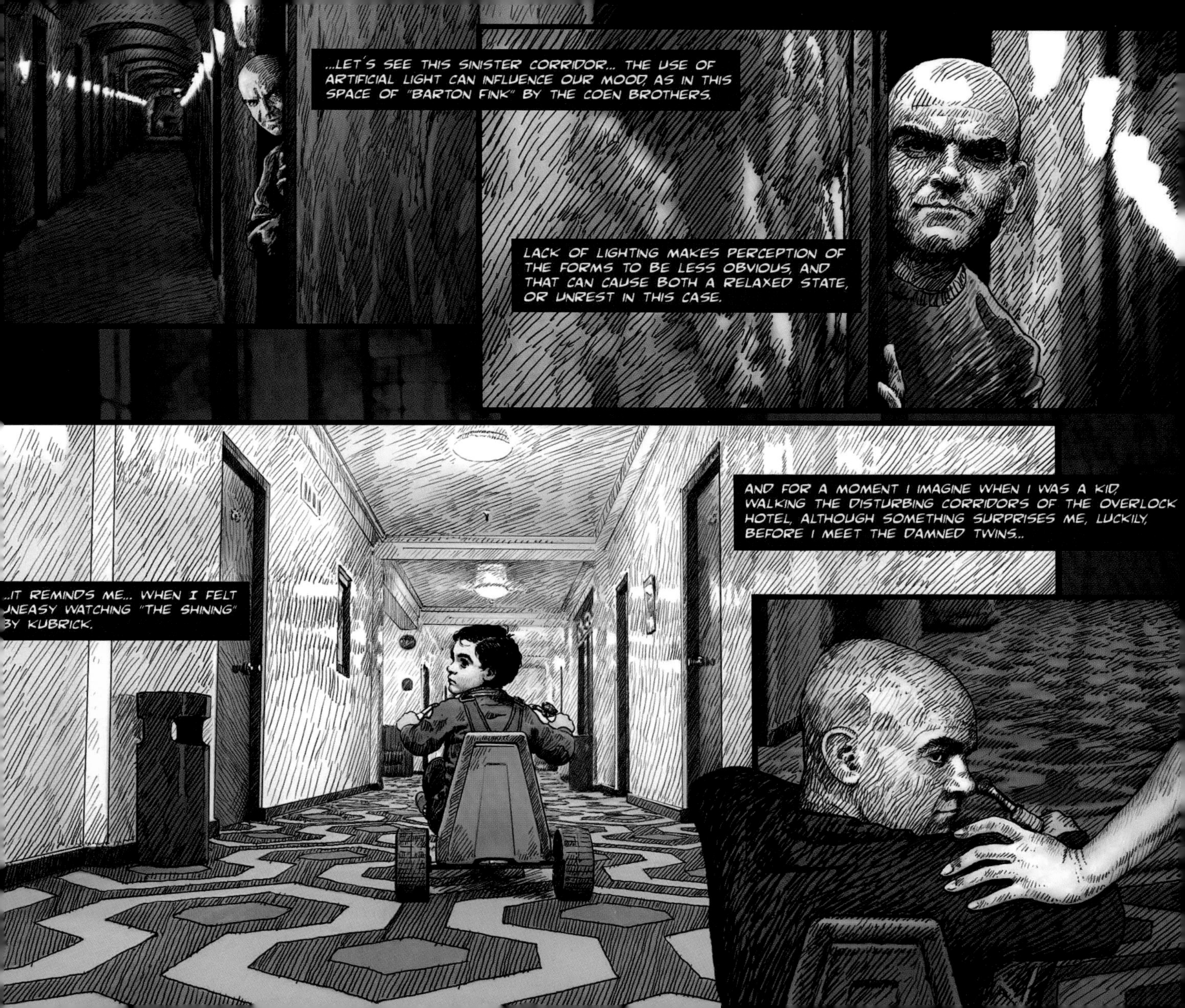
...LET'S SEE THIS SINISTER CORRIDOR... THE USE OF ARTIFICIAL LIGHT CAN INFLUENCE OUR MOOD, AS IN THIS SPACE OF "BARTON FINK" BY THE COEN BROTHERS.
LACK OF LIGHTING MAKES PERCEPTION OF THE FORMS TO BE LESS OBVIOUS, AND THAT CAN CAUSE BOTH A RELAXED STATE, OR UNREST IN THIS CASE.
..IT REMINDS ME... WHEN I FELT UNEASY WATCHING "THE SHINING" BY KUBRICK.
AND FOR A MOMENT I IMAGINE WHEN I WAS A KID, WALKING THE DISTURBING CORRIDORS OF THE OVERLOCK HOTEL, ALTHOUGH SOMETHING SURPRISES ME, LUCKILY, BEFORE I MEET THE DAMNED TWINS...

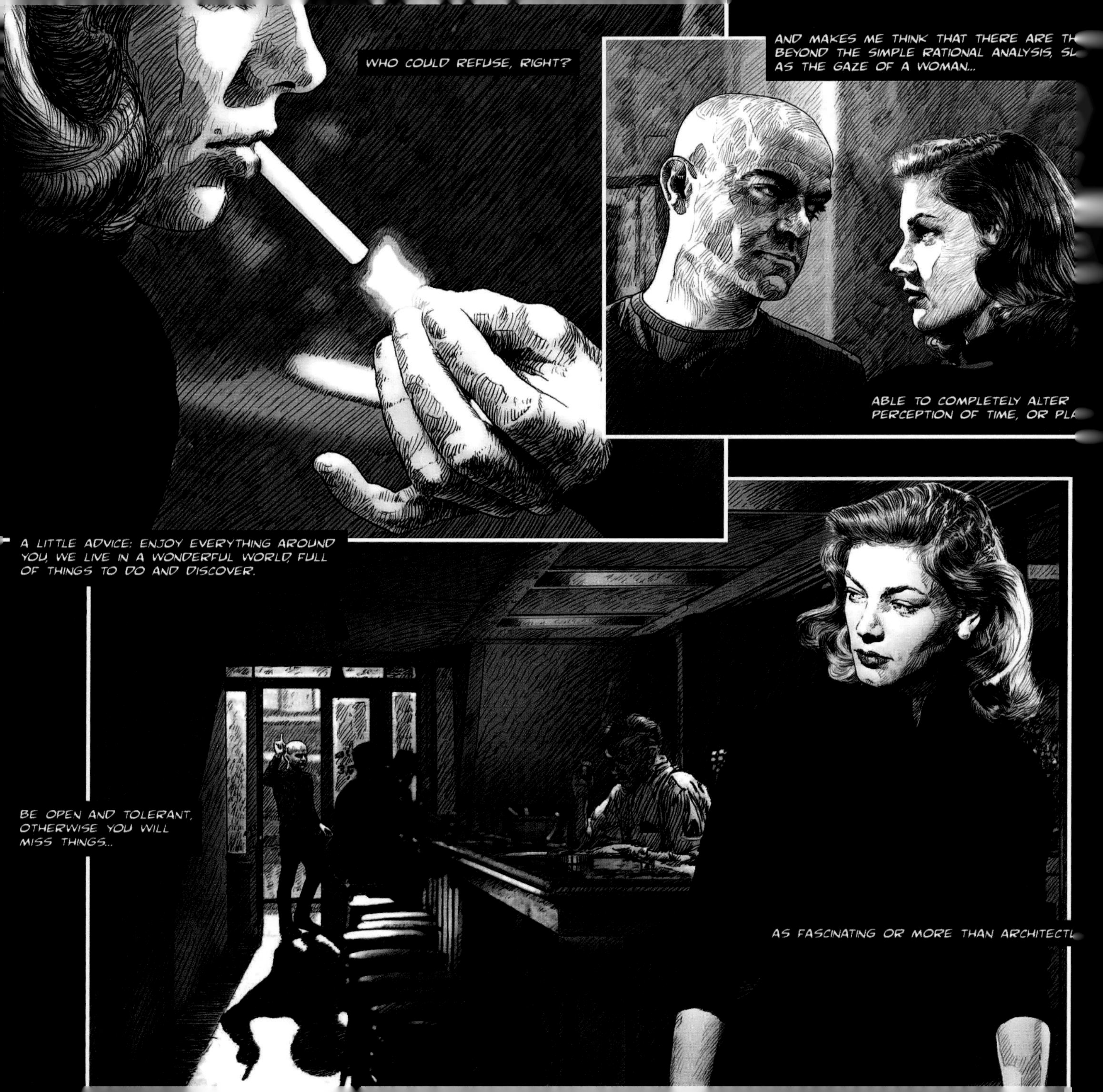
WHO COULD REFUSE, RIGHT?
AND MAKES ME THINK THAT THERE ARE TH BEYOND THE SIMPLE RATIONAL ANALYSIS, SU AS THE GAZE OF A WOMAN...
ABLE TO COMPLETELY ALTER PERCEPTION OF TIME, OR PLA
A LITTLE ADVICE: ENJOY EVERYTHING AROUND YOU, WE LIVE IN A WONDERFUL WORLD, FULL OF THINGS TO DO AND DISCOVER.
BE OPEN AND TOLERANT, OTHERWISE YOU WILL MISS THINGS...
AS FASCINATING OR MORE THAN ARCHITECTU

WE LEAVE THE INNER SPACE, AND RETURN TO THE STREET, AND WE FIND THIS FACADE, CHARACTERISTIC OF MANY CITIES. A FIRST READING SHOWS US JUST THE REPETITION OF WINDOWS WITH CLASSICAL ORDER, BUT THE PASSAGE OF TIME AFFECTS ARCHITECTURE IN AN UNPREDICTABLE WAY.

THE AGING OF MATERIALS, WEATHER CONDITIONS, POLLUTION AND HUMAN INTERVENTION...

CREATE A SERIES OF SUCCESSIVE LAYERS OF DIVERSE INFORMATION, WHICH END UP, TURNING UNIQUE EVERY OPENING, AND GIVING RISE TO A SET THAT TELLS US MANY DIFFERENT STORIES.

IT'S TIME TO LOOK FOR NEW SENSATIONS, BUT

ON A LARGER SCALE, WE CAN ALSO ENJOY THE VARIETY OF FORMS THAT THE CITY GIVES US.

VOLUMES OF DIFFERENT SIZE AND PROPORTIONS ARE ADDED, OVERLAP AND FIT TOGETHER, TO FILL UP TO THE LAST CUBIC METER THAT ENABLE REGULATIONS. BECAUSE THE OCCUPATION IN THE CITY SPACE IS CONDITIONED BY A NUMBER OF PARAMETERS, SUCH AS OCCUPATION IN PLANT, BUILDABILITY, THE SETBACKS, THE HEIGHT LIMITATION, AND A HOST OF RULES, WHETHER SUCCESSFUL OR NOT, ARE WHAT ULTIMATELY DETERMINE WHAT WE SEE..

RESULTING IN A COLORFUL PUZZLE OR TETRIS, LIVING IN IT ALL KINDS OF MATERIALS, COLORS AND TEXTURES.

WE LEAVE BEHIND THE VERTICAL CITY AND ITS INTERMEDIATE STOPS, AND THE SKY BEGINS TO TAKE INCREASINGLY GREATER PRESENCE.

BUILDINGS LOSE PRESENCE, AND BECOME PROGRESSIVELY, UNTIL WE ONLY SEE COMMUNICATION FLOWS AS ROADS AND BRIDGES...

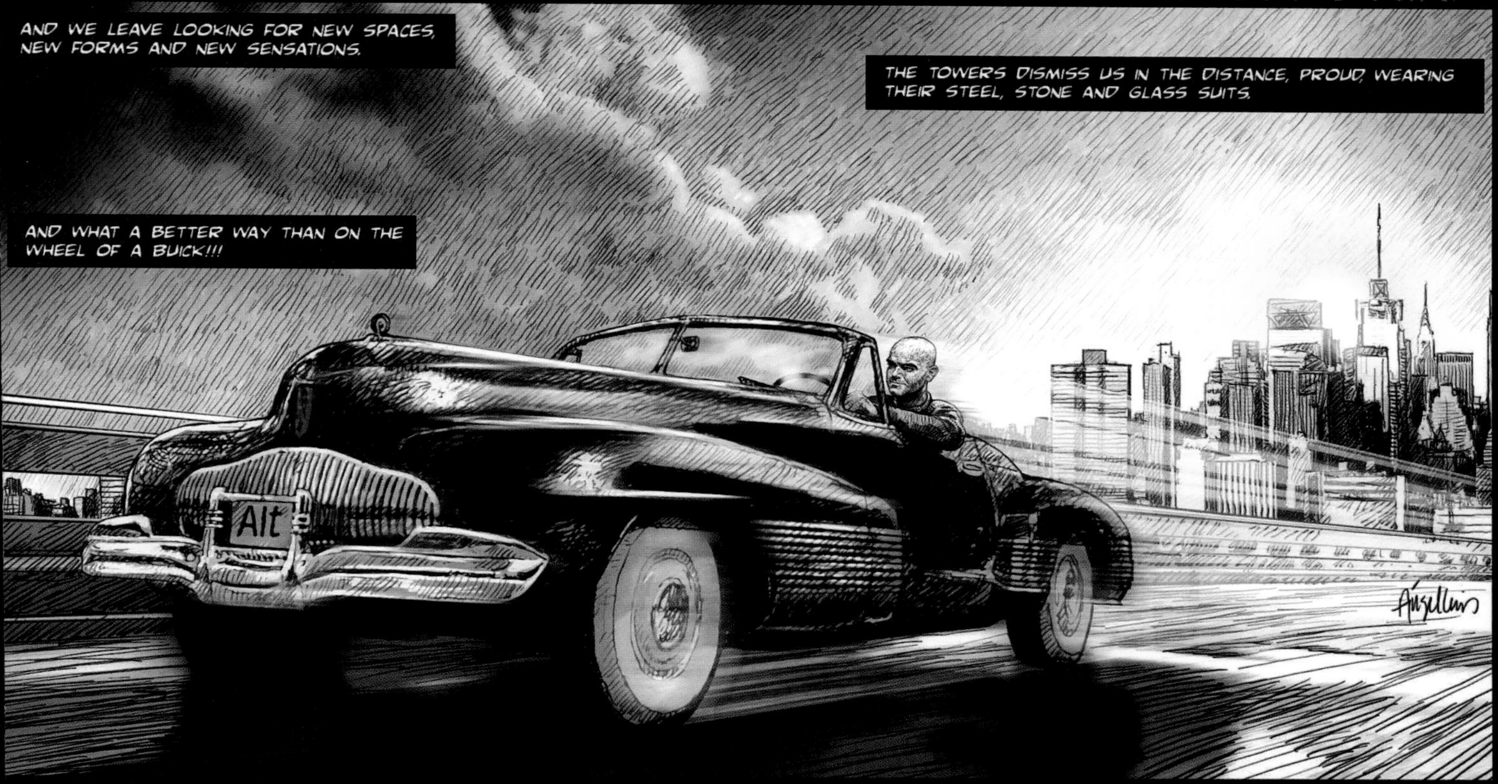
AND WE LEAVE LOOKING FOR NEW SPACES, NEW FORMS AND NEW SENSATIONS.
THE TOWERS DISMISS US IN THE DISTANCE, PROUD, WEARING THEIR STEEL, STONE AND GLASS SUITS.
AND WHAT A BETTER WAY THAN ON THE WHEEL OF A BUICK!!!
Alt

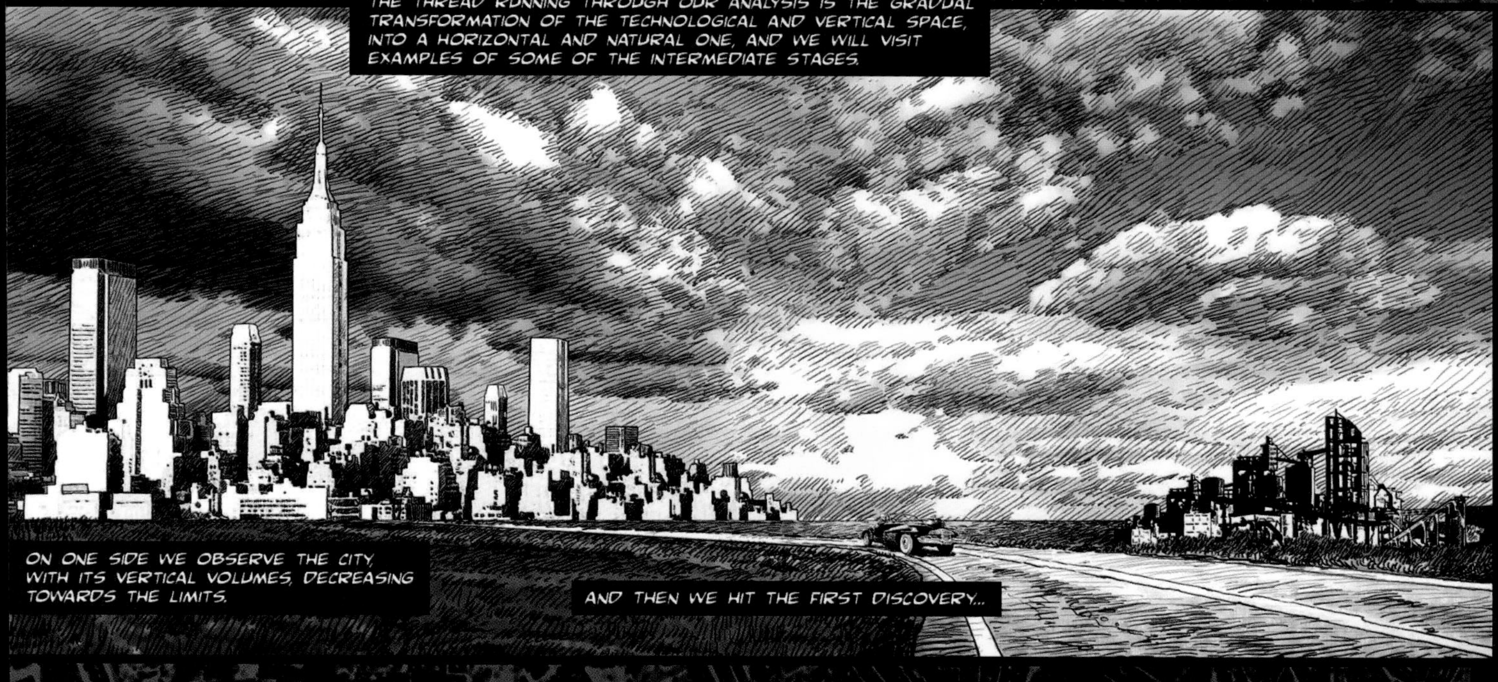
THE THREAD RUNNING THROUGH OUR ANALYSIS IS THE GRADUAL TRANSFORMATION OF THE TECHNOLOGICAL AND VERTICAL SPACE, INTO A HORIZONTAL AND NATURAL ONE, AND WE WILL VISIT EXAMPLES OF SOME OF THE INTERMEDIATE STAGES.
ON ONE SIDE WE OBSERVE THE CITY, WITH ITS VERTICAL VOLUMES, DECREASING TOWARDS THE LIMITS.
AND THEN WE HIT THE FIRST DISCOVERY...

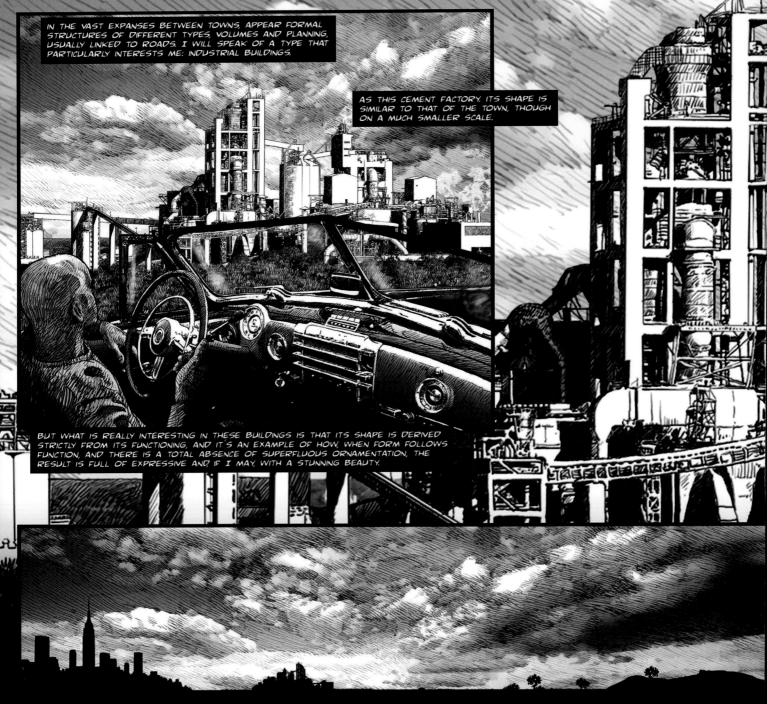

IN THE VAST EXPANSES BETWEEN TOWNS, APPEAR FORMAL STRUCTURES OF DIFFERENT TYPES, VOLUMES AND PLANNING, USUALLY LINKED TO ROADS. I WILL SPEAK OF A TYPE THAT PARTICULARLY INTERESTS ME: INDUSTRIAL BUILDINGS.

AS THIS CEMENT FACTORY. ITS SHAPE IS SIMILAR TO THAT OF THE TOWN, THOUGH ON A MUCH SMALLER SCALE.

BUT WHAT IS REALLY INTERESTING IN THESE BUILDINGS IS THAT ITS SHAPE IS DERIVED STRICTLY FROM ITS FUNCTIONING, AND IT'S AN EXAMPLE OF HOW, WHEN FORM FOLLOWS FUNCTION, AND THERE IS A TOTAL ABSENCE OF SUPERFLUOUS ORNAMENTATION, THE RESULT IS FULL OF EXPRESSIVE AND, IF I MAY, WITH A STUNNING BEAUTY.

CUT AT THE HORIZON WE CAN SEE AND COMPARE THE IMPACT OF THE HUMAN CONSTRUCTIONS ON THE ENVIRONMENT.

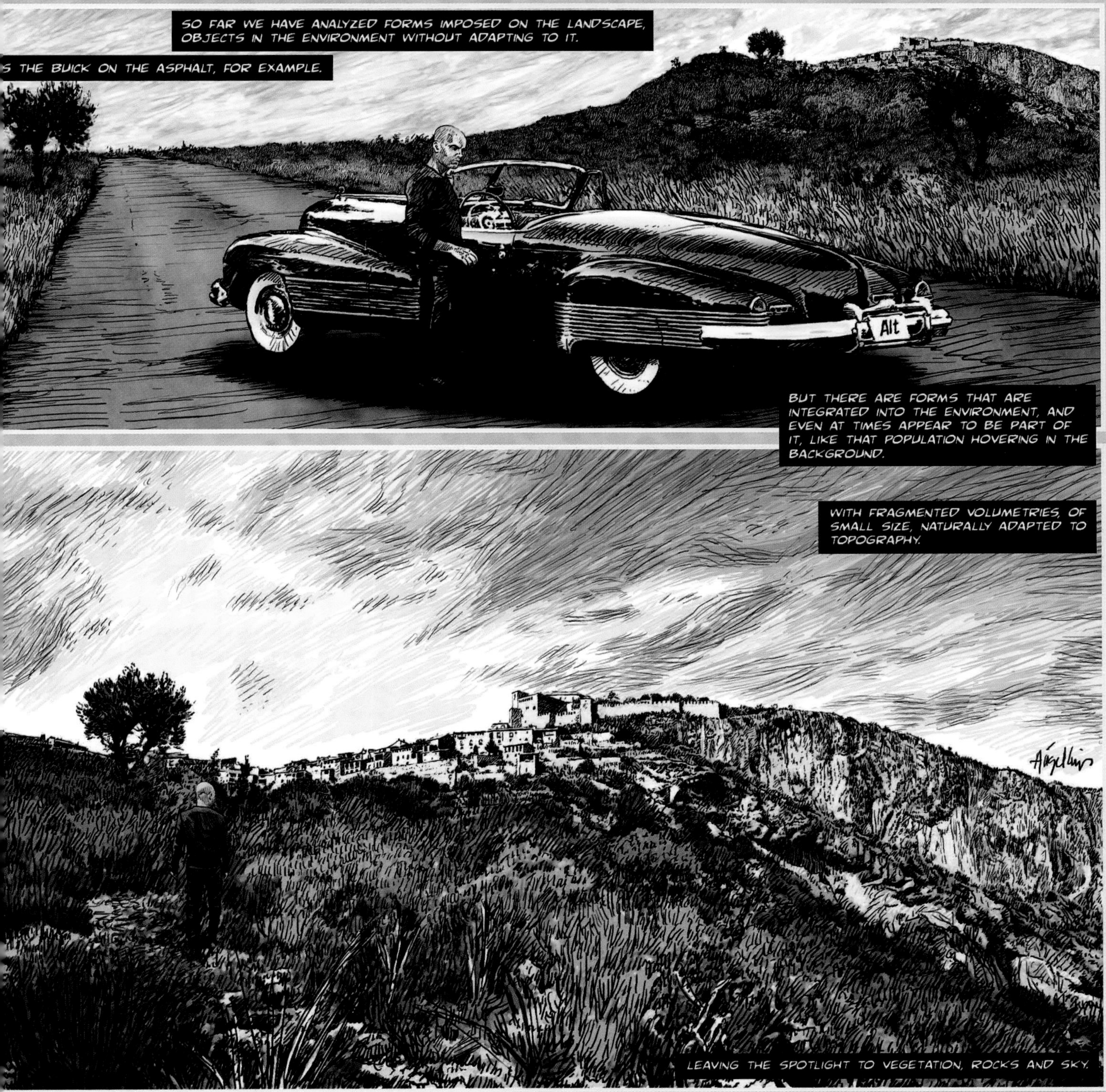
SO FAR WE HAVE ANALYZED FORMS IMPOSED ON THE LANDSCAPE, OBJECTS IN THE ENVIRONMENT WITHOUT ADAPTING TO IT.
S THE BUICK ON THE ASPHALT, FOR EXAMPLE.
Alt
BUT THERE ARE FORMS THAT ARE INTEGRATED INTO THE ENVIRONMENT, AND EVEN AT TIMES APPEAR TO BE PART OF IT, LIKE THAT POPULATION HOVERING IN THE BACKGROUND.
WITH FRAGMENTED VOLUMETRIES, OF SMALL SIZE, NATURALLY ADAPTED TO TOPOGRAPHY.
LEAVING THE SPOTLIGHT TO VEGETATION, ROCKS AND SKY.

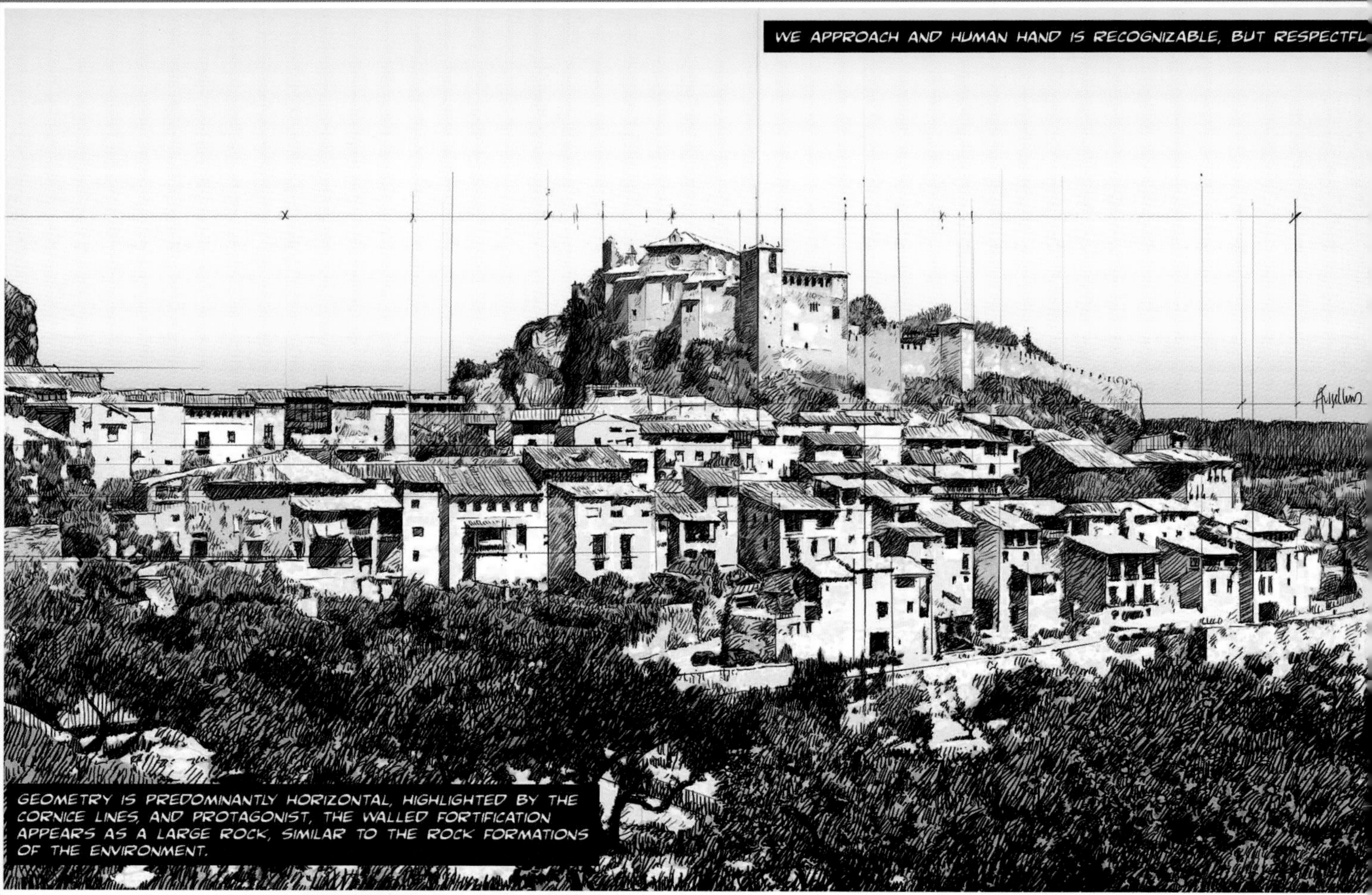
WE APPROACH AND HUMAN HAND IS RECOGNIZABLE, BUT RESPECTF
GEOMETRY IS PREDOMINANTLY HORIZONTAL, HIGHLIGHTED BY THE CORNICE LINES, AND PROTAGONIST, THE WALLED FORTIFICATION APPEARS AS A LARGE ROCK, SIMILAR TO THE ROCK FORMATIONS OF THE ENVIRONMENT.

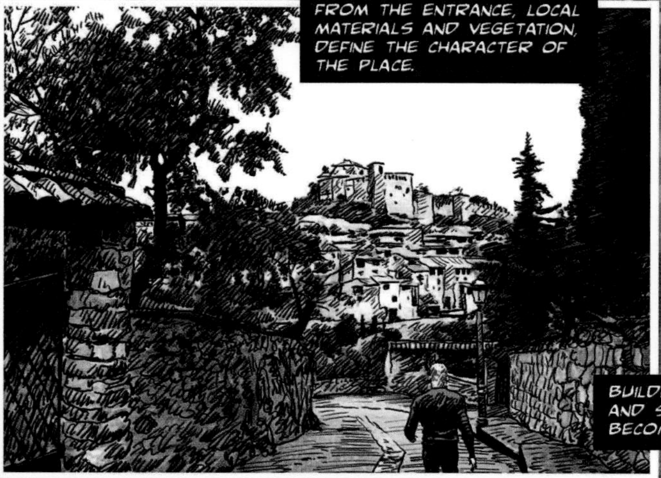
FROM THE ENTRANCE, LOCAL MATERIALS AND VEGETATION, DEFINE THE CHARACTER OF THE PLACE.

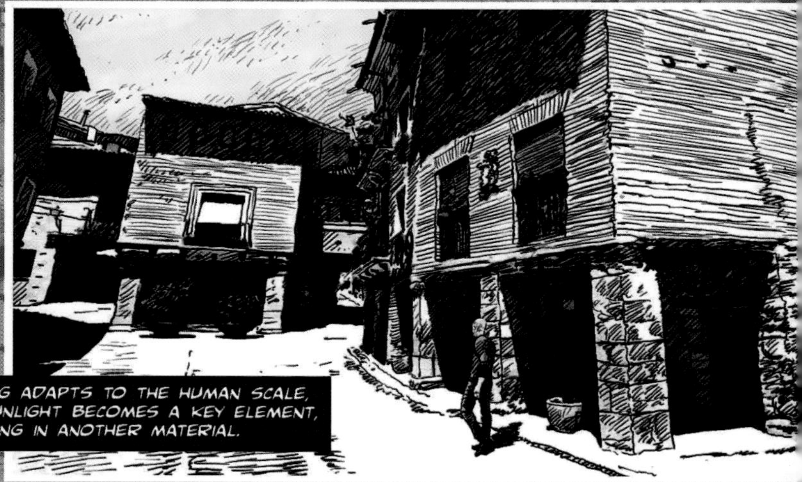
BUILDING ADAPTS TO THE HUMAN SCALE, AND SUNLIGHT BECOMES A KEY ELEMENT, BECOMING IN ANOTHER MATERIAL.

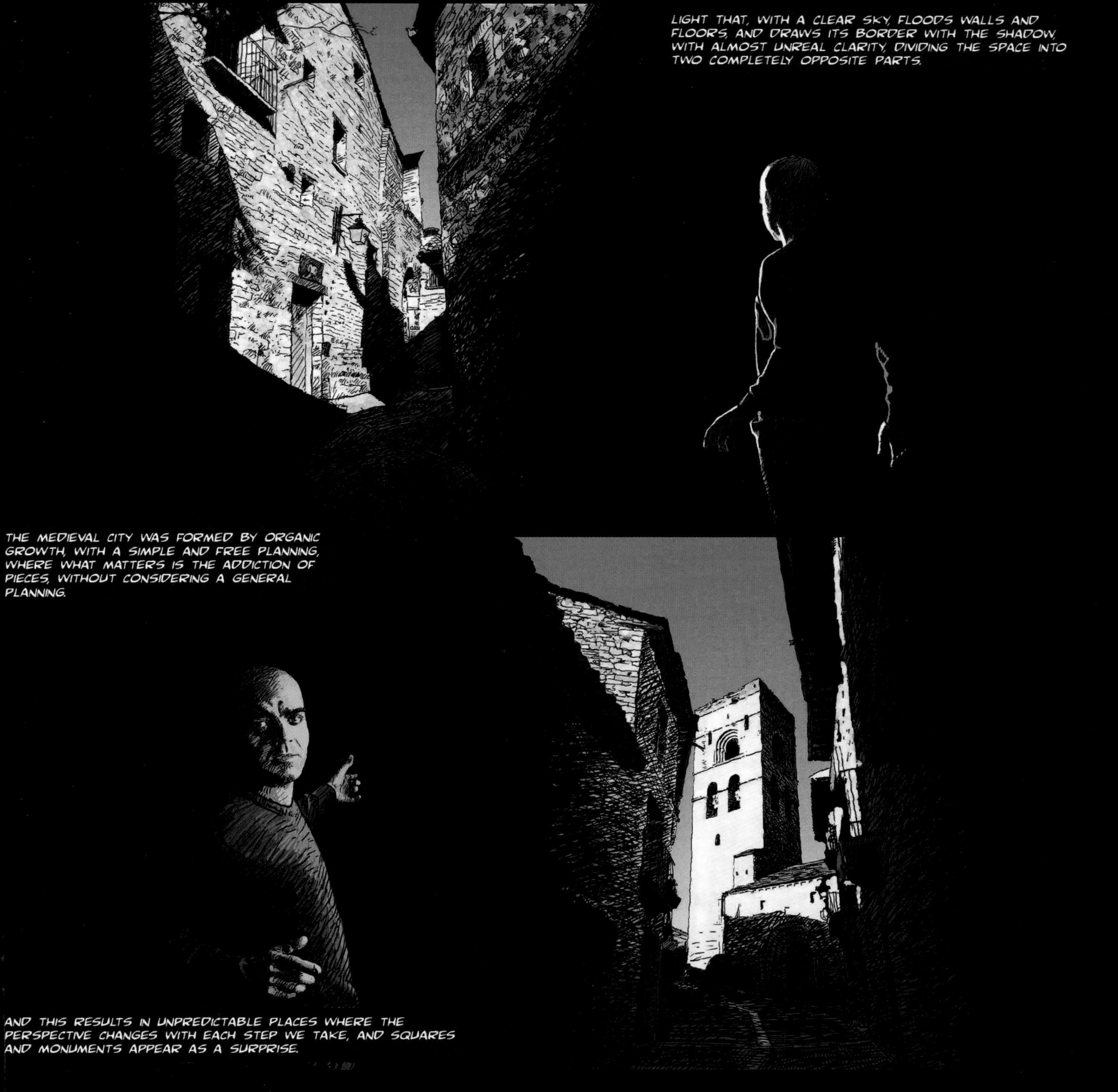
LIGHT THAT, WITH A CLEAR SKY, FLOODS WALLS AND FLOORS, AND DRAWS ITS BORDER WITH THE SHADOW, WITH ALMOST UNREAL CLARITY, DIVIDING THE SPACE INTO TWO COMPLETELY OPPOSITE PARTS.
THE MEDIEVAL CITY WAS FORMED BY ORGANIC GROWTH, WITH A SIMPLE AND FREE PLANNING, WHERE WHAT MATTERS IS THE ADDICTION OF PIECES, WITHOUT CONSIDERING A GENERAL PLANNING.
AND THIS RESULTS IN UNPREDICTABLE PLACES WHERE THE PERSPECTIVE CHANGES WITH EACH STEP WE TAKE, AND SQUARES AND MONUMENTS APPEAR AS A SURPRISE.

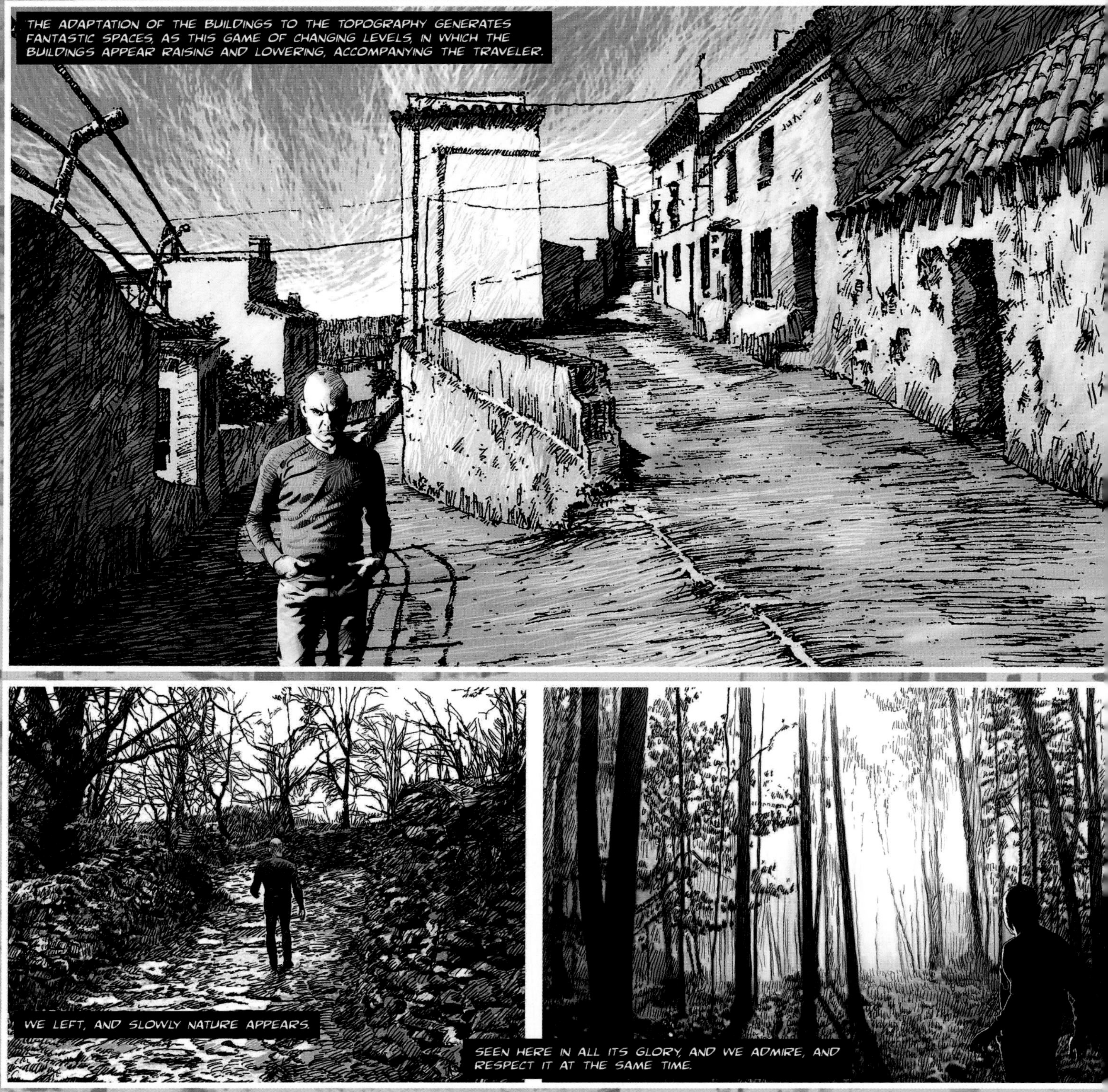
THE ADAPTATION OF THE BUILDINGS TO THE TOPOGRAPHY GENERATES FANTASTIC SPACES, AS THIS GAME OF CHANGING LEVELS, IN WHICH THE BUILDINGS APPEAR RAISING AND LOWERING, ACCOMPANYING THE TRAVELER.
WE LEFT, AND SLOWLY NATURE APPEARS.
SEEN HERE IN ALL ITS GLORY, AND WE ADMIRE, AND RESPECT IT AT THE SAME TIME.

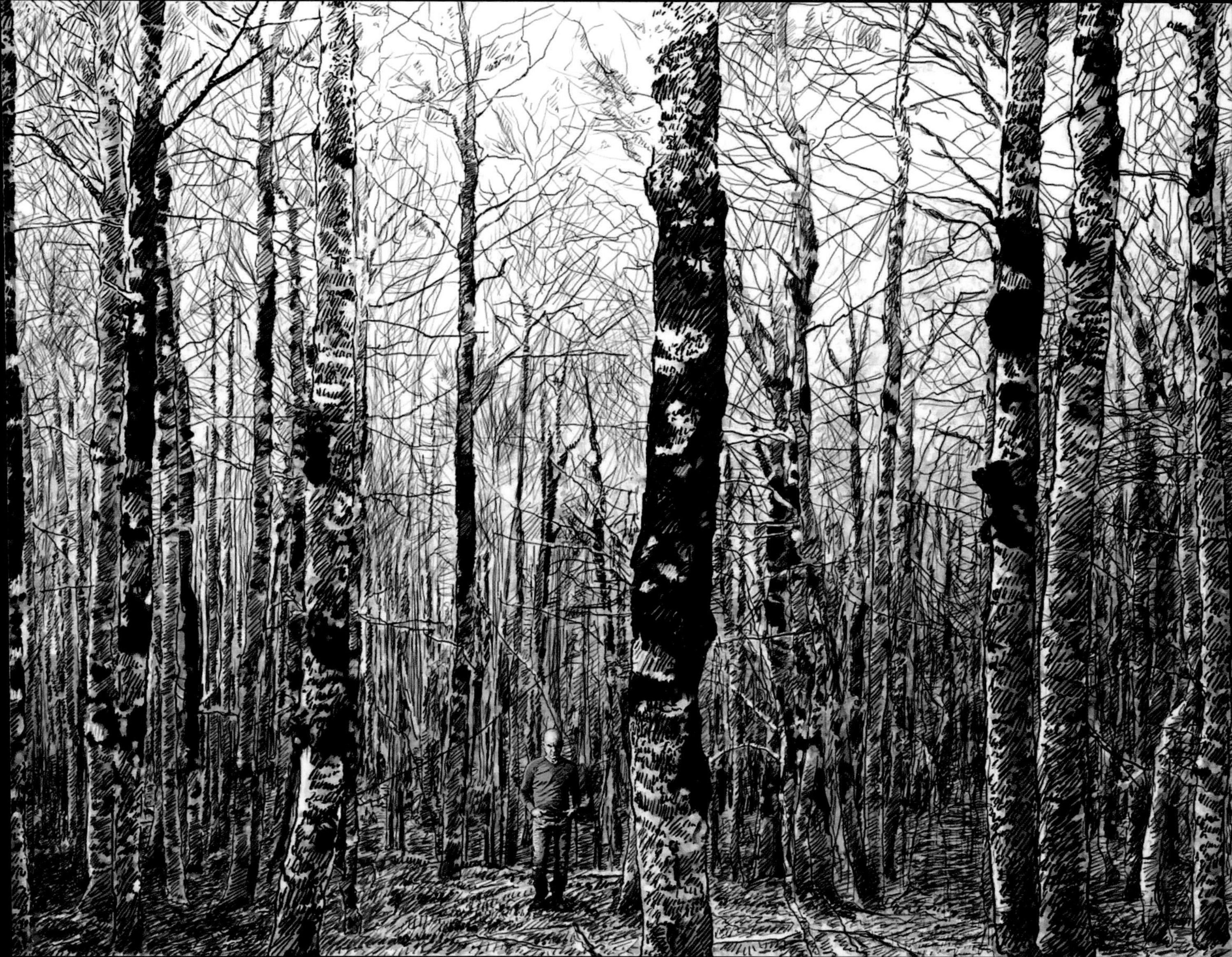

NATURE OVERWHELMS US AGAIN, REMINDING US THAT WE ARE INSIGNIFICANT, AS IN THIS BEECH FOREST WHERE TREES STAND PROUD, FULL OF LIFE, ORDERED AS HAUGHTY VERTICAL STRUCTURES, GENERATING A HIGHLY EXPRESSIVE SPACE.

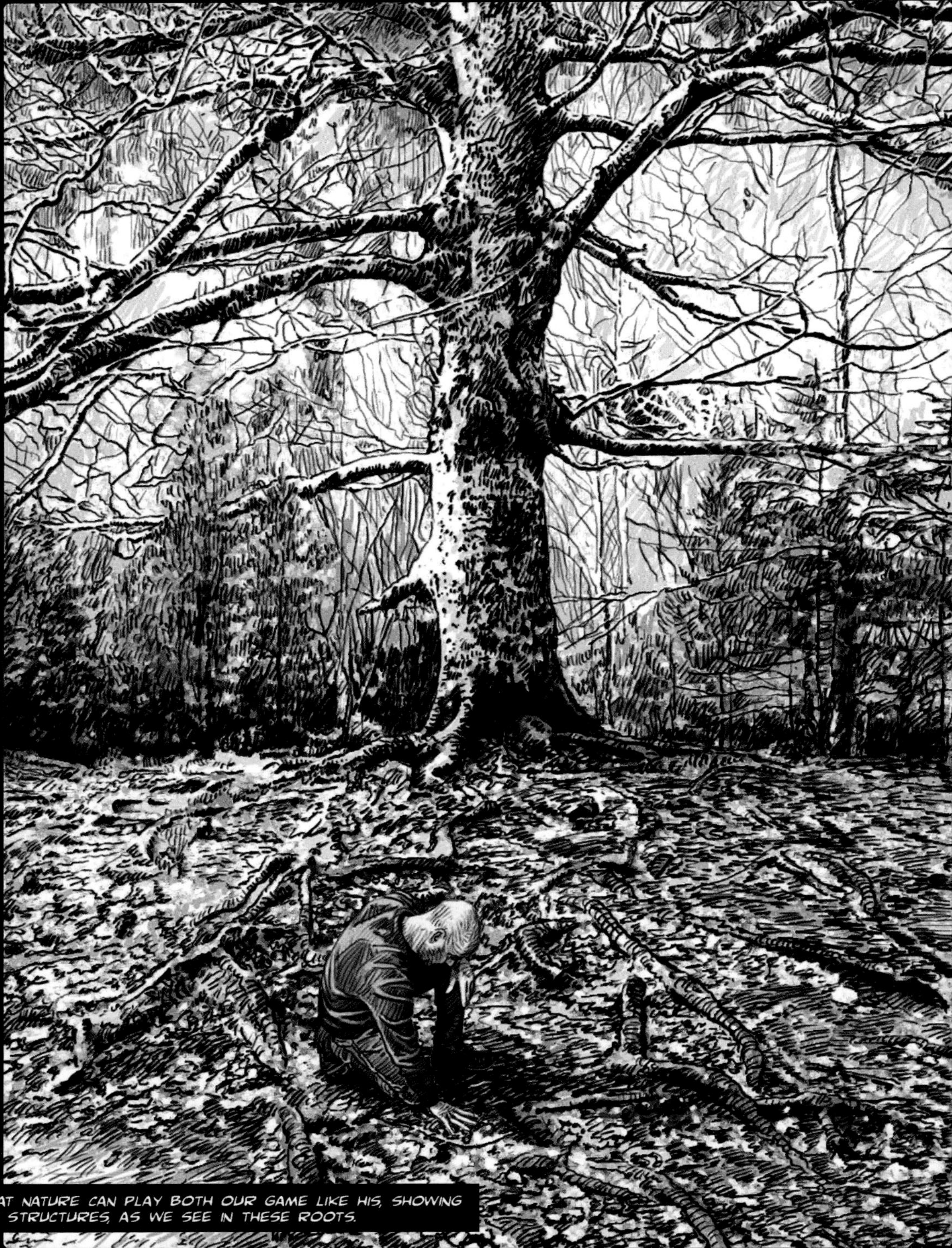
AND SHOWS THAT NATURE CAN PLAY BOTH OUR GAME LIKE HIS, SHOWING THEIR ORGANICS STRUCTURES, AS WE SEE IN THESE ROOTS.

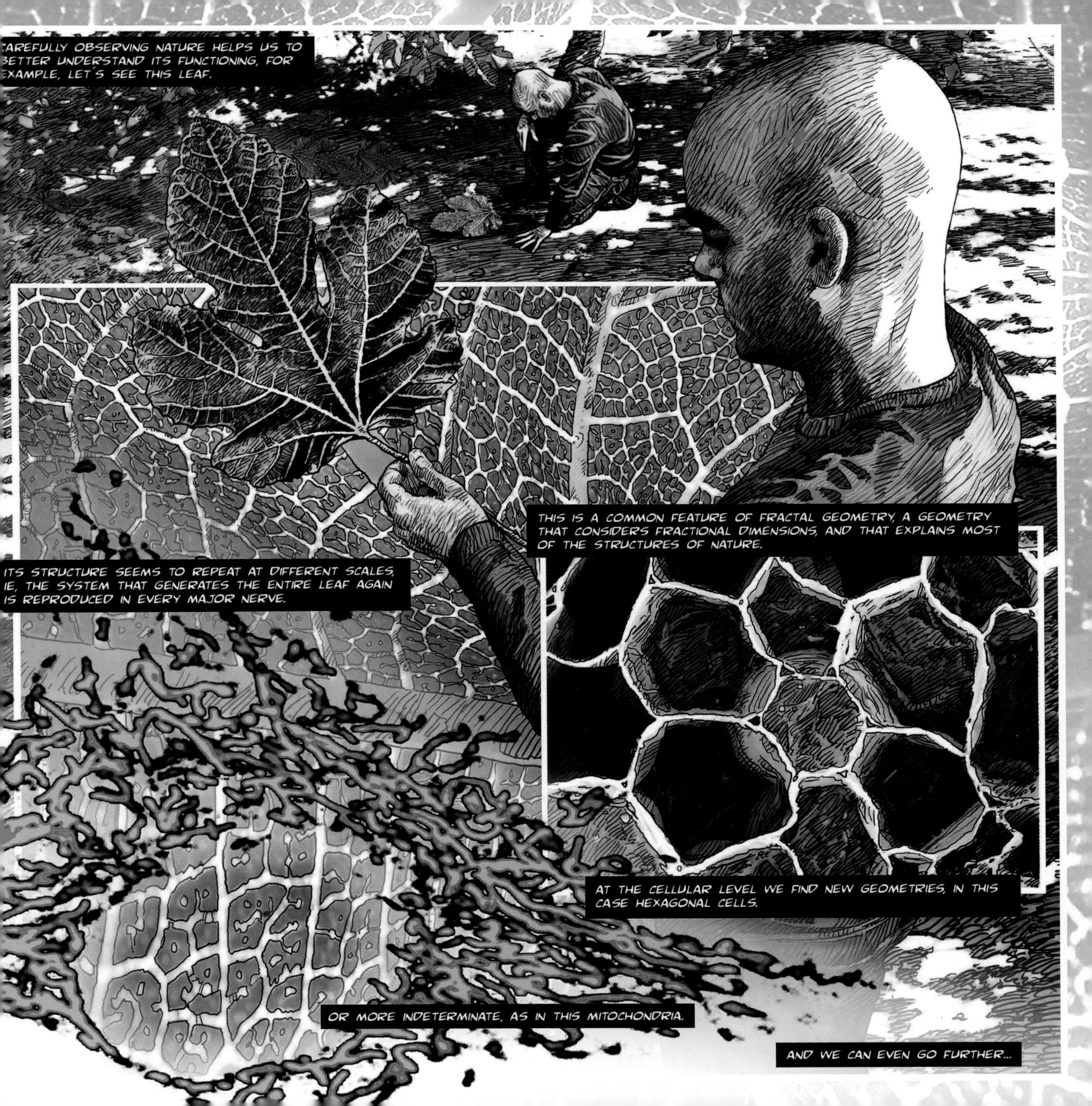
CAREFULLY OBSERVING NATURE HELPS US TO BETTER UNDERSTAND ITS FUNCTIONING, FOR EXAMPLE, LET'S SEE THIS LEAF.
ITS STRUCTURE SEEMS TO REPEAT AT DIFFERENT SCALES, IE, THE SYSTEM THAT GENERATES THE ENTIRE LEAF AGAIN IS REPRODUCED IN EVERY MAJOR NERVE.
THIS IS A COMMON FEATURE OF FRACTAL GEOMETRY, A GEOMETRY THAT CONSIDERS FRACTIONAL DIMENSIONS, AND THAT EXPLAINS MOST OF THE STRUCTURES OF NATURE.
AT THE CELLULAR LEVEL WE FIND NEW GEOMETRIES, IN THIS CASE HEXAGONAL CELLS.
OR MORE INDETERMINATE, AS IN THIS MITOCHONDRIA.
AND WE CAN EVEN GO FURTHER...

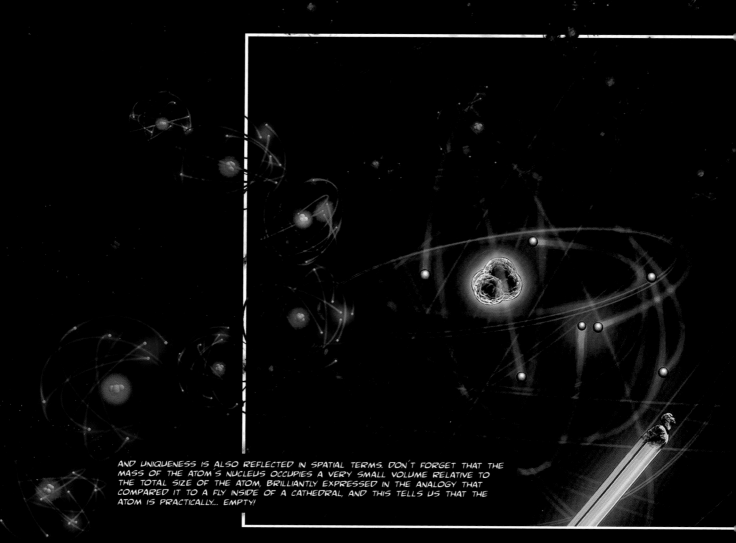

AT MOLECULAR AND ATOMIC LEVELS, WHERE
ENTIRELY DIFFERENT LAWS GOVERN.

CONCEPTS AS ELECTRIC POTENTIAL, VAN DER WAALS FORCES OR
HYDROGEN BONDS, ARE CRUCIAL IN THE FORMATION OF MATTER,
THOUGH THEY SOUND IRRELEVANT IN OUR EVERYDAY WORLD.

AND UNIQUENESS IS ALSO REFLECTED IN SPATIAL TERMS. DON'T FORGET THAT THE
MASS OF THE ATOM'S NUCLEUS OCCUPIES A VERY SMALL VOLUME RELATIVE TO
THE TOTAL SIZE OF THE ATOM, BRILLIANTLY EXPRESSED IN THE ANALOGY THAT
COMPARED IT TO A FLY INSIDE OF A CATHEDRAL, AND THIS TELLS US THAT THE
ATOM IS PRACTICALLY... EMPTY!

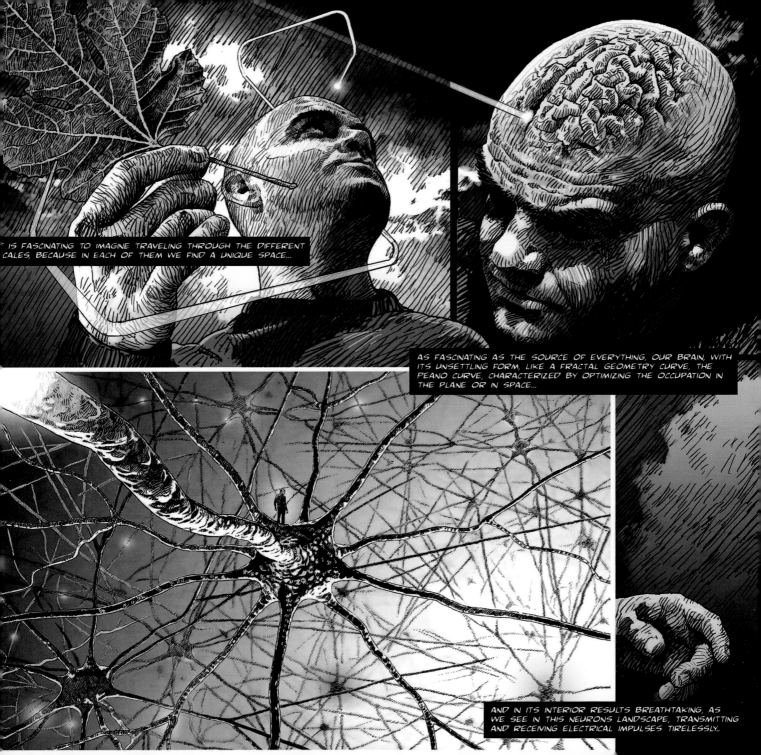

...IS FASCINATING TO IMAGINE TRAVELING THROUGH THE DIFFERENT SCALES, BECAUSE IN EACH OF THEM WE FIND A UNIQUE SPACE...

AS FASCINATING AS THE SOURCE OF EVERYTHING, OUR BRAIN, WITH ITS UNSETTLING FORM, LIKE A FRACTAL GEOMETRY CURVE, THE PEANO CURVE, CHARACTERIZED BY OPTIMIZING THE OCCUPATION IN THE PLANE OR IN SPACE...

AND IN ITS INTERIOR RESULTS BREATHTAKING, AS WE SEE IN THIS NEURONS LANDSCAPE, TRANSMITTING AND RECEIVING ELECTRICAL IMPULSES TIRELESSLY..

AND BACK TO REALITY, WE REALIZE THAT DESPITE
THE DIFFERENCES IN SCALE, SHAPE IS GOVERNED
BY SIMILAR PARAMETERS.

LIKE A TREE FORMATION, THAT CLEARLY REMINISCENT
IN ITS STRUCTURE, TO THE WORLD OF NEURONS WE
SAW PREVIOUSLY.

AND ONCE MORE, FRACTAL GEOMETRY IS BEHIND EACH FORM. IS SURPRISING TH
IT IS NOT SUBJECT OF STUDY IN SCHOOLS... FROM HERE, I HIGHLY RECOMMEND
READING "THE FRACTAL GEOMETRY OF NATURE" BY BENOIT MANDELBROT.

ANOTHER OBJECTIVE OF THIS TRIP IS TO SHOW HOW THE OBSERVATION OF OUR ENVIRONMENT,
PROVIDES EVERYTHING WE NEED TO UNDERSTAND OR MAKE ARCHITECTURE.

FOR EXAMPLE, IN THIS LANDSCAPE WE CAN EXTRACT WEALTH FROM A PERSPECTIV
FORMED BY ORGANIC ELEMENTS, AND HOW SHADOWS CAN BE AS IMPORTANT AS
THE ITEMS THAT ARE LINKED TO THEM, OR THE CONTRAST BETWEEN A COZY PLA
AND PROTECTED, AND A COMPLETELY OPEN ILLUMINATED SPACE.

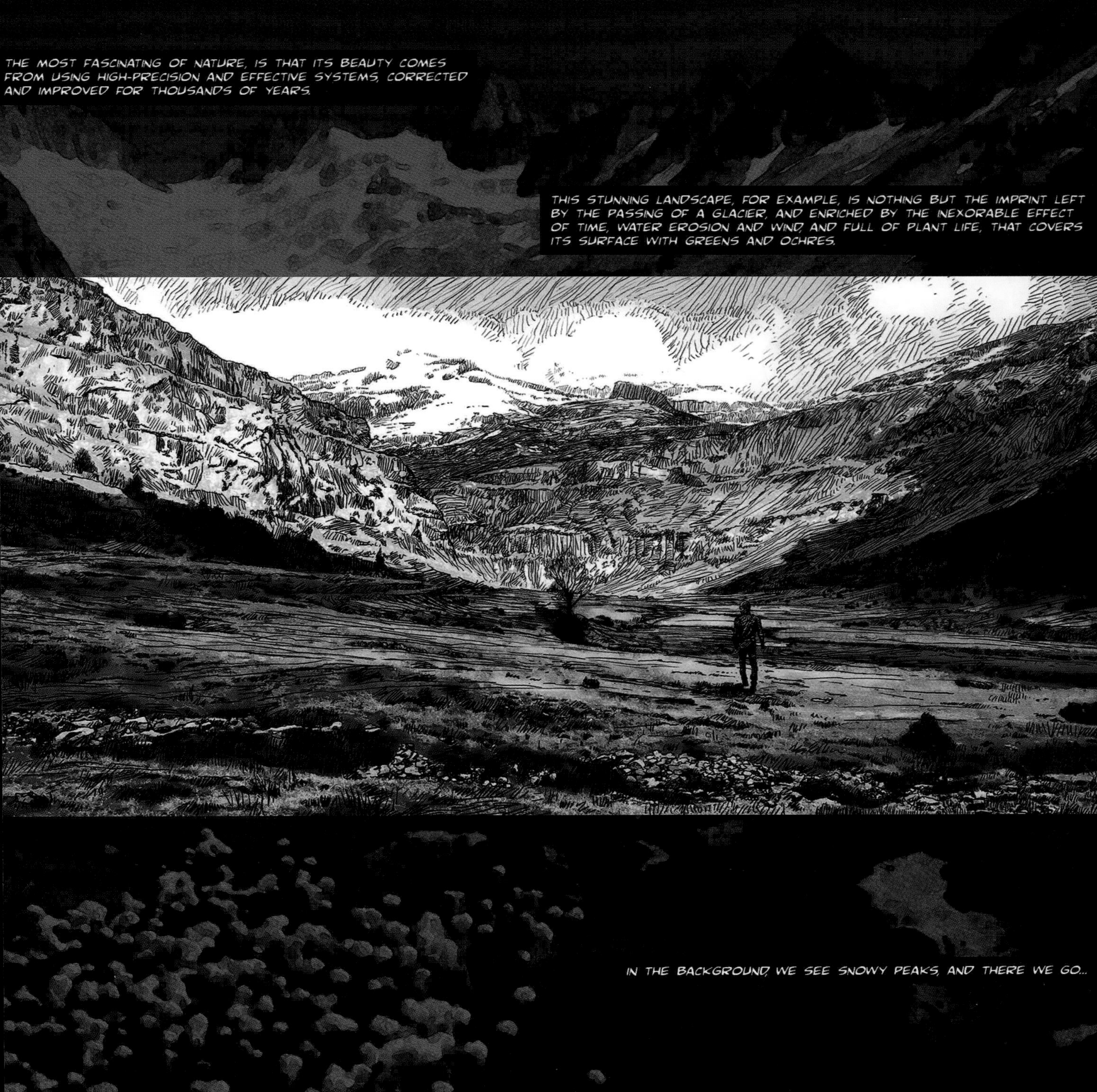
THE MOST FASCINATING OF NATURE, IS THAT ITS BEAUTY COMES FROM USING HIGH-PRECISION AND EFFECTIVE SYSTEMS, CORRECTED AND IMPROVED FOR THOUSANDS OF YEARS.
THIS STUNNING LANDSCAPE, FOR EXAMPLE, IS NOTHING BUT THE IMPRINT LEFT BY THE PASSING OF A GLACIER, AND ENRICHED BY THE INEXORABLE EFFECT OF TIME, WATER EROSION AND WIND, AND FULL OF PLANT LIFE, THAT COVERS ITS SURFACE WITH GREENS AND OCHRES.
IN THE BACKGROUND, WE SEE SNOWY PEAKS, AND THERE WE GO...

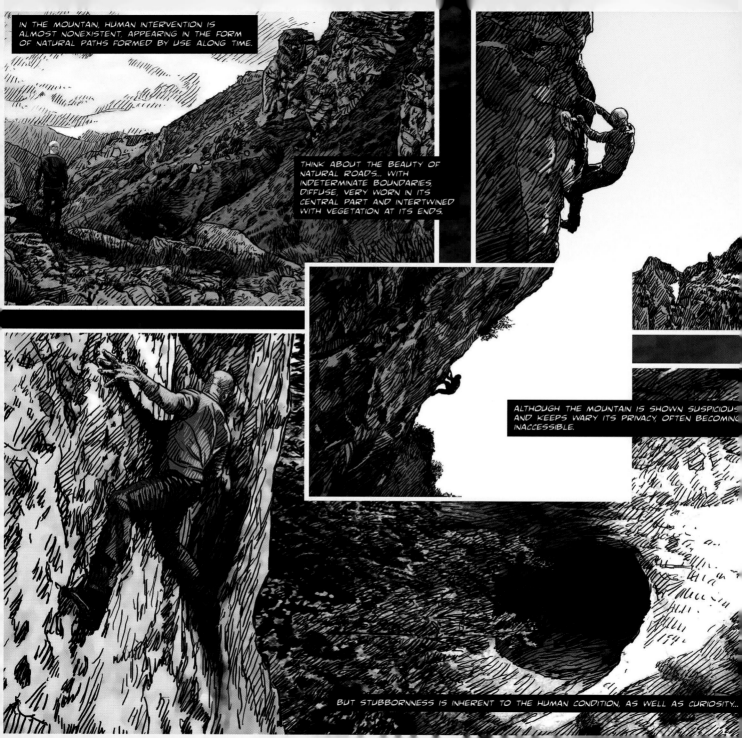

IN THE MOUNTAIN, HUMAN INTERVENTION IS ALMOST NONEXISTENT, APPEARING IN THE FORM OF NATURAL PATHS FORMED BY USE ALONG TIME.

THINK ABOUT THE BEAUTY OF NATURAL ROADS... WITH INDETERMINATE BOUNDARIES, DIFFUSE, VERY WORN IN ITS CENTRAL PART AND INTERTWINED WITH VEGETATION AT ITS ENDS.

ALTHOUGH THE MOUNTAIN IS SHOWN SUSPICIOUS AND KEEPS WARY ITS PRIVACY, OFTEN BECOMING INACCESSIBLE.

BUT STUBBORNNESS IS INHERENT TO THE HUMAN CONDITION, AS WELL AS CURIOSITY...

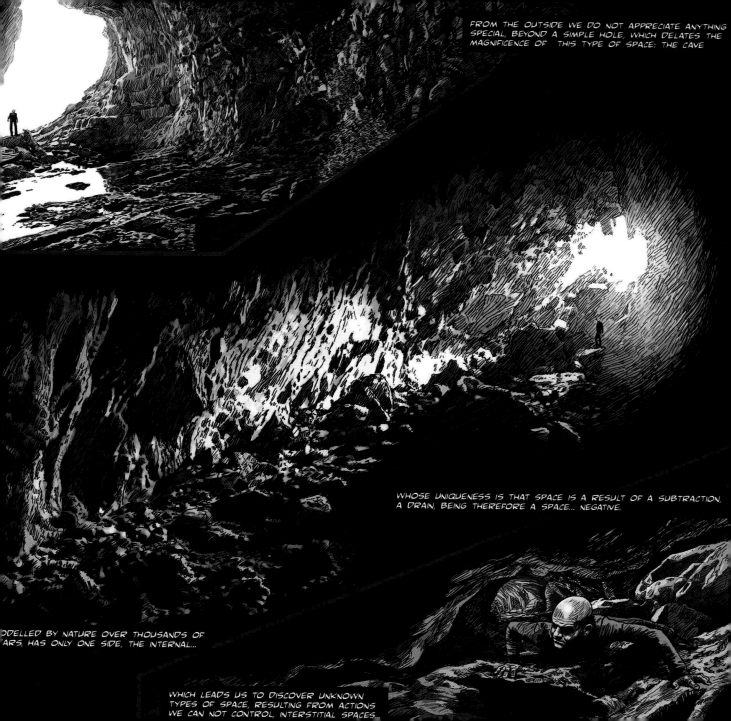

FROM THE OUTSIDE WE DO NOT APPRECIATE ANYTHING SPECIAL, BEYOND A SIMPLE HOLE, WHICH DELATES THE MAGNIFICENCE OF THIS TYPE OF SPACE: THE CAVE

WHOSE UNIQUENESS IS THAT SPACE IS A RESULT OF A SUBTRACTION, A DRAIN, BEING THEREFORE A SPACE... NEGATIVE.

...ODELLED BY NATURE OVER THOUSANDS OF ...ARS, HAS ONLY ONE SIDE, THE INTERNAL...

WHICH LEADS US TO DISCOVER UNKNOWN TYPES OF SPACE, RESULTING FROM ACTIONS WE CAN NOT CONTROL, INTERSTITIAL SPACES...

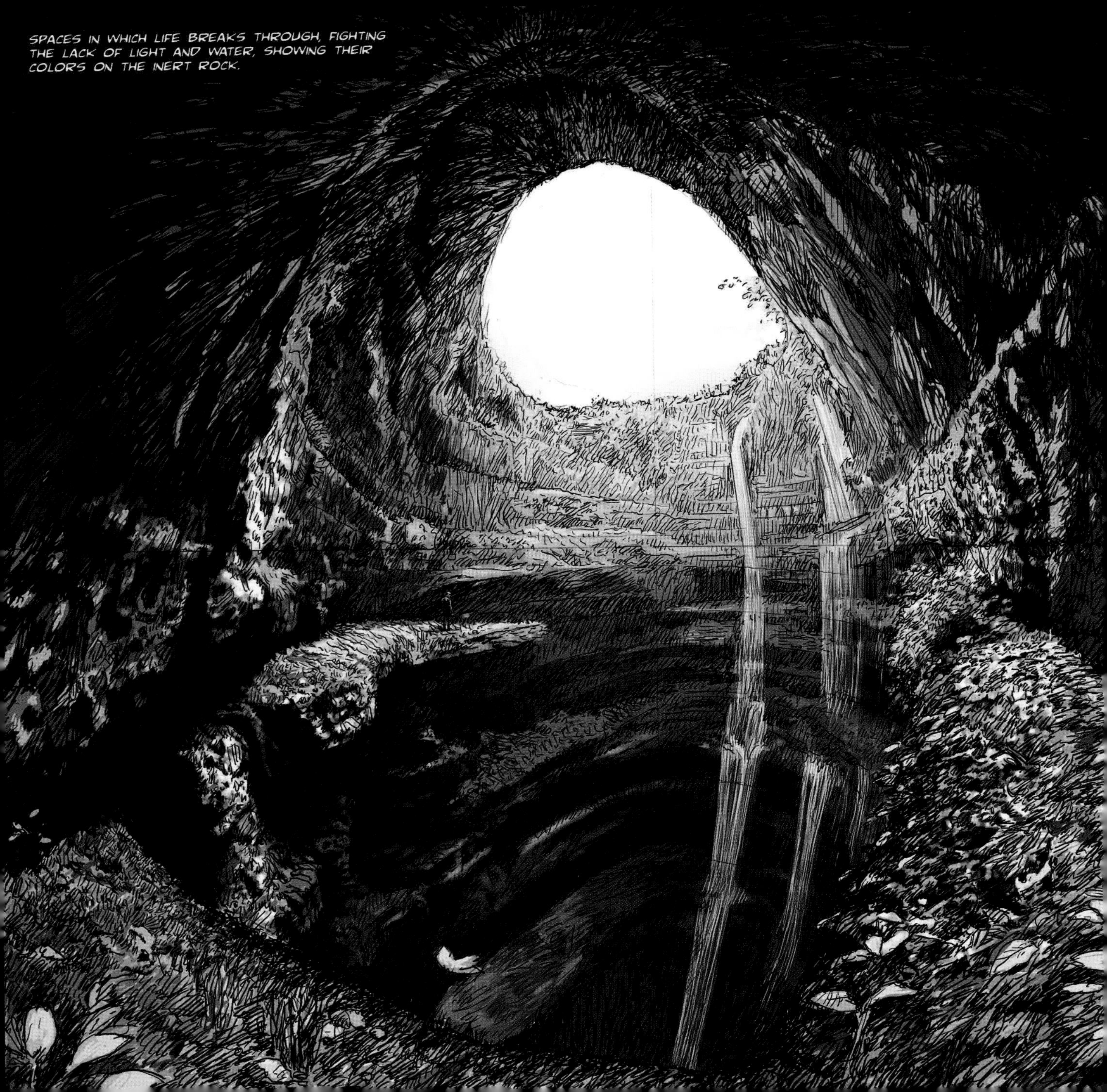
SPACES IN WHICH LIFE BREAKS THROUGH, FIGHTING THE LACK OF LIGHT AND WATER, SHOWING THEIR COLORS ON THE INERT ROCK.

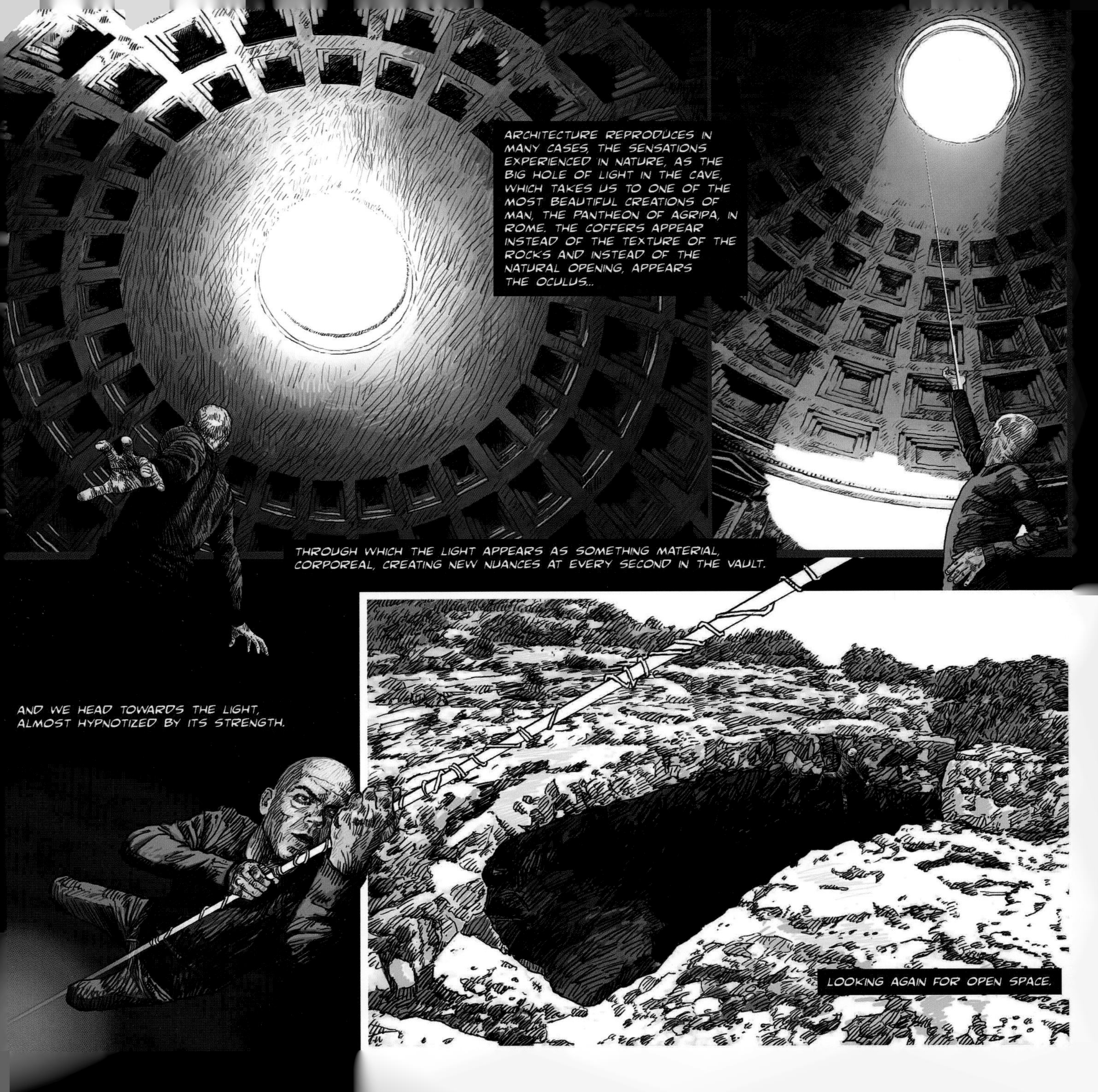
ARCHITECTURE REPRODUCES IN MANY CASES, THE SENSATIONS EXPERIENCED IN NATURE, AS THE BIG HOLE OF LIGHT IN THE CAVE, WHICH TAKES US TO ONE OF THE MOST BEAUTIFUL CREATIONS OF MAN, THE PANTHEON OF AGRIPA, IN ROME. THE COFFERS APPEAR INSTEAD OF THE TEXTURE OF THE ROCKS AND INSTEAD OF THE NATURAL OPENING, APPEARS THE OCULUS...
THROUGH WHICH THE LIGHT APPEARS AS SOMETHING MATERIAL, CORPOREAL, CREATING NEW NUANCES AT EVERY SECOND IN THE VAULT.
AND WE HEAD TOWARDS THE LIGHT, ALMOST HYPNOTIZED BY ITS STRENGTH.
LOOKING AGAIN FOR OPEN SPACE.

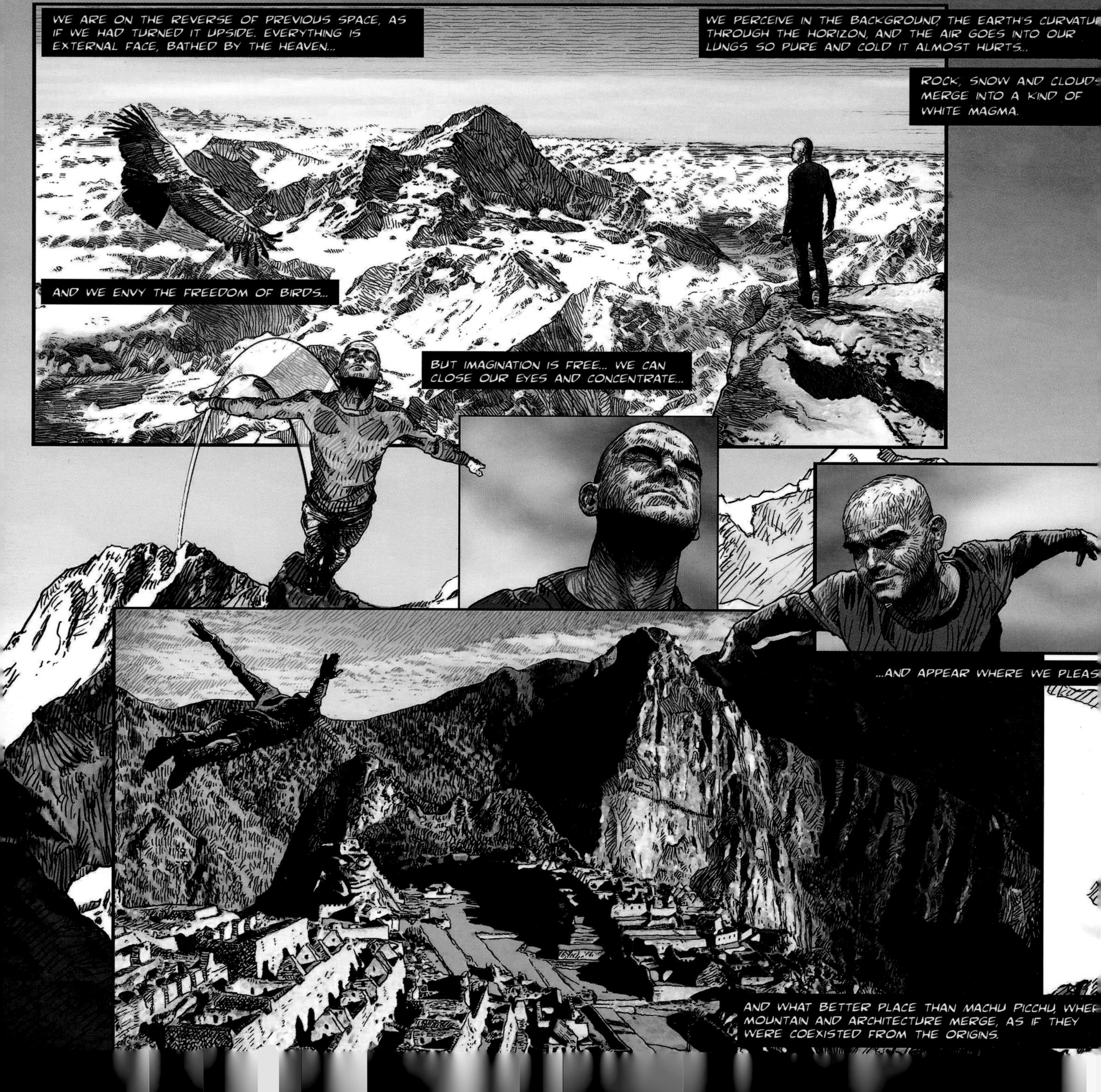
WE ARE ON THE REVERSE OF PREVIOUS SPACE, AS IF WE HAD TURNED IT UPSIDE. EVERYTHING IS EXTERNAL FACE, BATHED BY THE HEAVEN...
WE PERCEIVE IN THE BACKGROUND THE EARTH'S CURVATU THROUGH THE HORIZON, AND THE AIR GOES INTO OUR LUNGS SO PURE AND COLD IT ALMOST HURTS...
ROCK, SNOW AND CLOUDS MERGE INTO A KIND OF WHITE MAGMA.
AND WE ENVY THE FREEDOM OF BIRDS...
BUT IMAGINATION IS FREE... WE CAN CLOSE OUR EYES AND CONCENTRATE...
...AND APPEAR WHERE WE PLEAS
AND WHAT BETTER PLACE THAN MACHU PICCHU, WHER MOUNTAIN AND ARCHITECTURE MERGE, AS IF THEY WERE COEXISTED FROM THE ORIGINS.

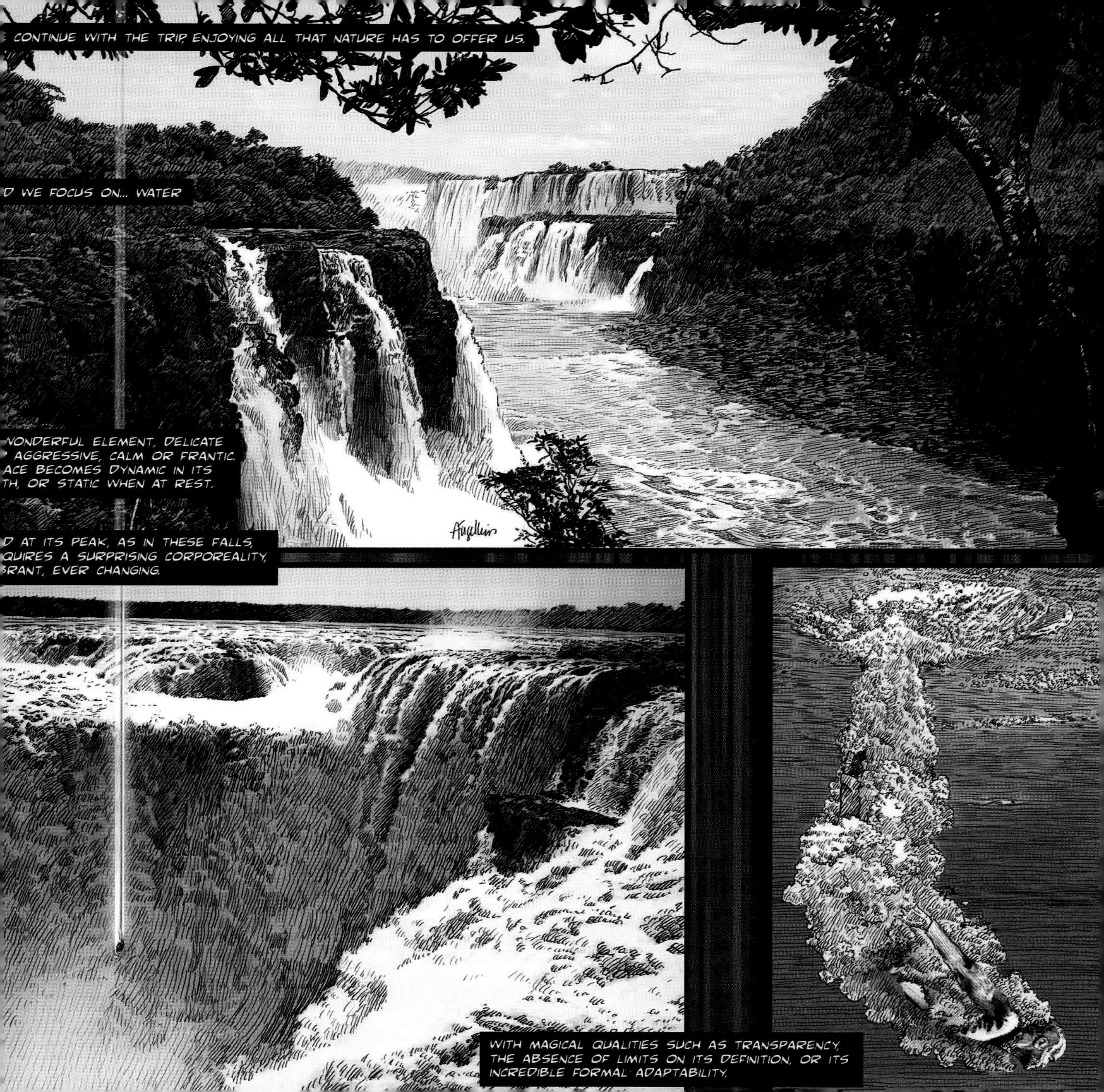
CONTINUE WITH THE TRIP, ENJOYING ALL THAT NATURE HAS TO OFFER US.
D WE FOCUS ON... WATER
WONDERFUL ELEMENT, DELICATE
AGGRESSIVE, CALM OR FRANTIC.
ACE BECOMES DYNAMIC IN ITS
TH, OR STATIC WHEN AT REST.
D AT ITS PEAK, AS IN THESE FALLS,
QUIRES A SURPRISING CORPOREALITY,
RANT, EVER CHANGING.
WITH MAGICAL QUALITIES SUCH AS TRANSPARENCY, THE ABSENCE OF LIMITS ON ITS DEFINITION, OR ITS INCREDIBLE FORMAL ADAPTABILITY.

AS WELL AS BEING VITAL TO THE EXISTENCE OF LIVING BEINGS.

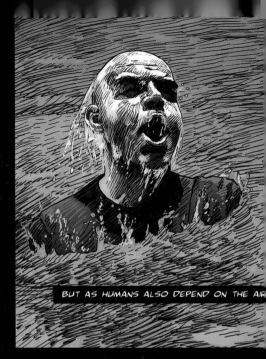

BUT AS HUMANS ALSO DEPEND ON THE AIR

OF ALL THAT WE HAVE SEEN IN NATURE, I DO NOT INTEND TO DISCOVER ANYTHING NEW, WE'VE ALL LIVED WITH HER SINCE WE CAN REMEMBER.

THE OBJECTIVE IS TO ANALYZE IT IN DEPTH, STUDY IT, LOVE IT AND UNDERSTAND IT, BECAUSE IT CONTAINS ALL THE SYSTEMS AND PROCESSES THAT ALLOW US TO CREATE, OR TO UNDERSTAND WHAT HAS BEEN CREATED.

FRACTALS, CREVICES, FLUIDS, FOLDS, LIGHTS AND SHADOWS, COLOR, ODOR, INDETERMINACY, PROBABILITY, CHAOS... IF WE UNDERSTAND ALL THAT NATURE OFFERS US, WE WILL EXPAND OUR MENTAL REPERTOIRE, IN ALL ASPECTS, TO UNSUSPECTED LIMITS

AND, TAKING ADVANTAGE OF THIS BEAUTIFUL SUNSET VIEW, I NOTE THAT IN THE SPACES AND FORMS, OR IN ARCHITECTURE, IT'S NOT ALL SCIENTIFIC KNOWLEDGE. AS HUMAN BEINGS WE HAVE A SPIRITUAL PART, AND WE ARE ABLE TO CREATE A TRANSCENDENT MEANING, AND WITH OUR CREATIONS WE SHOULD CAUSE... EMOTION.

BECAUSE, WHAT IS THE MEANING OF LIFE WITHOUT EMOTION?

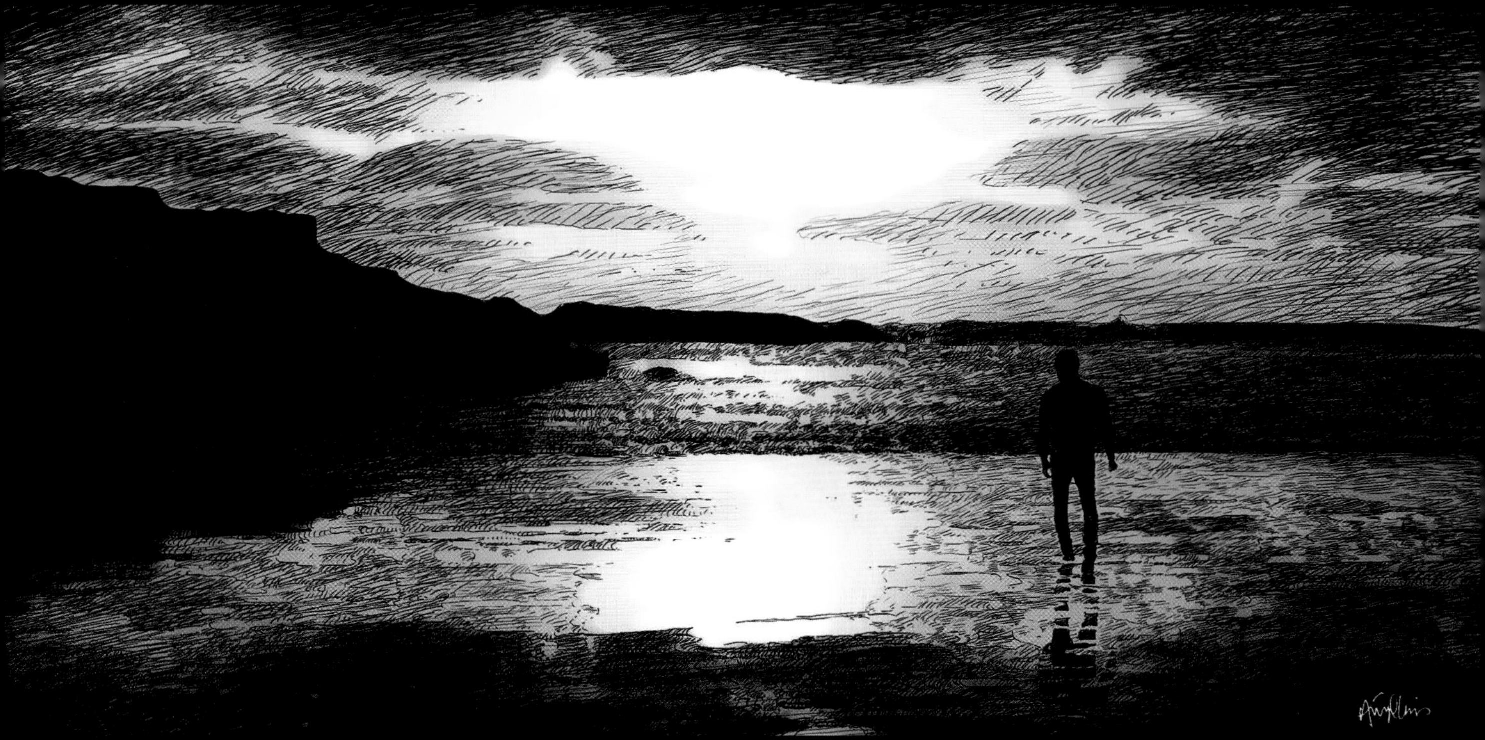

AND WHAT ABOUT ARCHITECTURE?

ARCHITECTURE IS A MEANINGFUL AND PURPOSEFUL ACTION, THAT OCCUPIES A PLACE IN SPACE AND INTERACTS INTEGRALLY WITH HUMANS. AND HAS TO BE ABLE TO GENERATE, CONSCIOUSLY, EMOTION IN USERS THEREOF. AND WE CAN EXTRACT THAT EMOTION FROM THE ANALYSIS AND REINTERPRETATION OF NATURAL PROCESSES.

AND FOR THAT MATTER, LET'S GO INTO THE OCEAN...

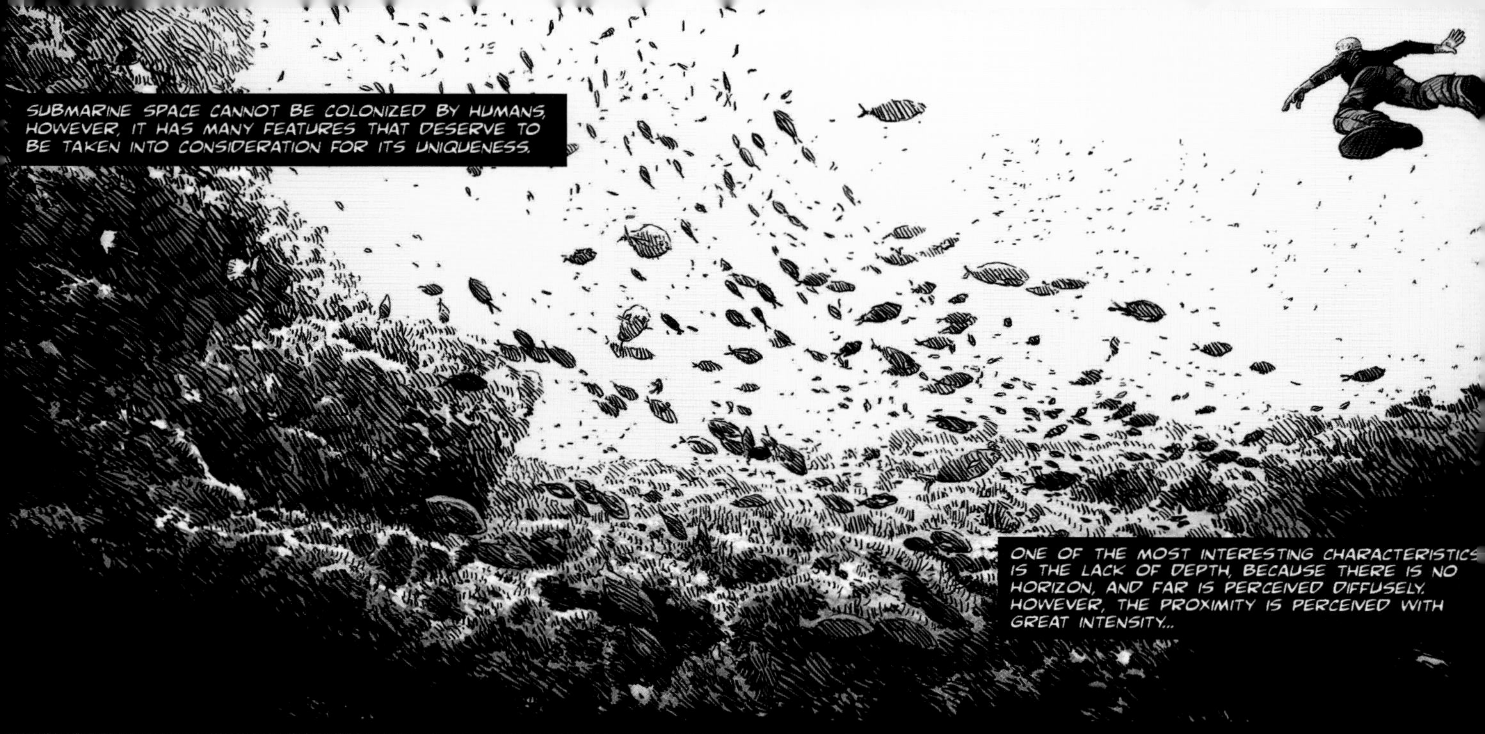
SUBMARINE SPACE CANNOT BE COLONIZED BY HUMANS, HOWEVER, IT HAS MANY FEATURES THAT DESERVE TO BE TAKEN INTO CONSIDERATION FOR ITS UNIQUENESS.
ONE OF THE MOST INTERESTING CHARACTERISTICS IS THE LACK OF DEPTH, BECAUSE THERE IS NO HORIZON, AND FAR IS PERCEIVED DIFFUSELY. HOWEVER, THE PROXIMITY IS PERCEIVED WITH GREAT INTENSITY...
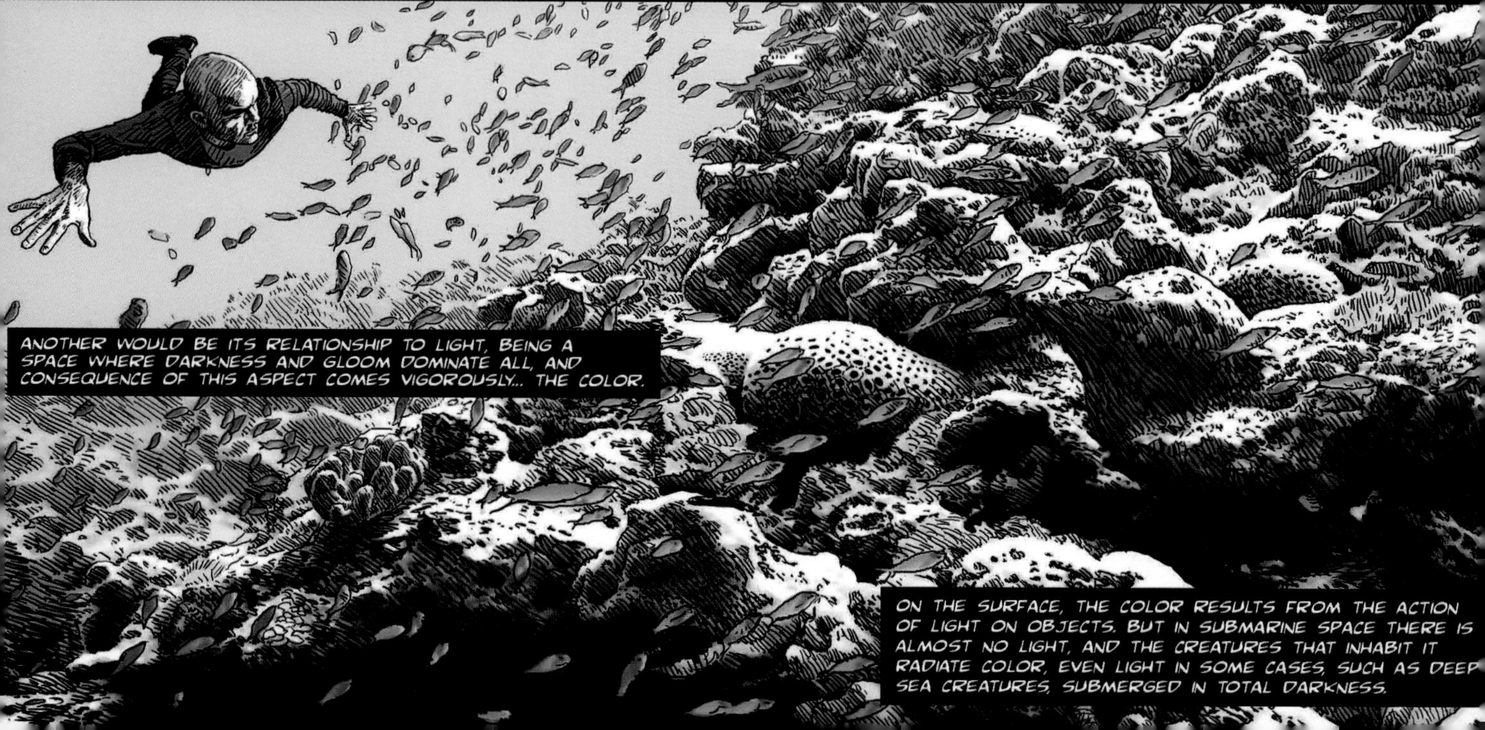
ANOTHER WOULD BE ITS RELATIONSHIP TO LIGHT, BEING A SPACE WHERE DARKNESS AND GLOOM DOMINATE ALL, AND CONSEQUENCE OF THIS ASPECT COMES VIGOROUSLY... THE COLOR.
ON THE SURFACE, THE COLOR RESULTS FROM THE ACTION OF LIGHT ON OBJECTS. BUT IN SUBMARINE SPACE THERE IS ALMOST NO LIGHT, AND THE CREATURES THAT INHABIT IT RADIATE COLOR, EVEN LIGHT IN SOME CASES, SUCH AS DEEP SEA CREATURES, SUBMERGED IN TOTAL DARKNESS.

THE LACK OF DEPTH IN THE SEABED CAN CAUSE EMOTIONS OF ENORMOUS INTENSITY, ONE OF THEM IS FEAR, BECAUSE WE CAN NOT ANTICIPATE WHAT LIES AHEAD IN THE DISTANCE, ACCENTUATED BY OUR CLUMSINESS UNDERWATER.

AND WHAT IS IF COMING IS A GREAT WHITE SHARK?

...NO, IT'S AN INOFFENSIVE BUT IMPOSING BLUE WHALE.

THIS CREATES ANOTHER STRONG EMOTION LINKED TO THE DIFFERENCE OF SCALE, AND THE SIZE OF THE HUGE WHALE OVERWHELMS US EVEN THOUGH WE KNOW THAT THERE IS NO DANGER.

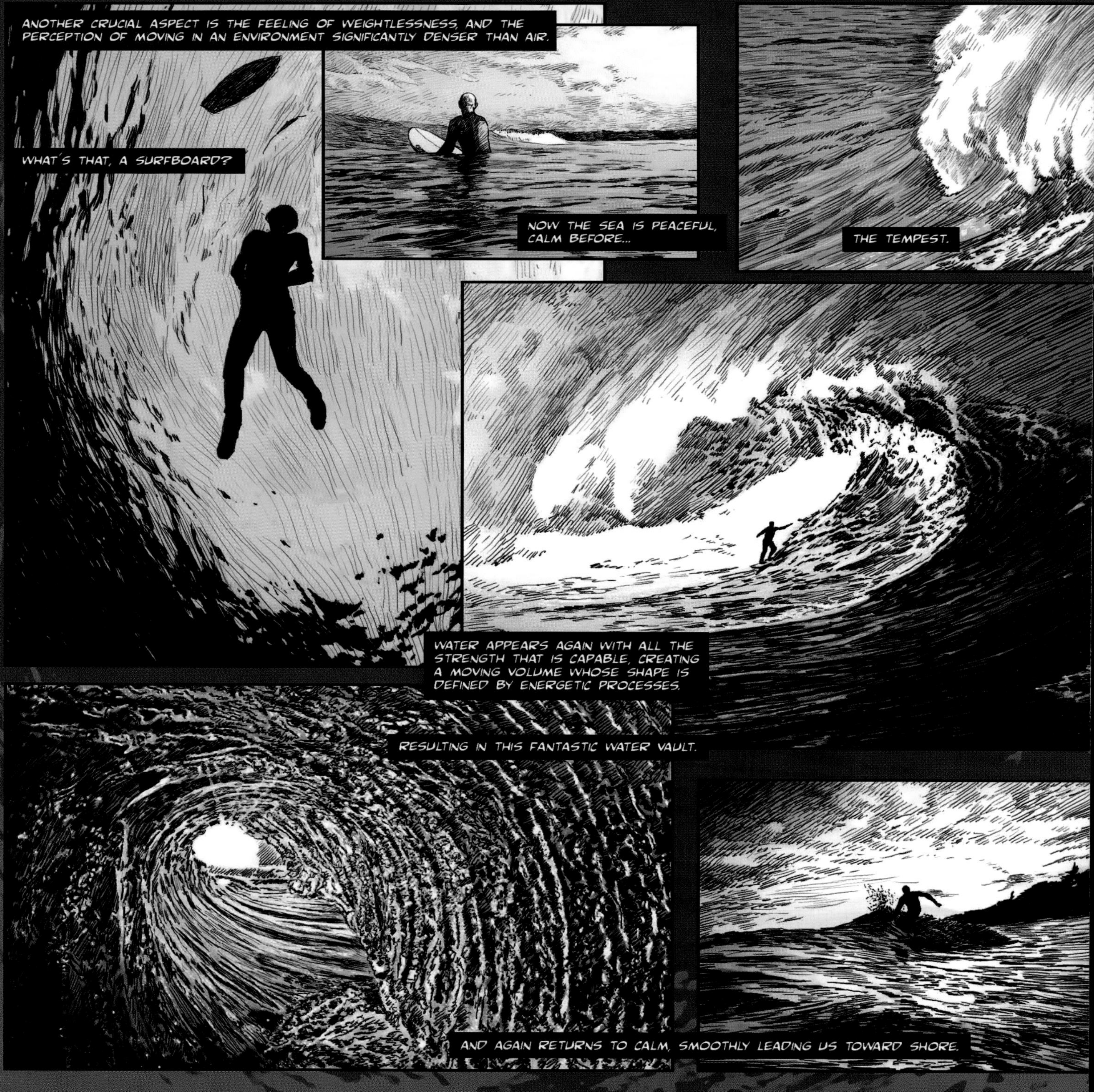
ANOTHER CRUCIAL ASPECT IS THE FEELING OF WEIGHTLESSNESS, AND THE PERCEPTION OF MOVING IN AN ENVIRONMENT SIGNIFICANTLY DENSER THAN AIR.
WHAT´S THAT, A SURFBOARD?
NOW THE SEA IS PEACEFUL, CALM BEFORE...
THE TEMPEST.
WATER APPEARS AGAIN WITH ALL THE STRENGTH THAT IS CAPABLE, CREATING A MOVING VOLUME WHOSE SHAPE IS DEFINED BY ENERGETIC PROCESSES.
RESULTING IN THIS FANTASTIC WATER VAULT.
AND AGAIN RETURNS TO CALM, SMOOTHLY LEADING US TOWARD SHORE.

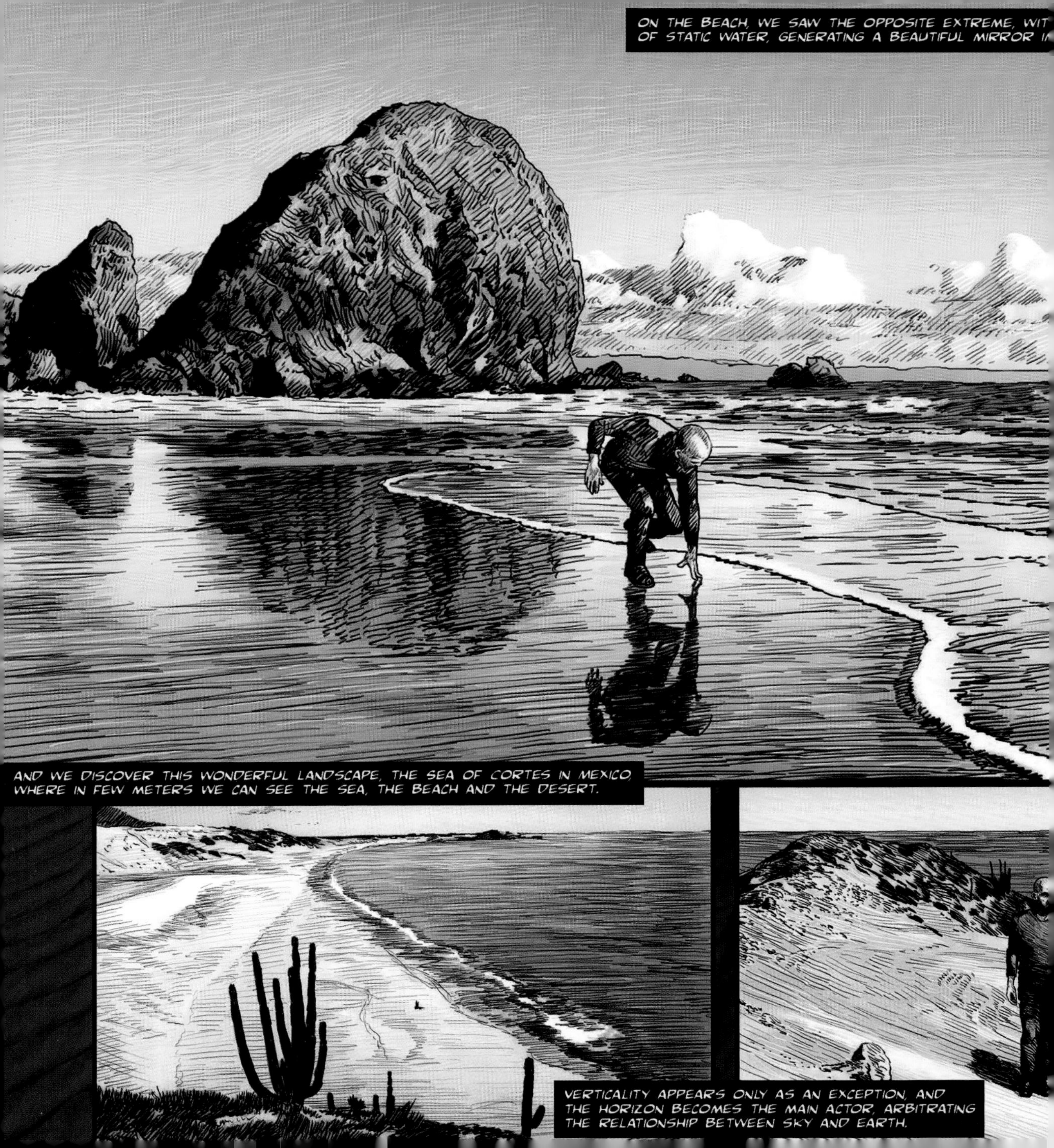
ON THE BEACH, WE SAW THE OPPOSITE EXTREME, WIT
OF STATIC WATER, GENERATING A BEAUTIFUL MIRROR I
AND WE DISCOVER THIS WONDERFUL LANDSCAPE, THE SEA OF CORTES IN MEXICO, WHERE IN FEW METERS WE CAN SEE THE SEA, THE BEACH AND THE DESERT.
VERTICALITY APPEARS ONLY AS AN EXCEPTION, AND THE HORIZON BECOMES THE MAIN ACTOR, ARBITRATING THE RELATIONSHIP BETWEEN SKY AND EARTH.

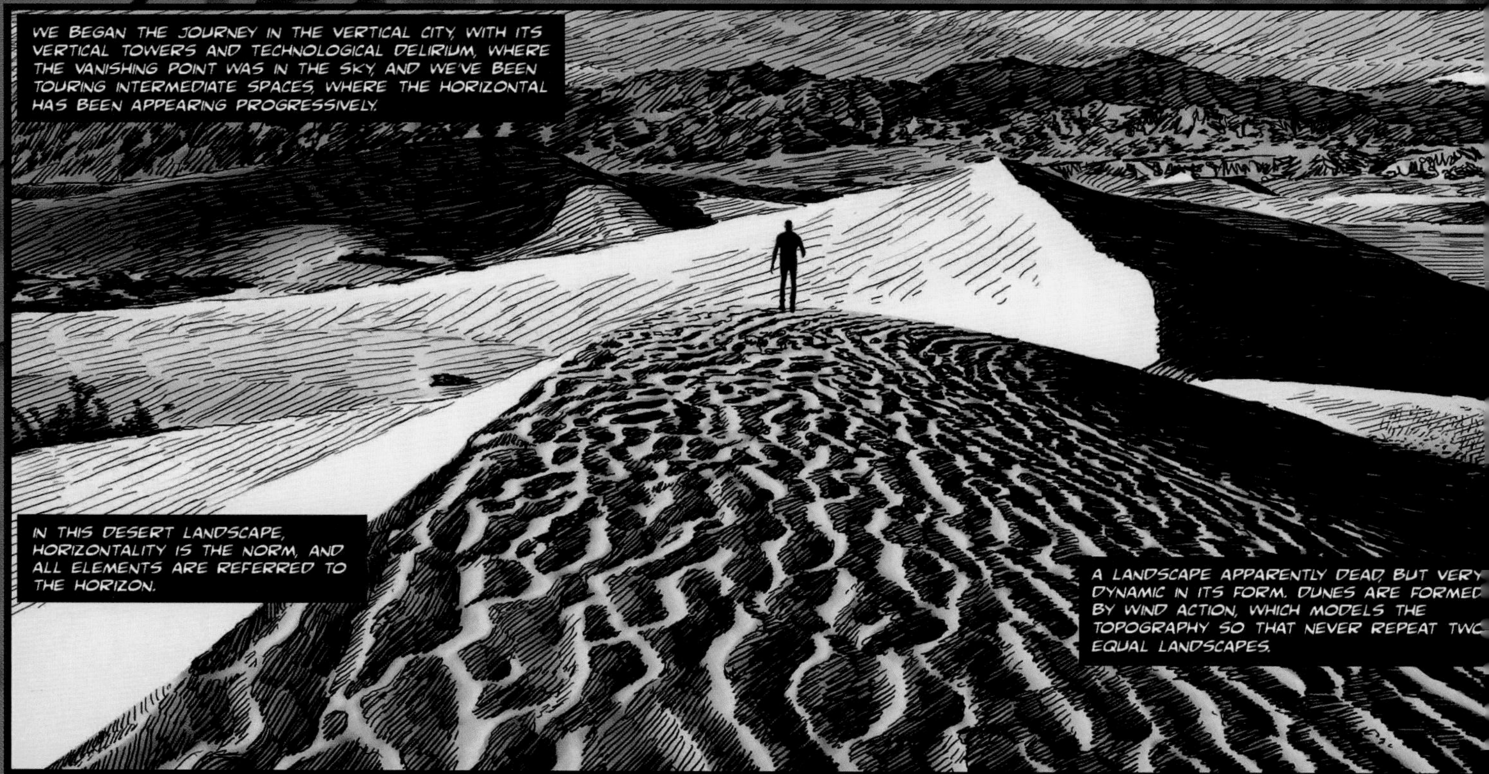
WE BEGAN THE JOURNEY IN THE VERTICAL CITY, WITH ITS VERTICAL TOWERS AND TECHNOLOGICAL DELIRIUM, WHERE THE VANISHING POINT WAS IN THE SKY, AND WE'VE BEEN TOURING INTERMEDIATE SPACES, WHERE THE HORIZONTAL HAS BEEN APPEARING PROGRESSIVELY.
IN THIS DESERT LANDSCAPE, HORIZONTALITY IS THE NORM, AND ALL ELEMENTS ARE REFERRED TO THE HORIZON.
A LANDSCAPE APPARENTLY DEAD, BUT VERY DYNAMIC IN ITS FORM. DUNES ARE FORMED BY WIND ACTION, WHICH MODELS THE TOPOGRAPHY SO THAT NEVER REPEAT TWO EQUAL LANDSCAPES.

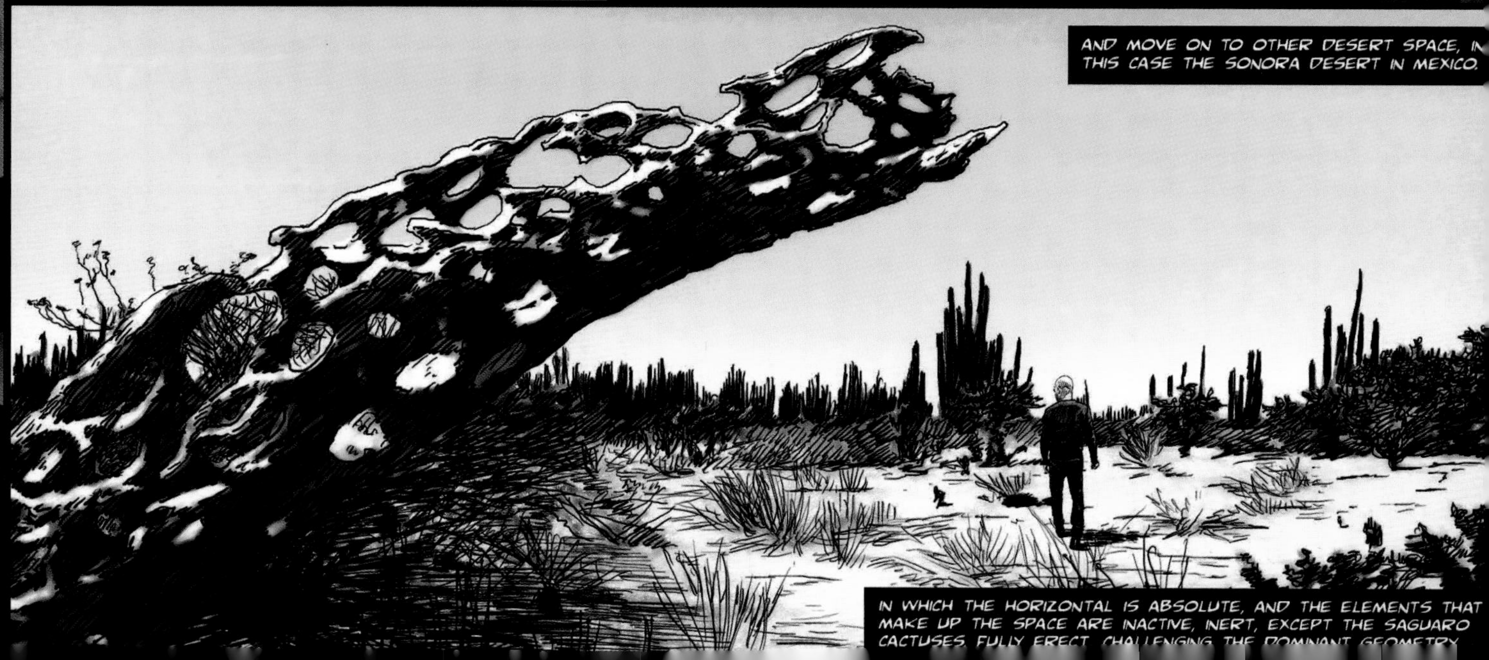
AND MOVE ON TO OTHER DESERT SPACE, IN THIS CASE THE SONORA DESERT IN MEXICO.
IN WHICH THE HORIZONTAL IS ABSOLUTE, AND THE ELEMENTS THAT MAKE UP THE SPACE ARE INACTIVE, INERT, EXCEPT THE SAGUARO CACTUSES, FULLY ERECT, CHALLENGING THE DOMINANT GEOMETRY.

BUT EVEN VEGETATION DISAPPEARS
AND THERE IS ONLY ROCK AND DUST.

TWO GREAT AMORPHOUS MASSES DEFINE SPACE, HEAVEN AND
EARTH, SEPARATED BY A STRAIGHT LINE, THE HORIZON.

AND AS A LAST FORMAL GESTURE, THE COLOSSAL ROCK FORMATIONS OF
MONUMENT VALLEY APPEAR, AS HUGE DOORS TO THE INDETERMINATE, THE UNKNOWN...

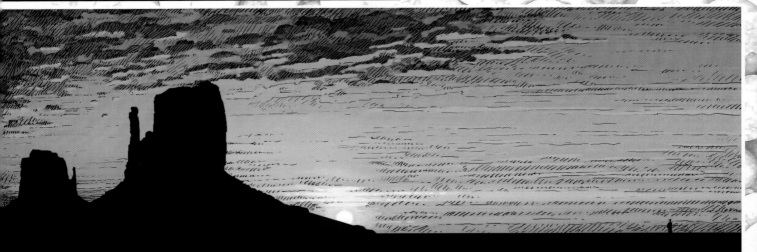

...THE HORIZON BECOMES TINGED WITH RED AND THE
SPACE IS REDUCED TO ITS MINIMUM EXPRESSION...

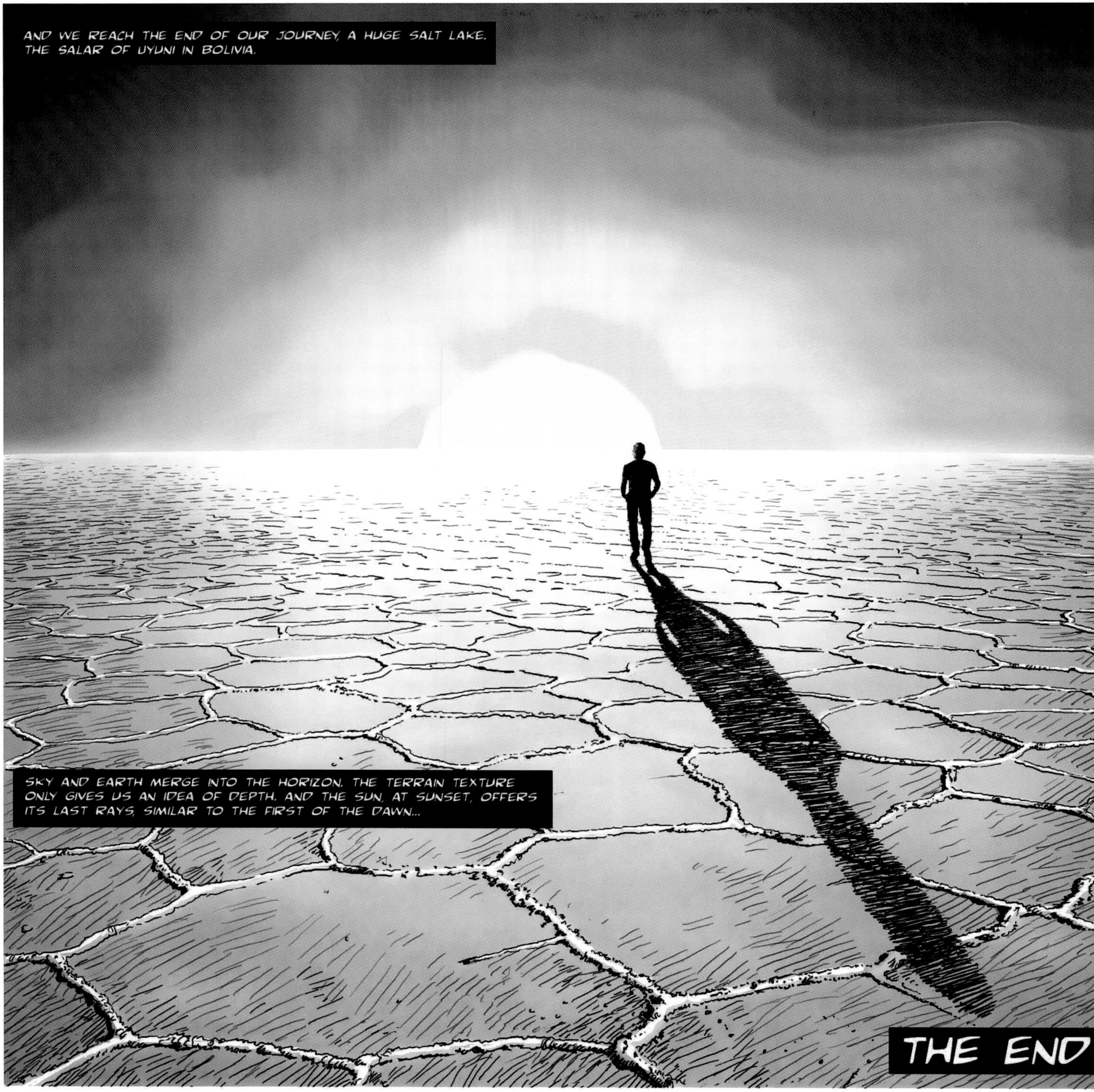
AND WE REACH THE END OF OUR JOURNEY, A HUGE SALT LAKE. THE SALAR OF UYUNI IN BOLIVIA.
SKY AND EARTH MERGE INTO THE HORIZON. THE TERRAIN TEXTURE ONLY GIVES US AN IDEA OF DEPTH. AND THE SUN, AT SUNSET, OFFERS ITS LAST RAYS, SIMILAR TO THE FIRST OF THE DAWN...
THE END

And this is all... for now.

What you have seen is the result of six months of hard work. Over four hundred handmade drawings and more than two thousand hours drawing. But I enjoyed every line and it has been tremendously rewarding. After thirty years drawing I think that, thanks to this work, I draw now much better than six months ago.

I would have continued if it were not my other passion, architecture, also requires a lot of dedication. At least for me, drawing is also architecture, and I don´t conceive designning without drawing. Both in the process of creation and development.

Many years ago, when I began to develop as a future architect, we did not have the technology of today, and we had no choice but to draw everything by hand. Then the new technologies came, 3d programs, Cad, which represented a huge contribution and advancement to facilitate our work. But these tools are complementary and should not ever replace the hand drawing.

The drawing is the purest way to express what we think, and it comes directly from the impulses that our brain transmits to our hand, without intermediaries. An architect is forged solving problems in the construction, and there is no better tool than the sketch by hand, to clarify any doubts, and to improvise solutions or new ideas effectively.

It allows us to capture the emotions that produce environmental observation and through the frame, lines, colors..., select what we want to empower to convey these emotions.

And that's what I've tried to capture through drawings and texts in this work: emotion. If I have succeeded, even if it´s only with one of the drawings, the effort will have been worthwhile.

I hope this is the first of many works, where I will try to complete the issues covered and introduce new ones.

This is a point and followed so sure we'll meet again.

A big hug!

Ángel Luis Tendero (ALT)

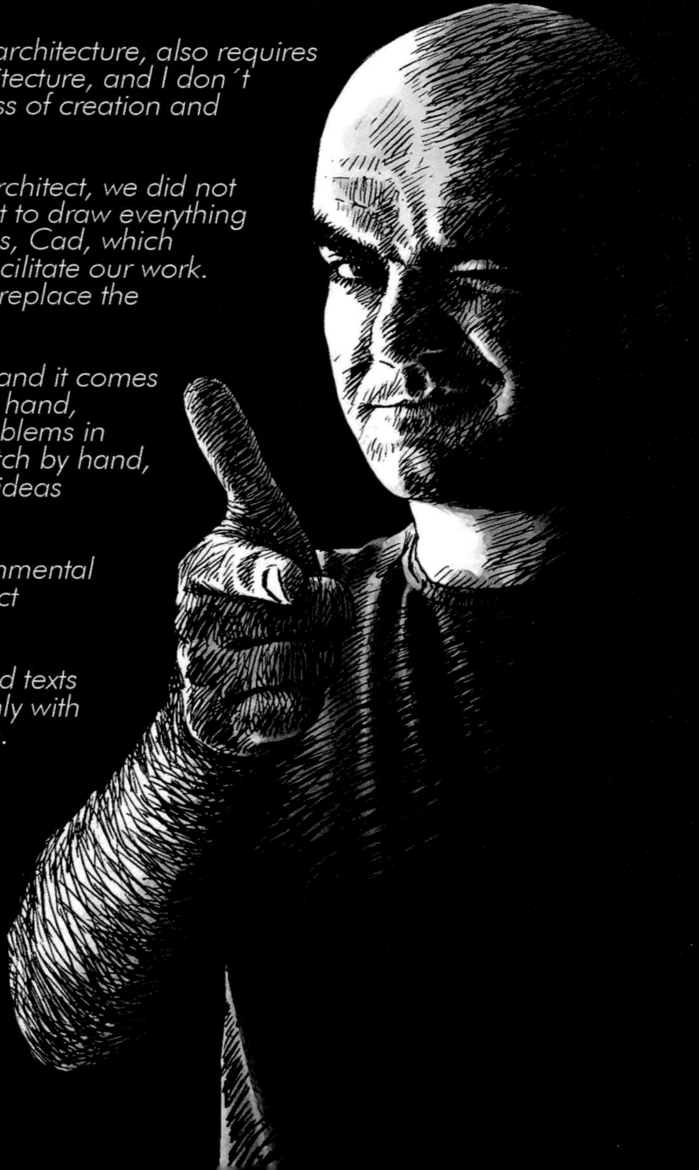

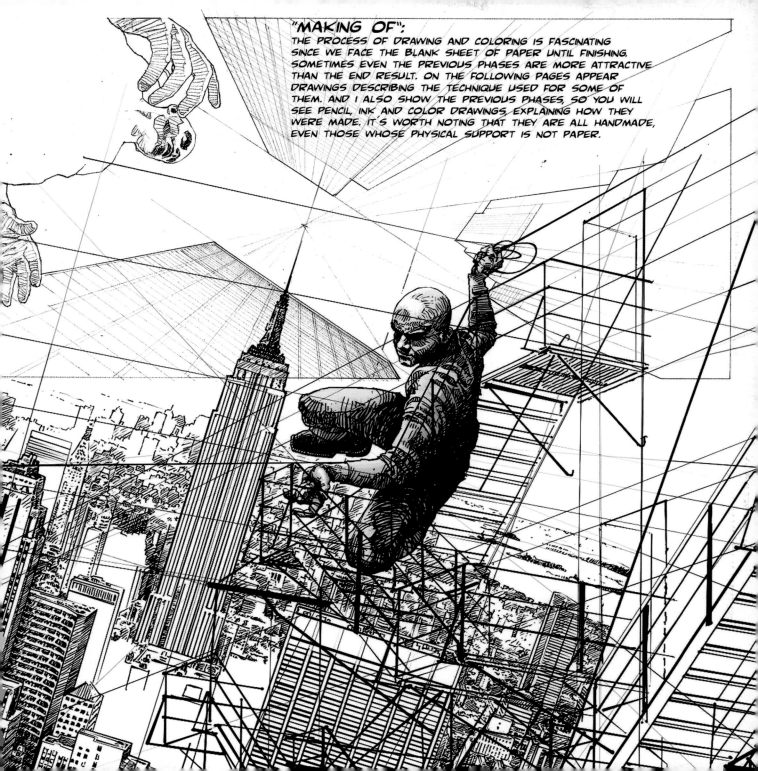

"MAKING OF":
THE PROCESS OF DRAWING AND COLORING IS FASCINATING
SINCE WE FACE THE BLANK SHEET OF PAPER UNTIL FINISHING.
SOMETIMES EVEN THE PREVIOUS PHASES ARE MORE ATTRACTIVE
THAN THE END RESULT. ON THE FOLLOWING PAGES APPEAR
DRAWINGS DESCRIBING THE TECHNIQUE USED FOR SOME OF
THEM. AND I ALSO SHOW THE PREVIOUS PHASES, SO YOU WILL
SEE PENCIL, INK AND COLOR DRAWINGS EXPLAINING HOW THEY
WERE MADE. IT'S WORTH NOTING THAT THEY ARE ALL HANDMADE,
EVEN THOSE WHOSE PHYSICAL SUPPORT IS NOT PAPER.

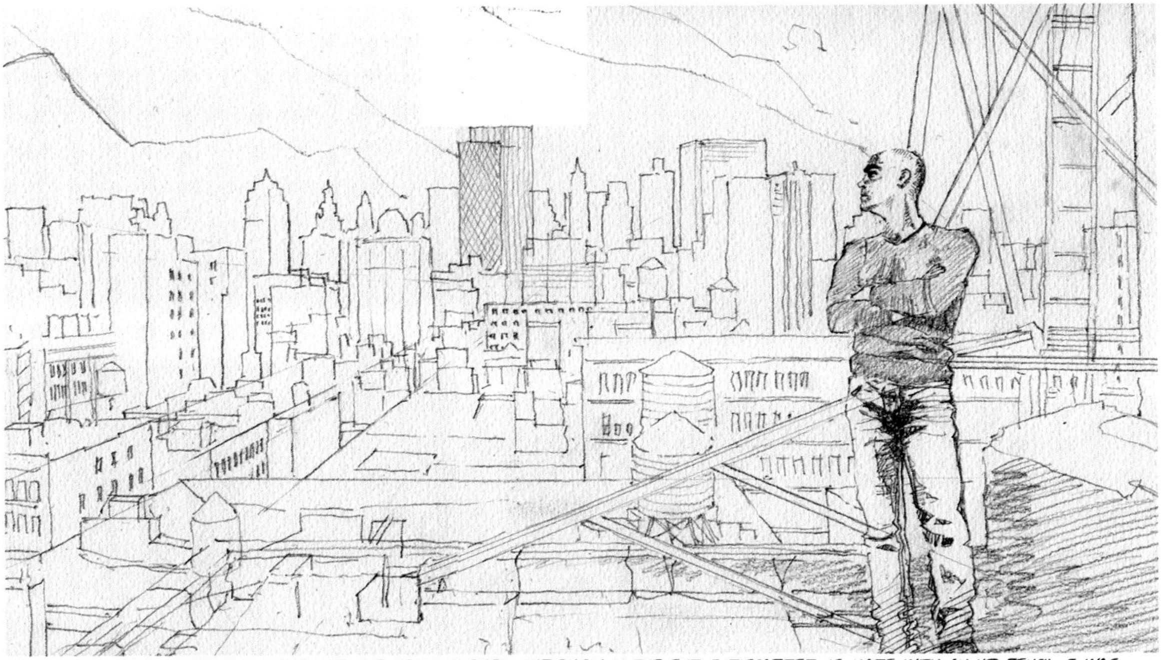

THIS IS THE FIRST DRAWING I MADE FOR THE COMIC THOUGH, CURIOUSLY, IN THE END I DISCARDED. IS MADE WITH AN HB PENCIL. I WAS FINDING THE STYLE OF THE WHOLE COMIC, AND THIS DID NOT FIT WITH THE REST. THE DISTINGUISHING FEATURE IS THAT IT IS MADE ENTIRELY FREEHAND, WITHOUT USING RULES, SO I THINK IT HAS A SPECIAL CHARM.

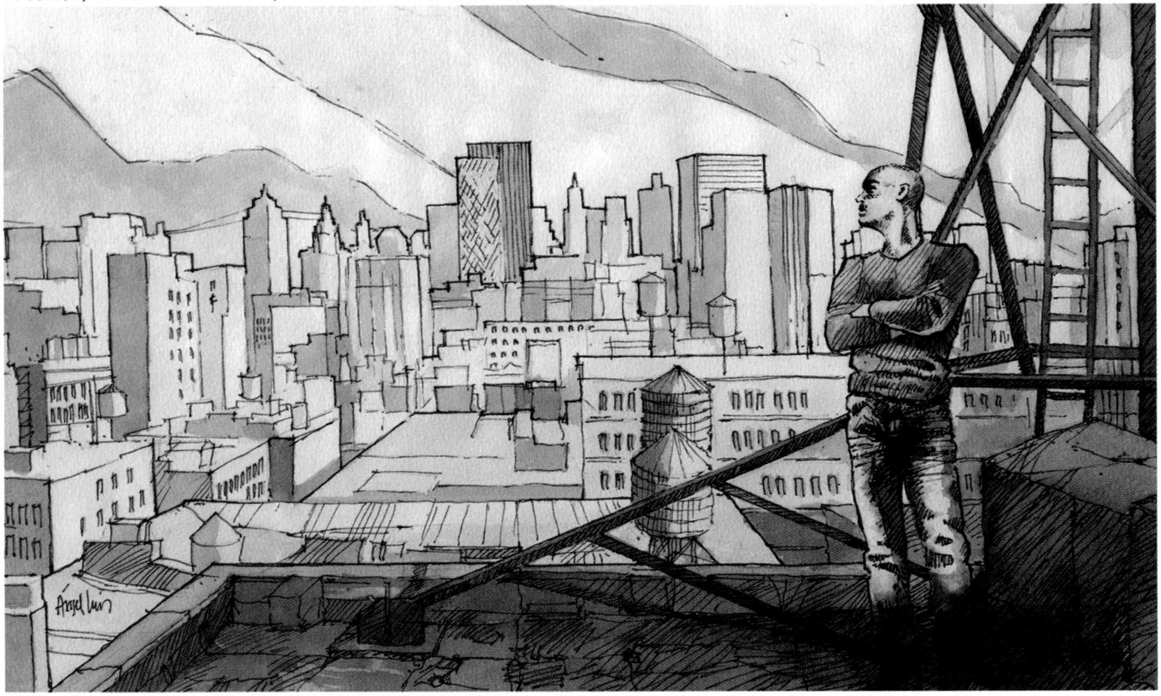

AND COLOR APPLIED TO WATERCOLOR, DIGITAL UNRETOUCHED, GIVE IT AN AIR SOMEWHAT "NAIF" THAT ATTRACTED ME A LOT. ON THE NEXT PAGE YOU CAN SEE HOW I MADE THE SAME PICTURE, WITH SOME CHANGES, BUT WITH THE OVERALL STYLE OF THE OTHER DRAWINGS.

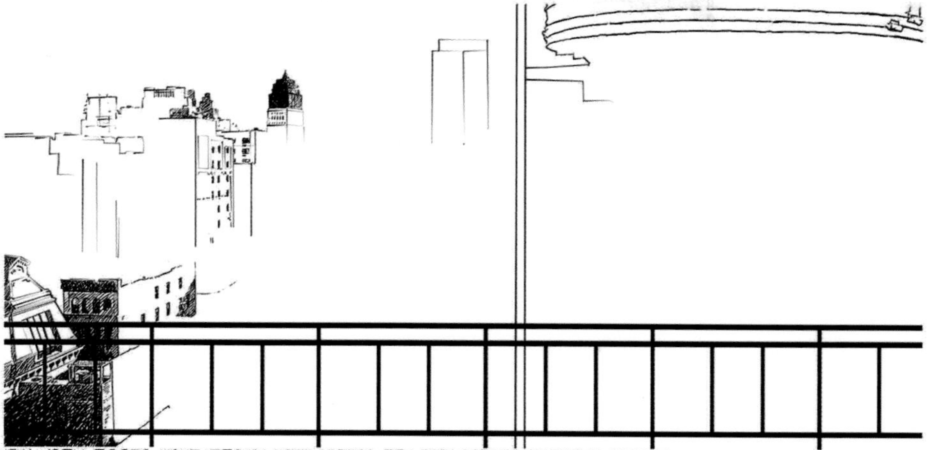

NEW YORK ROOFS. HAND DRAWN WITH DIGITAL PEN AND TABLET. DRAWING STAGES.
INITIAL. DRAWING MADE BY DEFINING RANDOMIZED COMPLETE SECTORS.

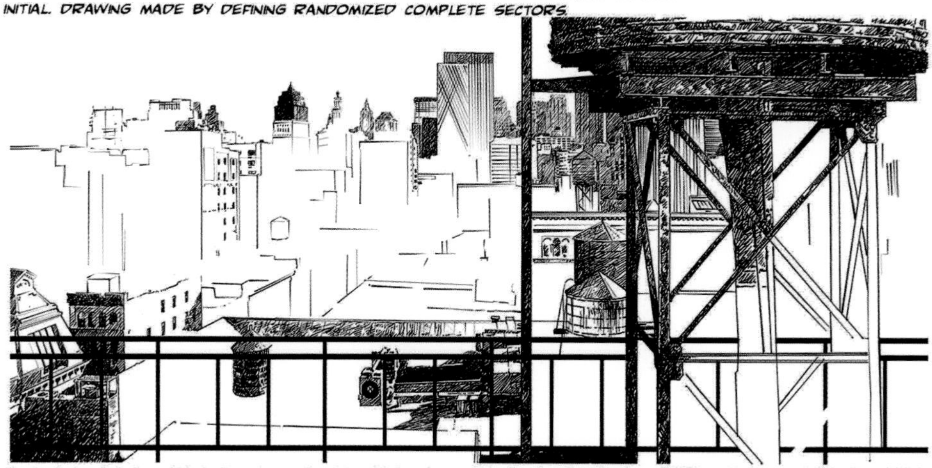

THIS IS A WAY OF DRAWING THAT I ENJOY VERY MUCH. TRYING TO DEFINE WITH GREAT DETAIL INDEPENDENT PARTS. LEAVING THE REST NEARLY BLANK.

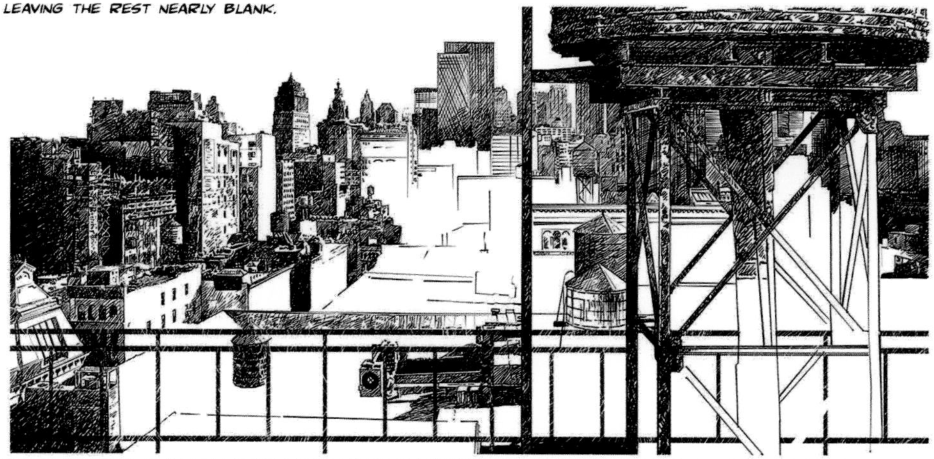

THE TEXTURE IS ACHIEVED BY DIFFERENT KINDS OF STRIPED, AND THE NUANCES APPLYING EACH TYPE ARE RESPONSIBLE FOR CAUSING GREATER SENSE OF DEPTH AND VOLUME.

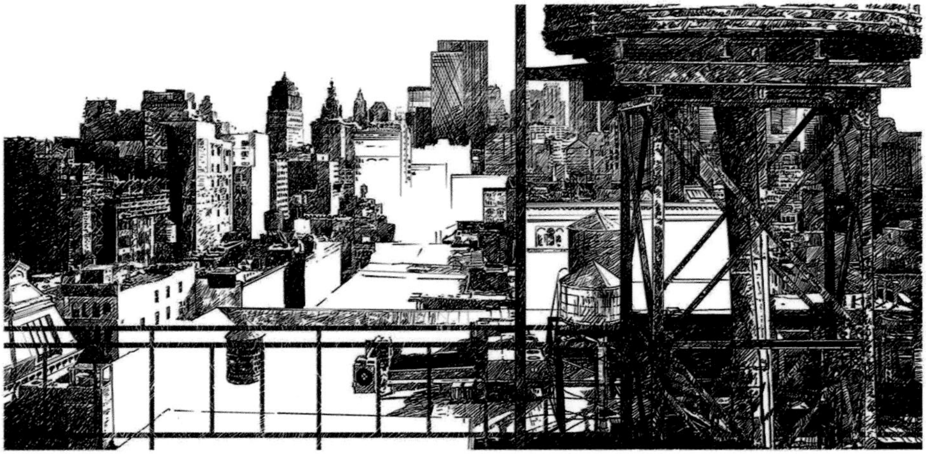

EXHAUSTIVE DEFINITION OF THE WATER TANK IN THE FOREGROUND INCREASES THE FEELING OF DEPTH. IT IS VERY IMPORTANT TO APPLY SMALL THICKNESS TO DEFINE THE FARTHER OBJECTS.

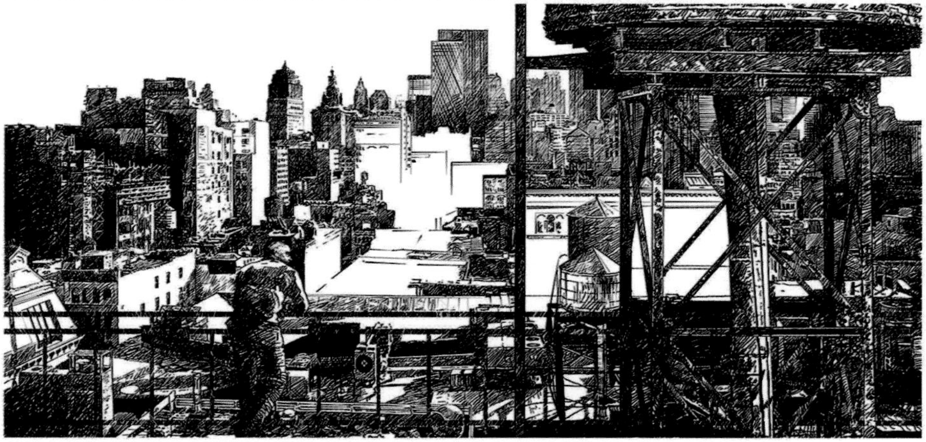

THE CHARACTER WAS INCLUDED LATER, ONE OF THE GREAT ADVANTAGES OF DOING THE DRAWING IN DIGITAL FORMAT.

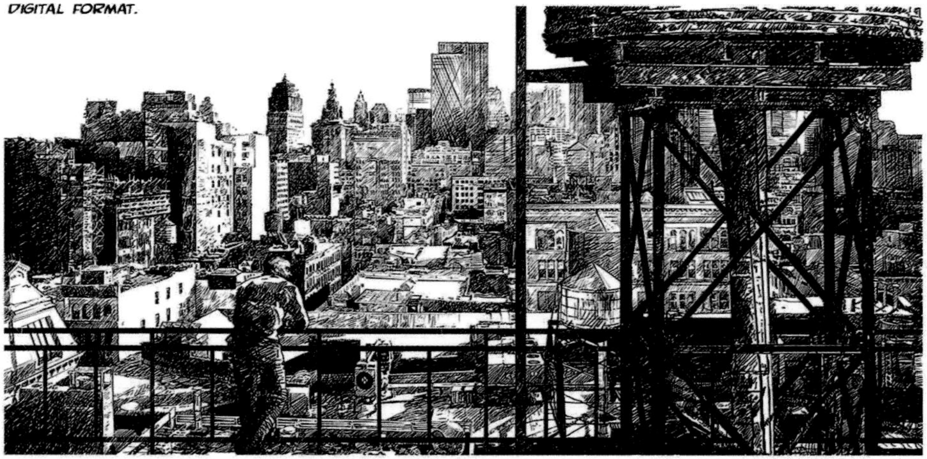

FINISHED DRAWING. ONCE WE HAVE SEEN THE RESULT, I ENHANCED THE DEPTH EFFECT WITH A NEW STRIPED PHASE, WHICH ALSO ALLOWS TO GIVE UNIFORMITY TO THE WHOLE.

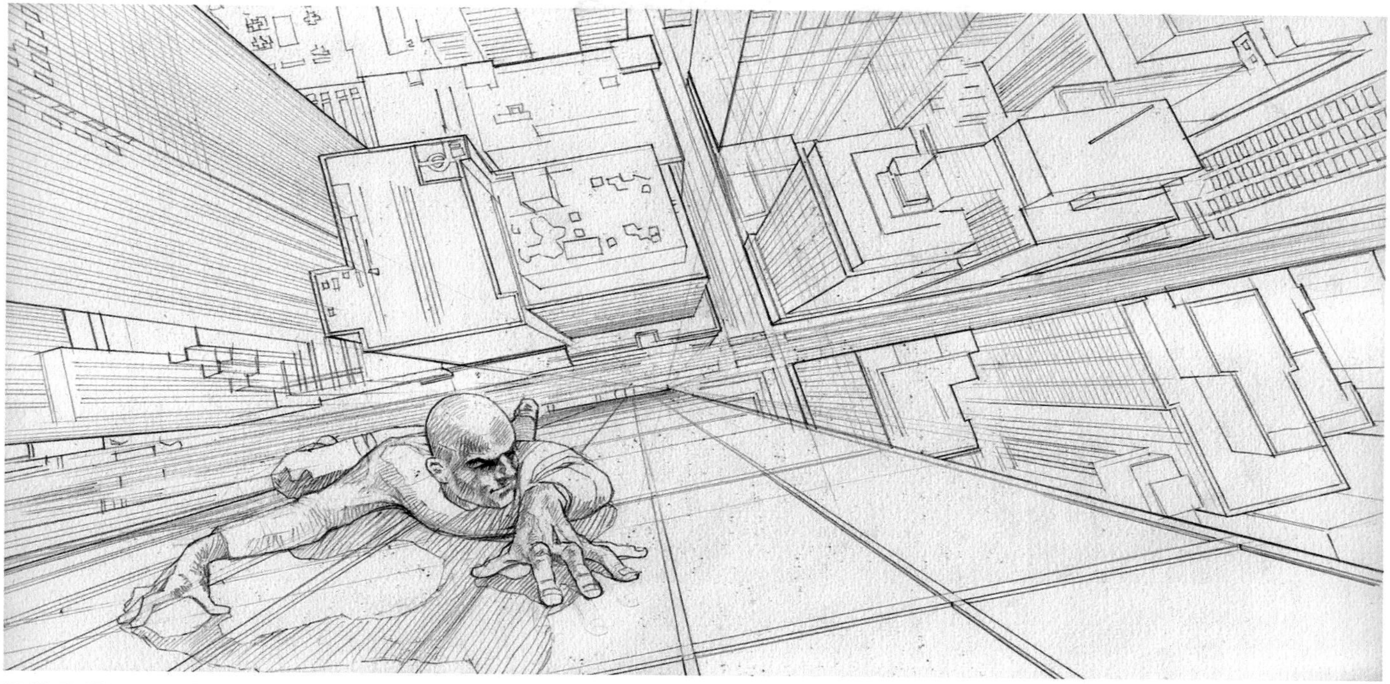

CLIMBING. PENCIL 2H. ANGLE SHOT. THE VANISHING POINT LIES BELOW THE HORIZON PLANE. THE OVERALL COMPOSITION IS IN THE FORM OF A CROSS AND IS DETERMINED BY THE DIRECTIONS OF TWO MAIN STREETS. I LINED THE STREETS TO CREATE THE SENSATION OF VEHICLES MOVING.

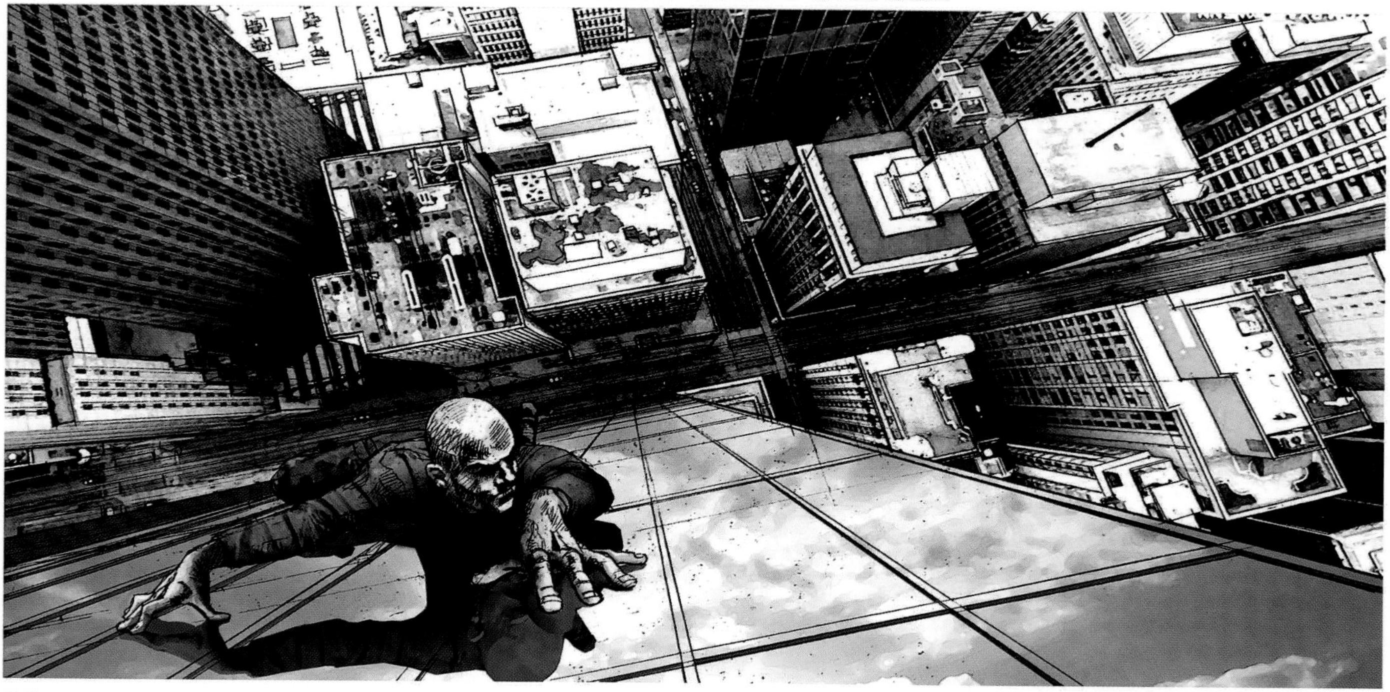

INKED WITH STYLUS PILOT V5 AND V7, WATERCOLOR COLORED. DIGITALLY RETOUCHED WITH A FILTER THAT DILUTE THE COLOR. I ALSO USED OVEREXPOSURE AND UNDEREXPOSURE TOOLS TO GIVE NUANCES TO SURFACES. THE REFLECTION IN THE GLASS FACADE IS A DESATURATED SYMMETRY OF THE CHARACTER.

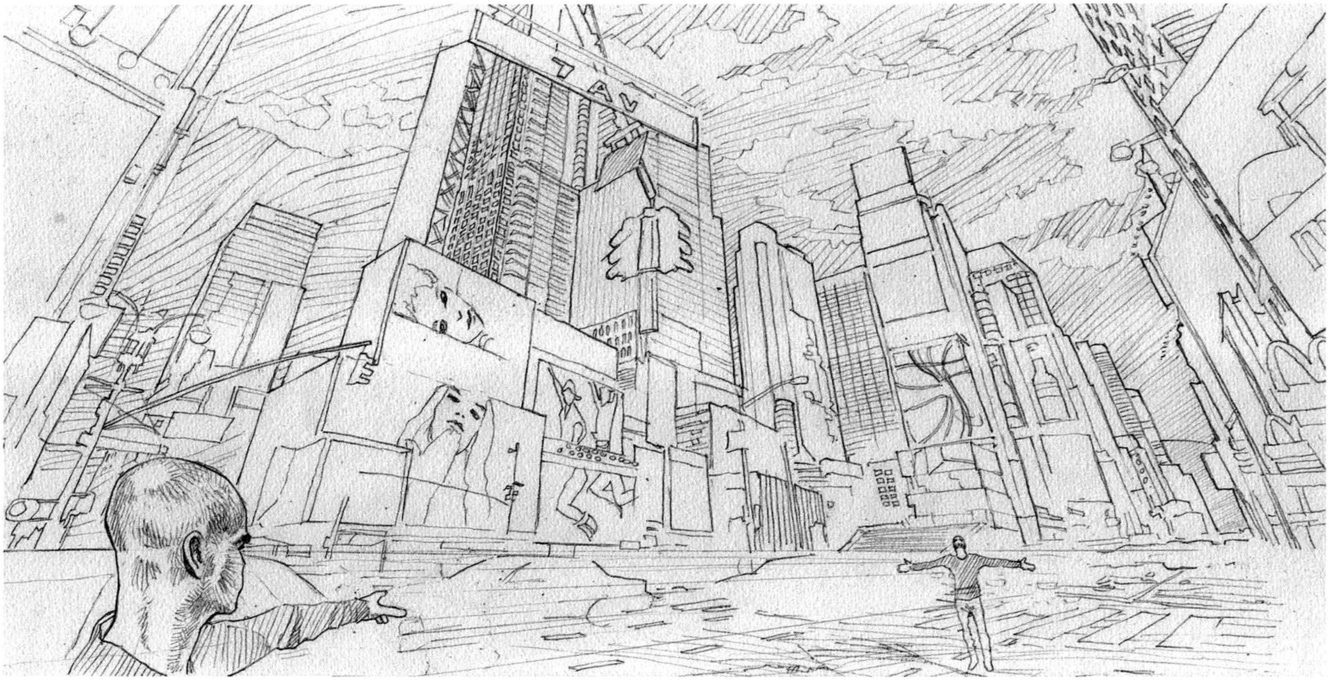
7 AV

TIMES SQUARE. PENCIL 2H. IT´S A FORCED PERSPECTIVE WITH THREE VANISHING POINTS, TWO ON THE HORIZON AND ONE IN THE SKY. AERIAL VANISHING POINT CREATES A ENVELOPING ATMOSPHERE. I DREW UNFOCUSED VEHICLES TO GIVE THE ILLUSION OF SPEED.

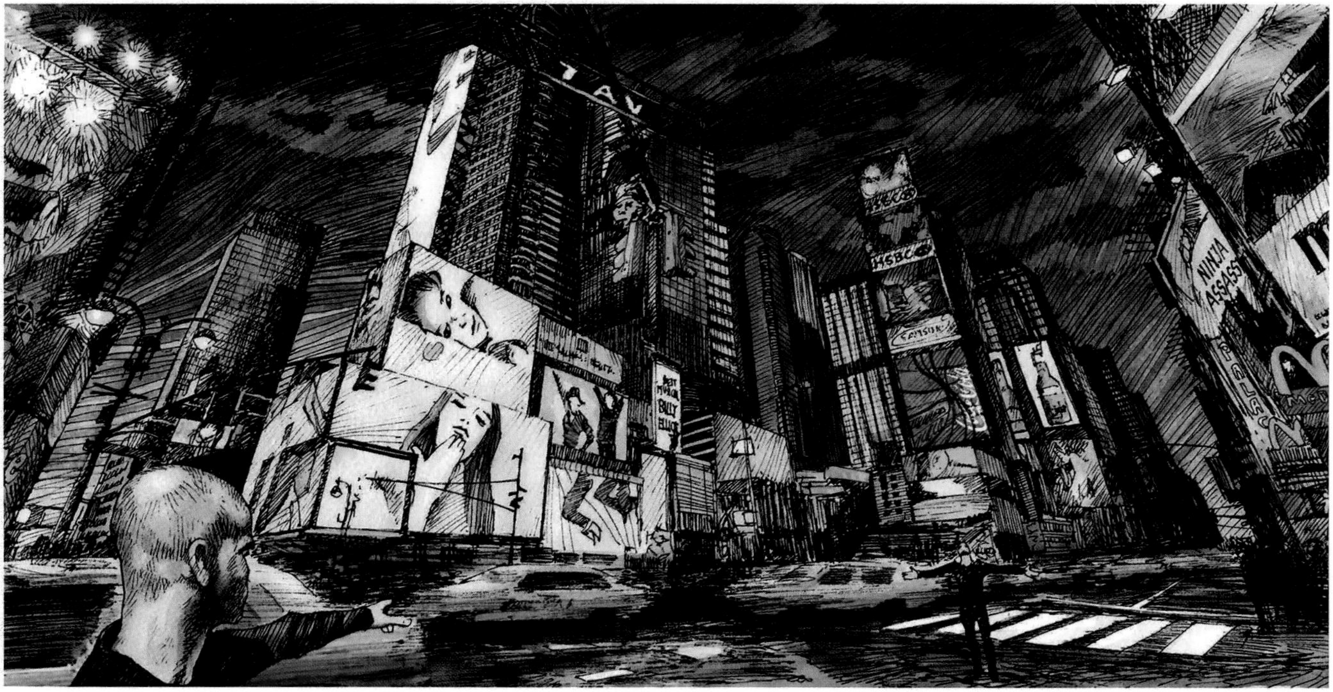
7 AV
NINJA ASSASS

INKED WITH STYLUS PILOT V5 AND V7 WATERCOLOR AND COLORED. DIGITALLY RETOUCHED TO INCREASE THE CONTRAST OF BLACK AND THE COLORS. I HAVE MARKED A LOT THE STROKE IN THE SKY AND I GAVE IT MOVEMENT, TO GIVE MORE EXPRESSION TO THE SCENE.

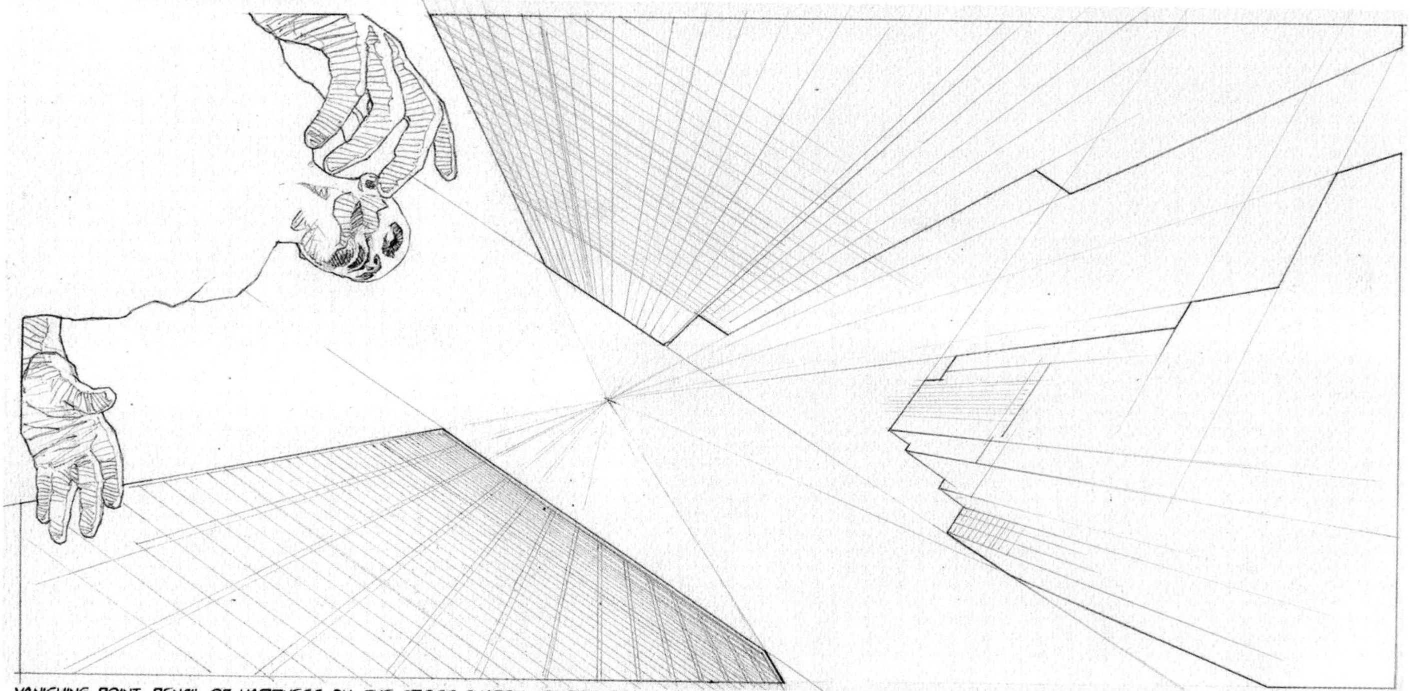

VANISHING POINT. PENCIL OF HARDNESS 2H. THE CROSS-SHAPED COMPOSITION IS DETERMINED BY THE VOID BETWEEN THE BUILDINGS. VANISHING POINT ATTRACTS TO ITSELF ALL LINES, AND THE EFFECT OF FLIGHT TO THE SKY IS ACCENTUATED BY THE SINGULAR POINT OF VIEW OF THE HUMAN FIGURE.

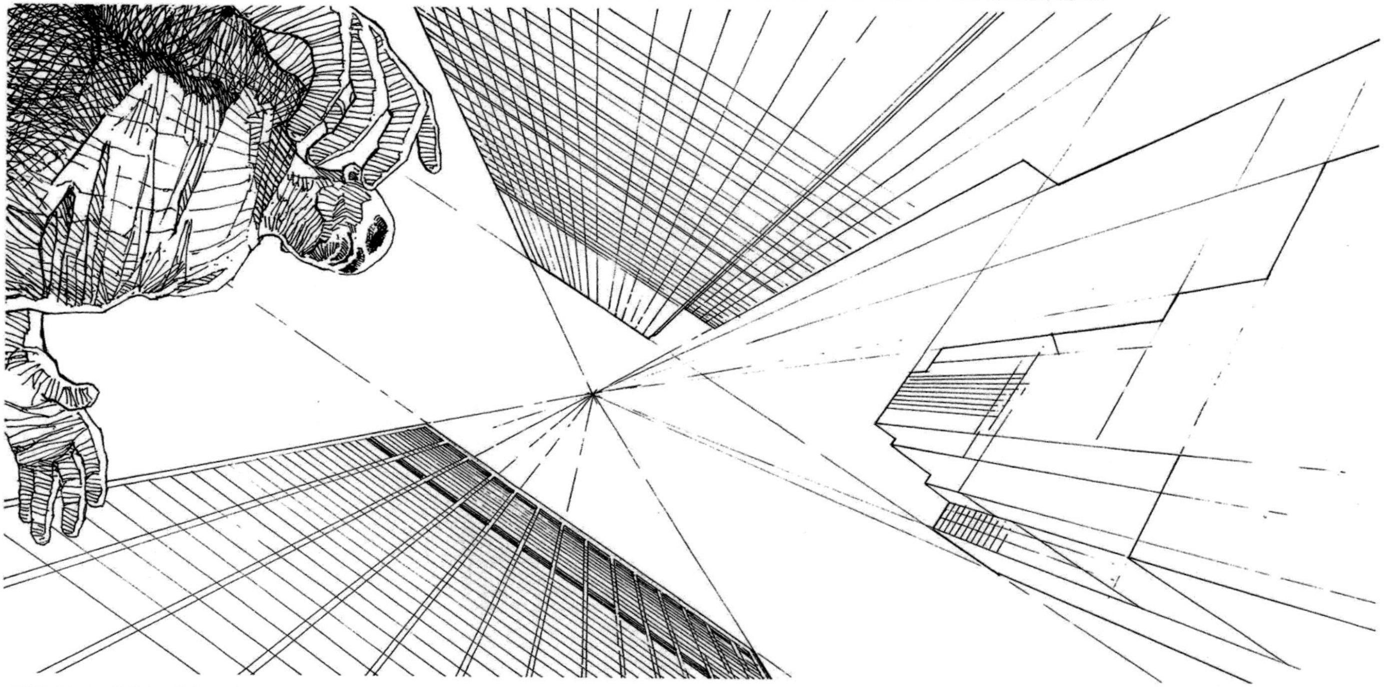

INKED WITH STYLUS PILOT V5 AND V7. I REVIEWED MORE INTENSELY REAL ELEMENTS, DEFINING THE HUMAN FIGURE WITH A STROKE IN WHICH I TRIED TO AVOID EXCESSIVE REALISM. FEW SIMPLE LINES DEFINE THE FACADES. I ALSO WANTED TO HIGHLIGHT THE VANISHING POINT EVEN IN THE FINAL RESULT.

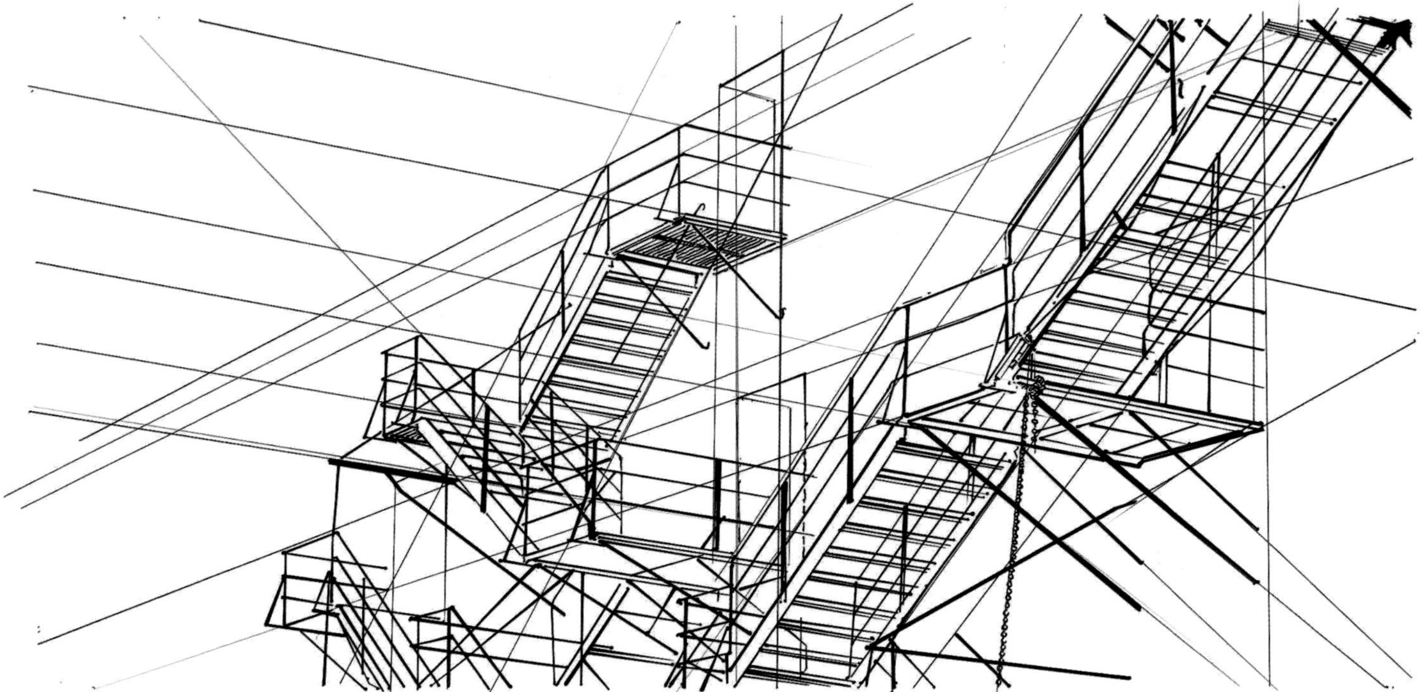

FIRE ESCAPE. TWO VANISHING POINT PERSPECTIVE. STYLUS PILOT HI-TECPOINT V5 AND V7. I WANTED TO DO A DRAWING IN WHICH THE SHAPE APPEARED FROM THE FUSION OF ALL THE CONFIGURATION LINES. LINES THAT LEAK TO INFINITY WITHOUT INTERRUPTION AND THAT CROSS IN MANY DIRECTIONS.

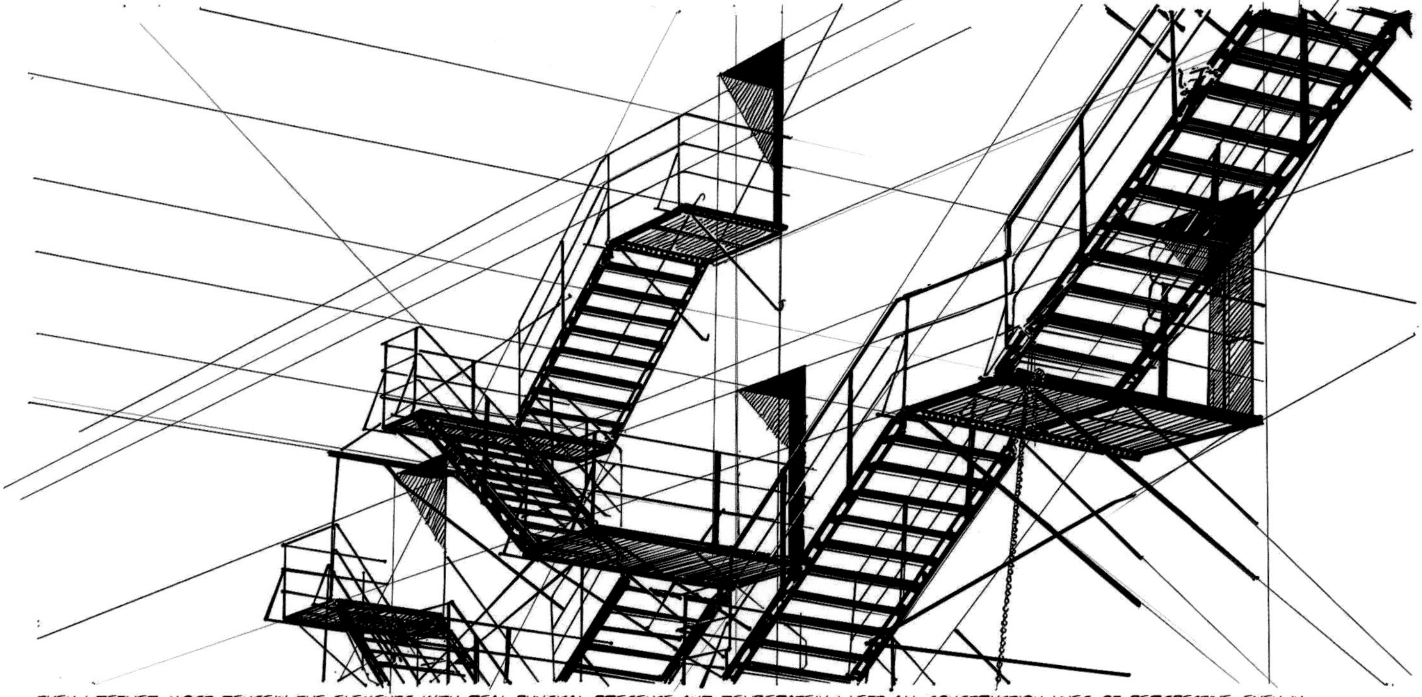

THEN I DEFINED MOST DENSELY THE ELEMENTS WITH REAL PHYSICAL PRESENCE AND DELIBERATELY, I LEFT ALL CONSTRUCTION LINES OF PERSPECTIVE, EVEN IN THE FINAL COLORED DRAWING.

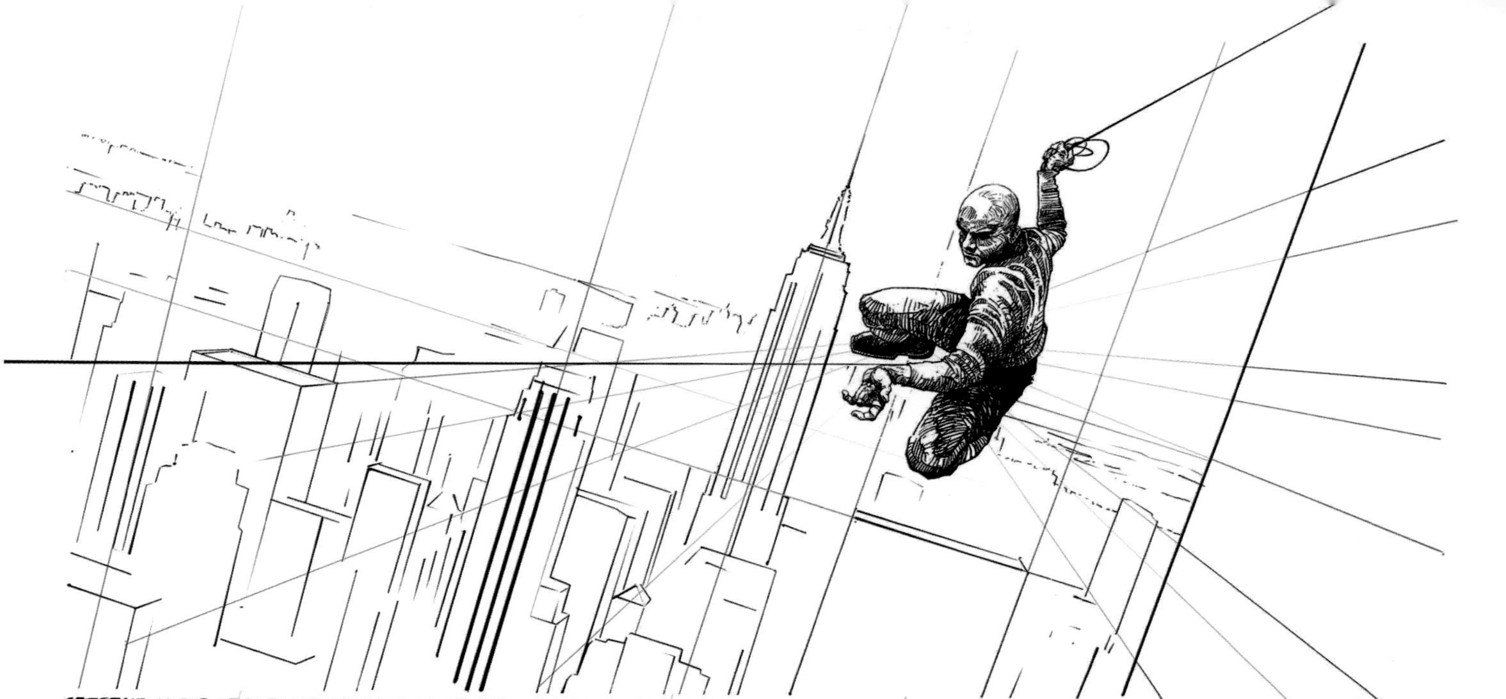

SPIDERALT. IN THE FIRST PHASE DECISIONS OF GENERAL COMPOSITION ARE TAKEN . IN THIS CASE THE DRAWING TURNS AROUND THE CHARACTER. THE NET THROWN IN A STRAIGHT PARALLEL LINE TO THE EDGES OF THE DRAWING AND THE INCLINED VIEW OF THE CITY DO THE REST.

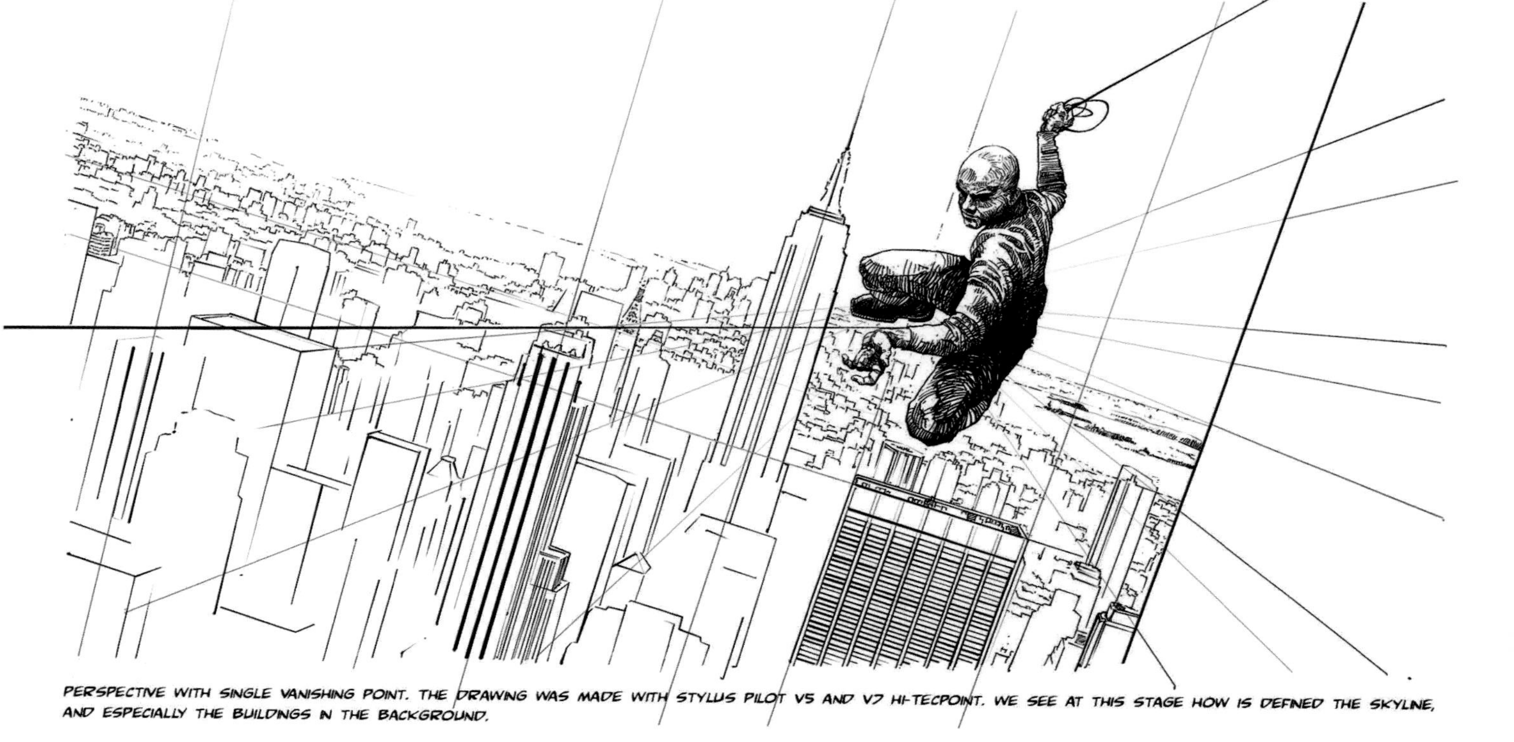

PERSPECTIVE WITH SINGLE VANISHING POINT. THE DRAWING WAS MADE WITH STYLUS PILOT V5 AND V7 HI-TECPOINT. WE SEE AT THIS STAGE HOW IS DEFINED THE SKYLINE, AND ESPECIALLY THE BUILDINGS IN THE BACKGROUND.

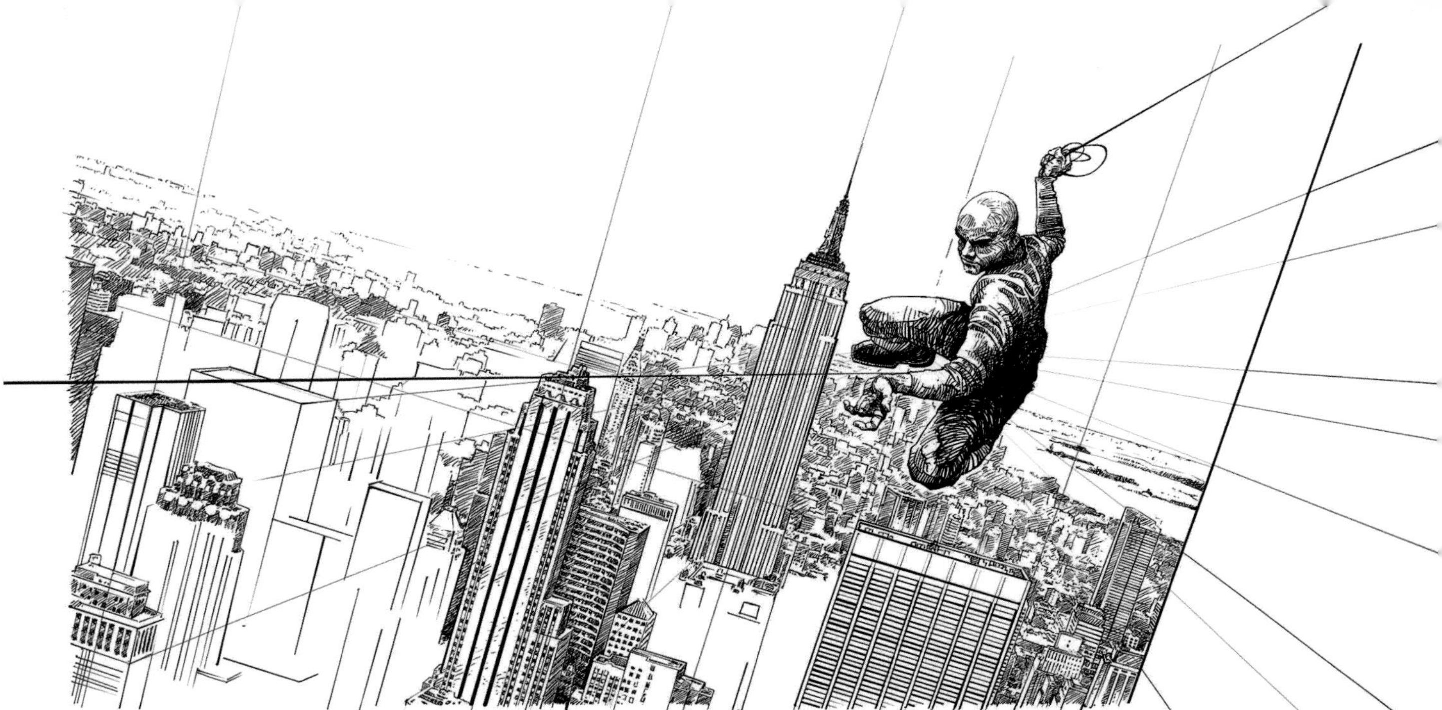

THE TEXTURES OF THE BUILDINGS ARE APPLIED FOR ADDED REALISM AND VOLUME. NEARBY BUILDINGS ARE DEFINED IN GREATER STROKE WEIGHT, AND THE LEVEL OF DETAIL IS DECREASING THE LONGER THE DISTANCE.

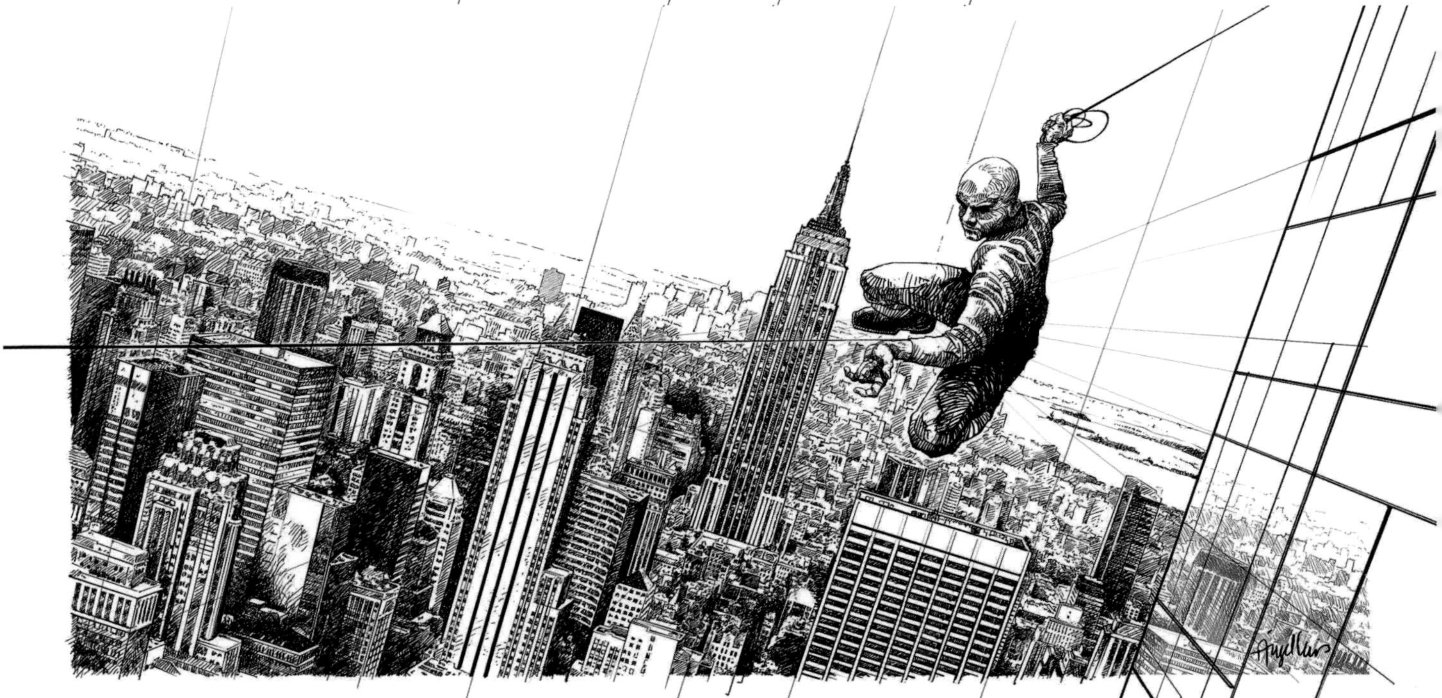

THIS IS THE FINISHED INK DRAWING. I SCANNED AND DELETED ON THE COMPUTER WHITES SO ONLY REMAIN THE BLACK AND GRAY INK. SYMMETRY IS CREATED IN THE REFLECTION IN THE GLASS FACADE, AND THEN GIVING A LOWER OPACITY GIVES REALISM TO THE SURFACE.

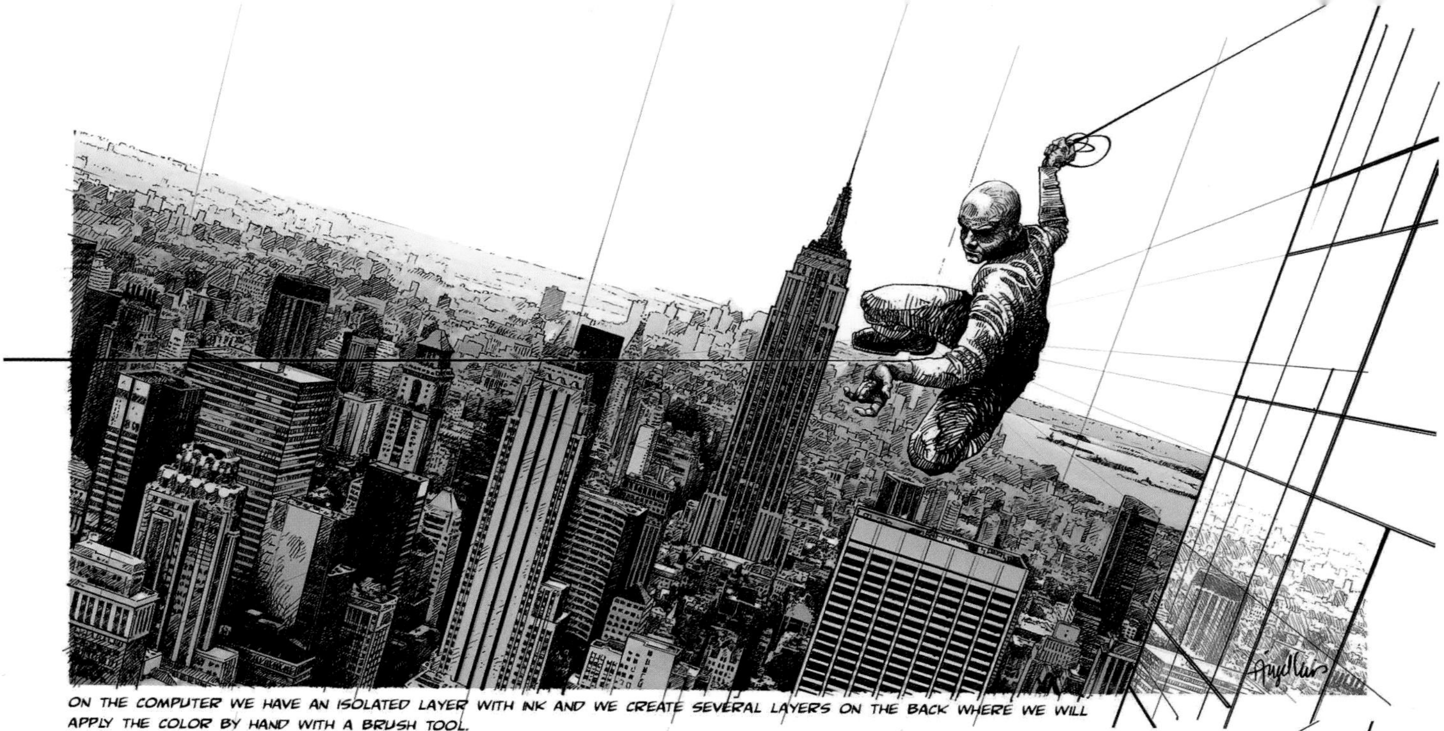

ON THE COMPUTER WE HAVE AN ISOLATED LAYER WITH INK AND WE CREATE SEVERAL LAYERS ON THE BACK WHERE WE WILL APPLY THE COLOR BY HAND WITH A BRUSH TOOL.

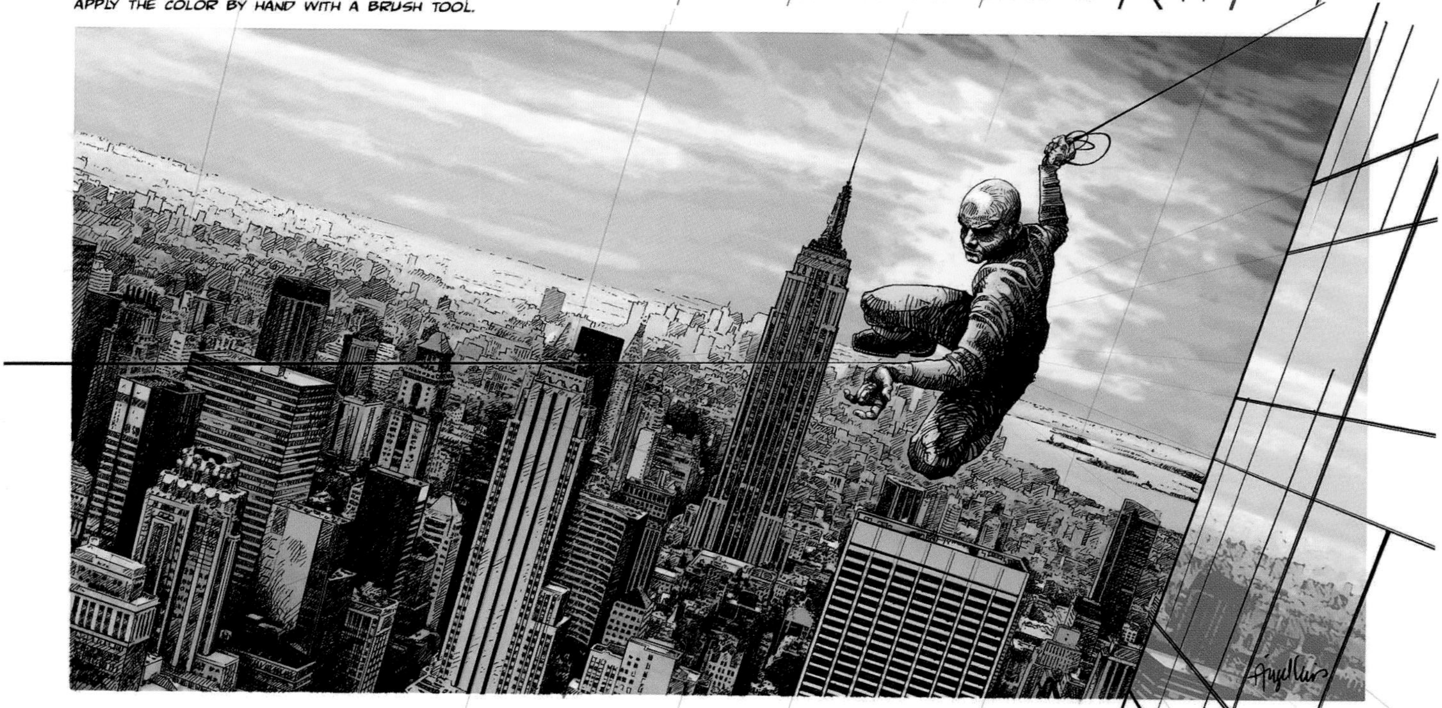

THE SKY WAS COLORED IN A SEPARATE LAYER AND I APPLIED A GAUSSIAN BLUR TO ACCENTUATE ITS REMOTENESS. FINALLY I REVIEWED ALL COLOR GROUND WITH OVEREXPOSURE AND UNDEREXPOSURE TOOLS TO GIVE NUANCES TO SURFACES.

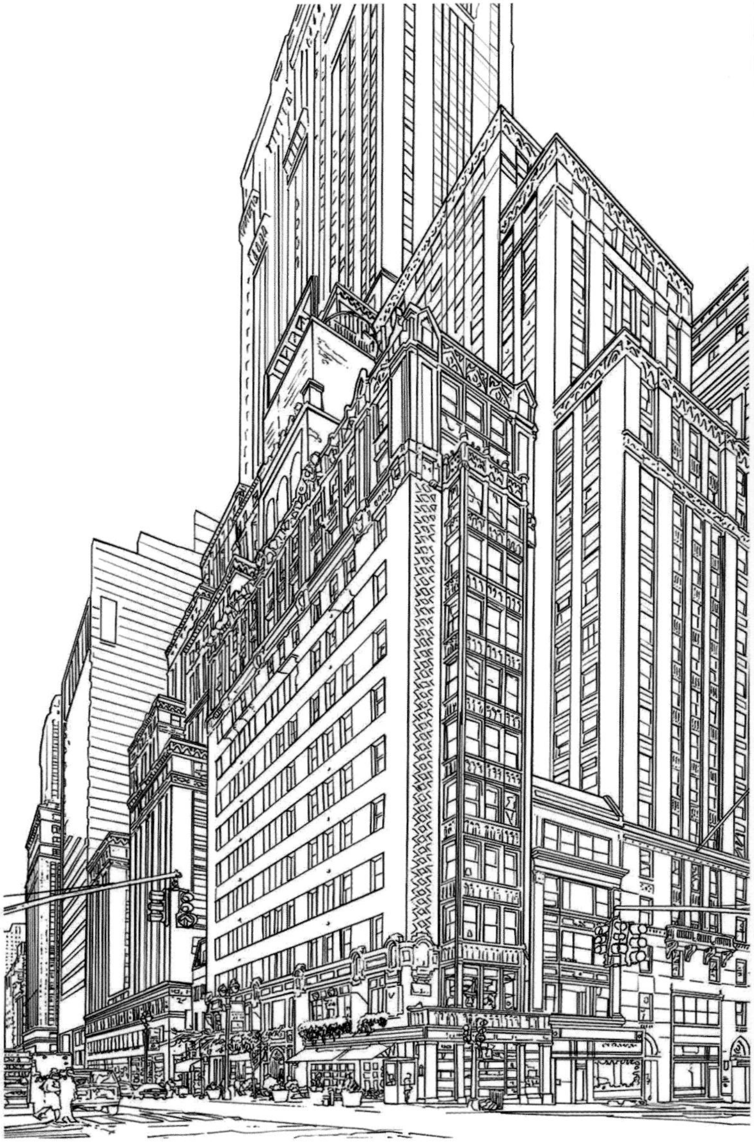

NEW YORK CORNER. DRAWN WITH STYLUS PILOT V5 AND V7 HI-TECPOINT. DOUBLE VANISHING POINT. BUILDING OCCUPIES ALMOST ALL FROM THE IMAGE FOR ACCENTUATE THE ROUNDNESS OF THE VOLUMES.

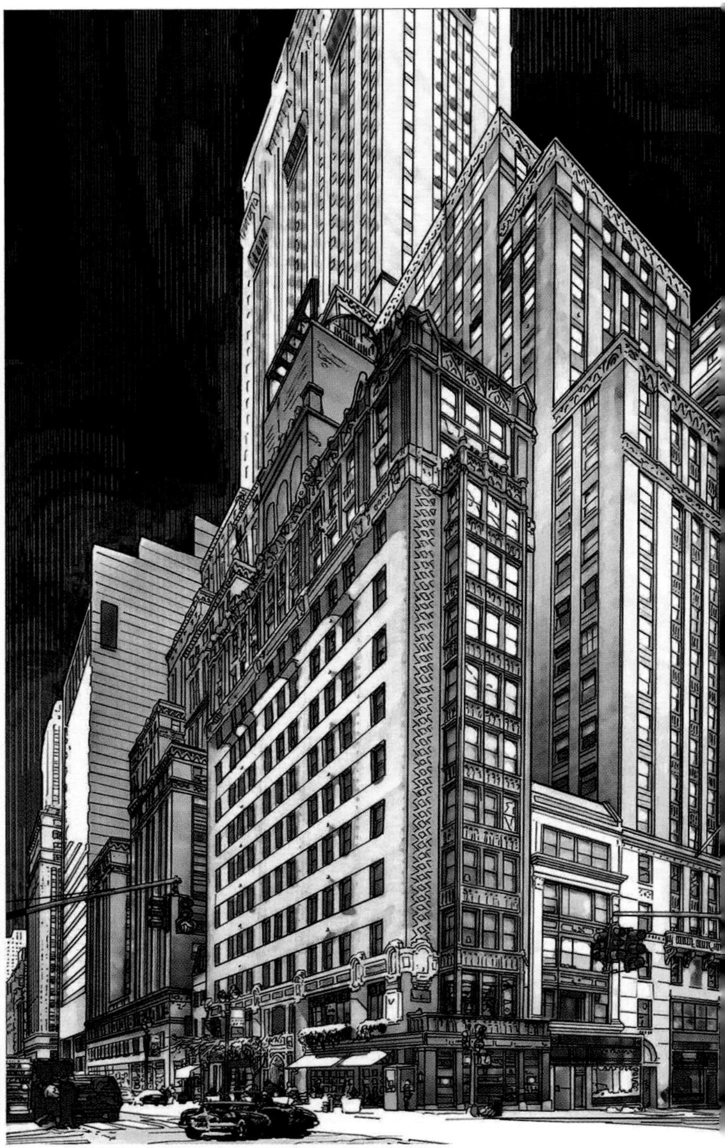

I ISOLATED THE INK DRAWING ON ONE LAYER AND APPLY THE COLOR IN BACK LAYERS B HAND, WITH DIGITAL PEN. THEN I MATICE SUBSEQUENTLY SURFACES WITH OVEREXPOSURE UNDEREXPOSURE TOOLS. I APPLIED A FILTER TO HEAVEN, A STRIPED PATTERN VERY CLO TOGETHER CREATING A MOIRÉ EFFECT.

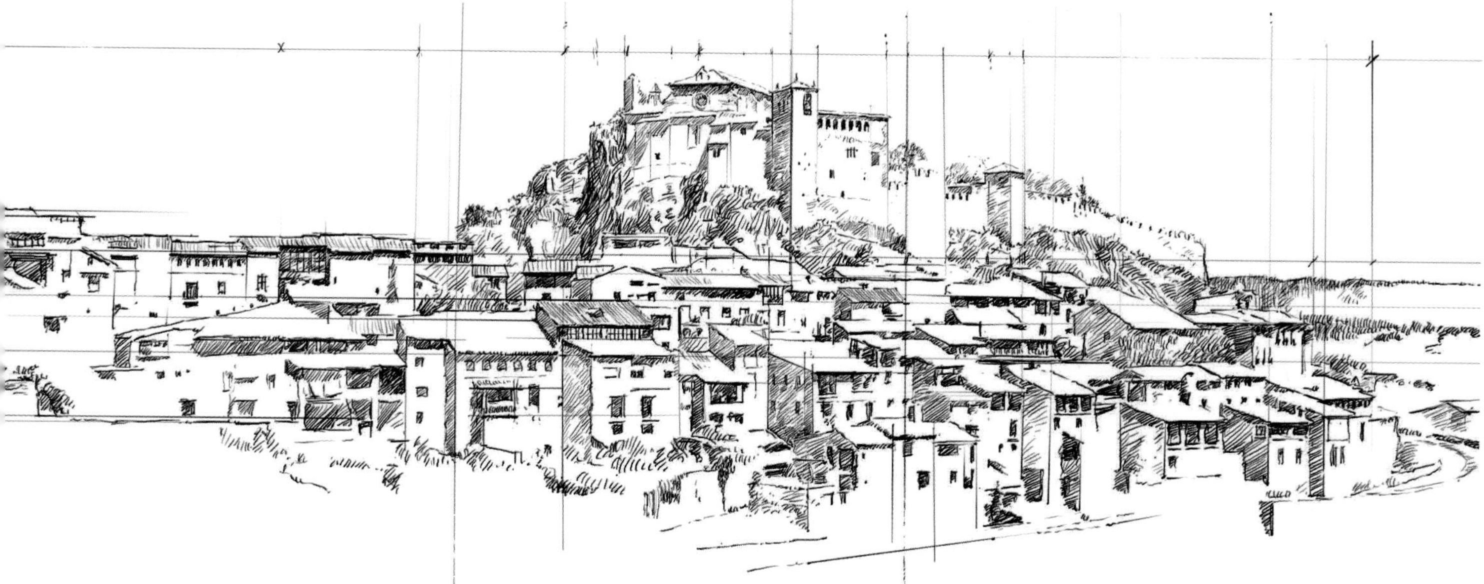

VILLAGE. DRAWN WITH STYLUS V5 AND V7. STRUCTURING DRAWING PHASE. YOU CAN SEE THE CONSTRUCTION LINES. VERTICAL AND HORIZONTAL AXES, ON WHICH ARE POSITIONED REFERENCES TO PROVIDE PROPORTION TO THE DRAWING. IN THIS CASE I WANTED TO ACCENTUATE THE HORIZONTAL LINES IN CONTRAST TO THE ORGANIC PROFILE OF THE FORTRESS.

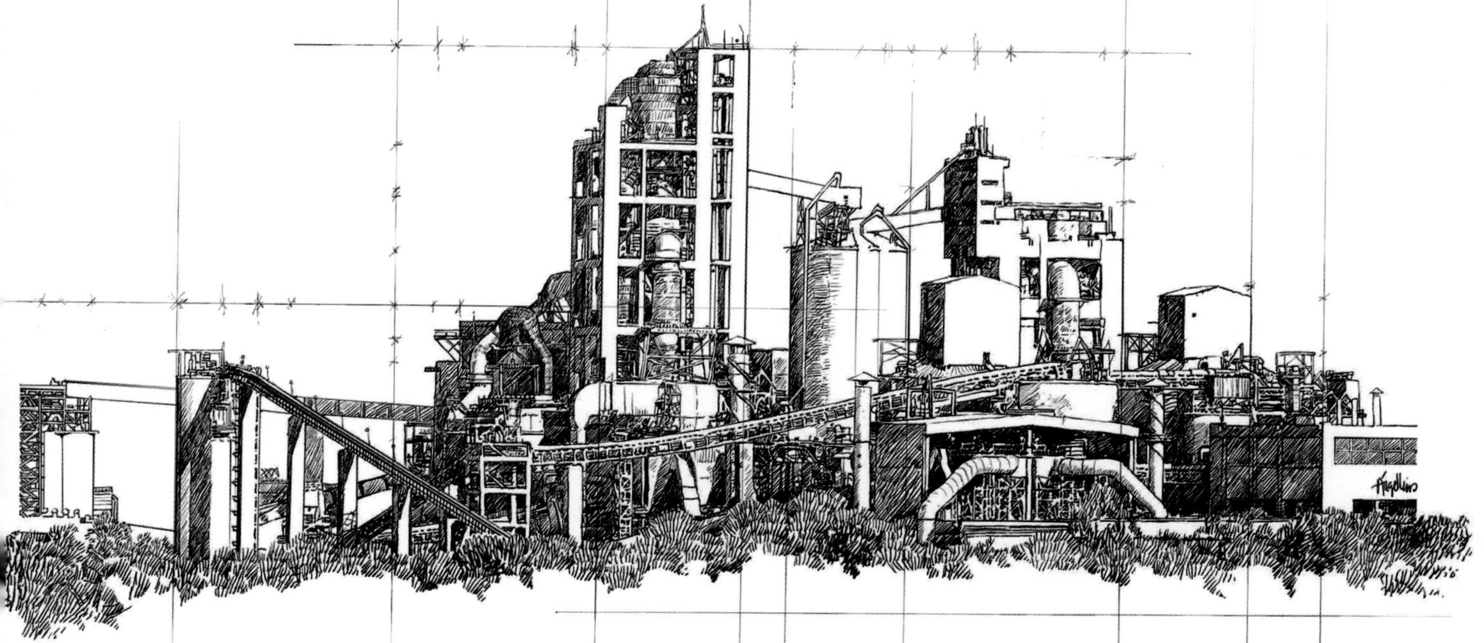

CEMENT FACTORY. DRAWN WITH STYLUS V5 AND V7. THE COMPOSITION ATTEMPTS TO CONTRAST THE ORTHOGONAL PARTS AS WALKWAYS WITH THE FREE GEOMETRY OF PIPES. THE DRAWING IS FINISHED AT THE BOTTOM, WITH THE VEGETATION ABRUPTLY CUT AGAINST WHITE BACKGROUND, LOOKING FOR THE CONTRAST BETWEEN THE NATURAL AND THE ARTIFICIAL.

STAIRS. DRAWING WITH STYLUS V5 AND V7. IT´S A PERSPECTIVE
OF A SINGLE VANISHING POINT, THAT COMBINED WITH THE SWASTIKA
COMPOSITION, GIVES THE WHOLE A ROTARY MOVEMENT IN A
ENDLESS HELIX. THE COMPOSITION HAS BEEN FORCED, AND THE
MAIN LINES GO TO THE VERTICES OF THE BACKGROUND SQUARE,
LOOKING TO CREATE A TENSION BETWEEN DRAWING AND LIMITS.
THE MASSES OF BLACK WERE ADDED DIGITALLY.

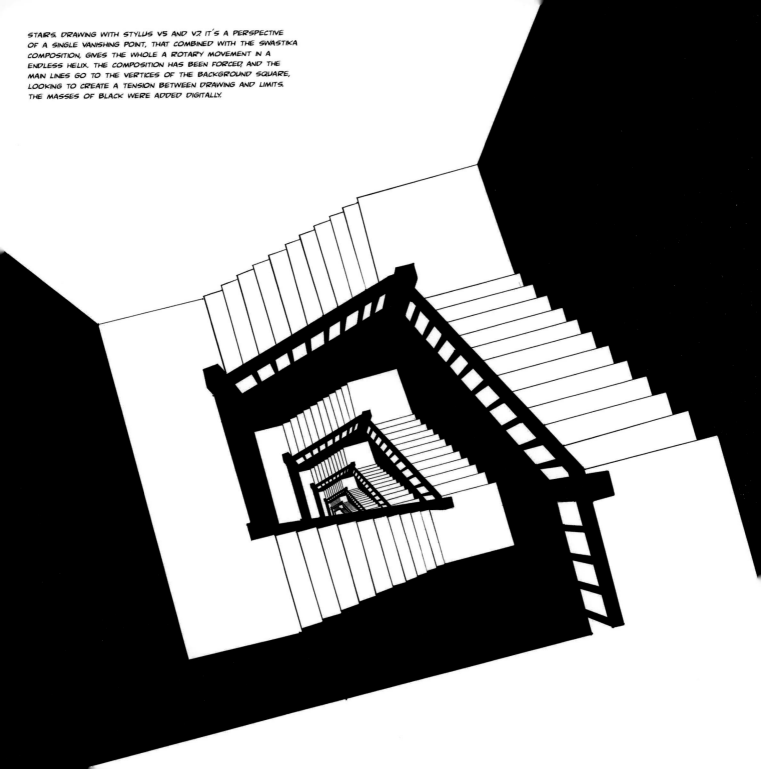

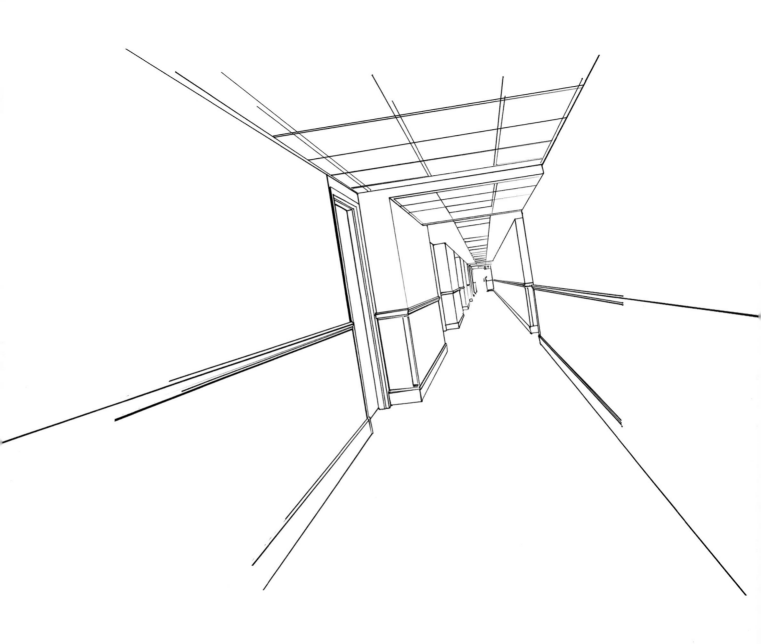

CORRIDOR. DRAWING WITH PEN. V5 AND V7 IS A PERSPECTIVE OF A SINGLE VANISHING POINT. THE SLIGHT
TURN TO THE LEFT OF THE COMPOSITION SEEKS TO CREATE A SENSE OF RESTLESSNESS. THIS IS A
RESOURCE THAT IS COMMONLY USED IN CINEMATOGRAPHIC PLANNING.

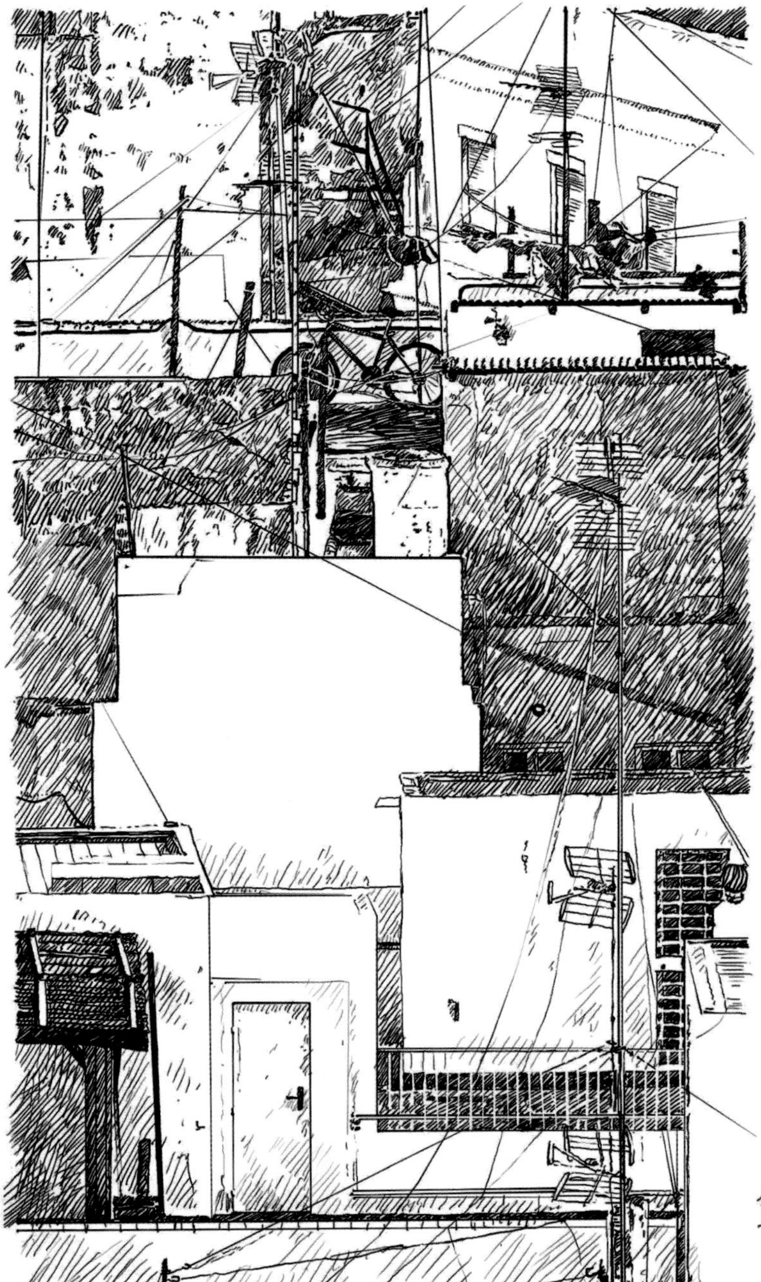

ROOFS. DRAWN WITH STYLUS PILOT V5 AND V7. IT'S AN ORTHOGONAL COMPOSITION. A COLLAGE OF WALLS AND FLOORS IN WHICH, INTENTIONALLY, HAS BEEN AVOIDED THE PRESENCE OF VANISHING LINES THAT DEFINE A CONICAL PERSPECTIVE. THE GAME OF BOXES ARE "SEWN" BY SUPPORTING ELEMENTS OF THE SCENE, SUCH AS CABLES, ANTENNAS, RAILINGS...

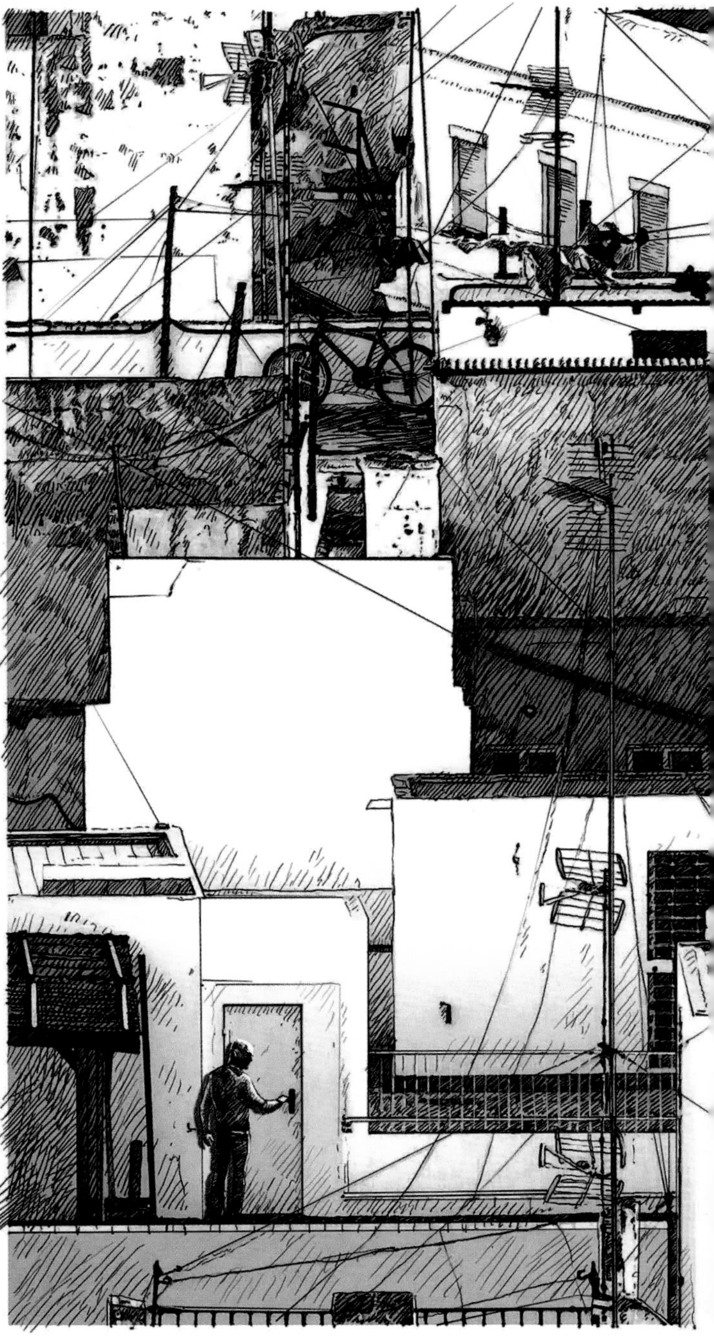

I DIDN'T GIVE DEPTH TO THE PERSPECTIVE SO I USED COLOR FOR THIS PURPOSE. THE DIFFERENT LEVELS FROM LIGHTING AND SHADOWS BETWEEN VOLUMES, ALONG WITH THE NUANCES OF COLOR, GET THAT EACH PLANE IS UNDERSTOOD WITH DIFFERENTIATED DEPTH. I USED, TO GIVE MORE REALISTIC, DIGITAL TOOLS AS OVEREXPOSURE AND UNDEREXPOSURE.

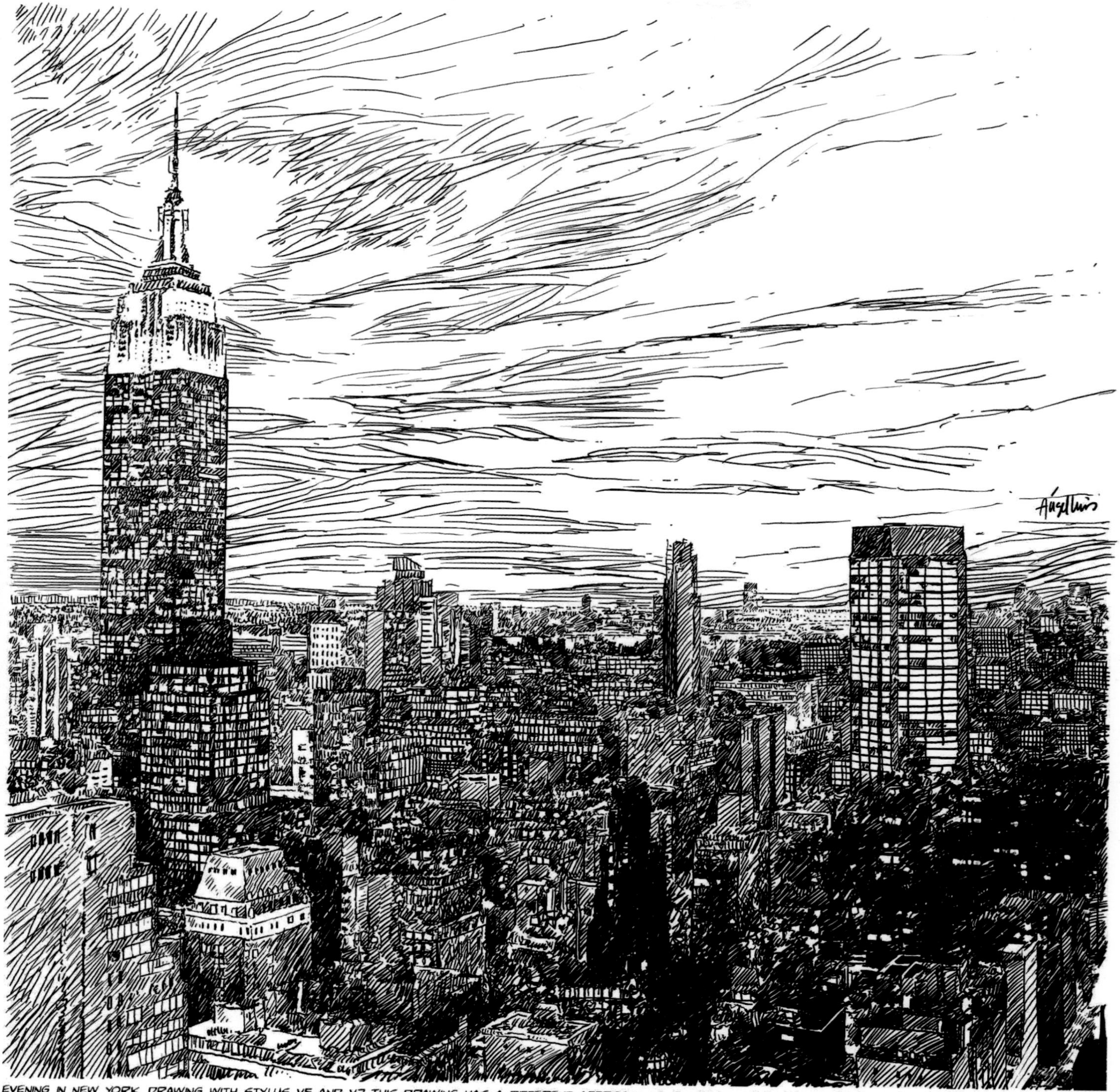

EVENING IN NEW YORK. DRAWING WITH STYLUS V5 AND V7. THIS DRAWING HAS A DIFFERENT APPROACH TO OTHERS. IF YOU LOOK, LINES OF FLIGHT ARE NOT APPRECIATED (ALTHOUGH THERE ARE, OF COURSE...). THE INTENTION WAS TO GENERATE A NEARLY AMORPHOUS MASS OF BLACK SPOTS, SMALL STRIPES AND WHITE PIXELS, CREATING A CHAOTIC MAGMA IN APPEARANCE, BUT ENTIRELY RECOGNIZABLE.

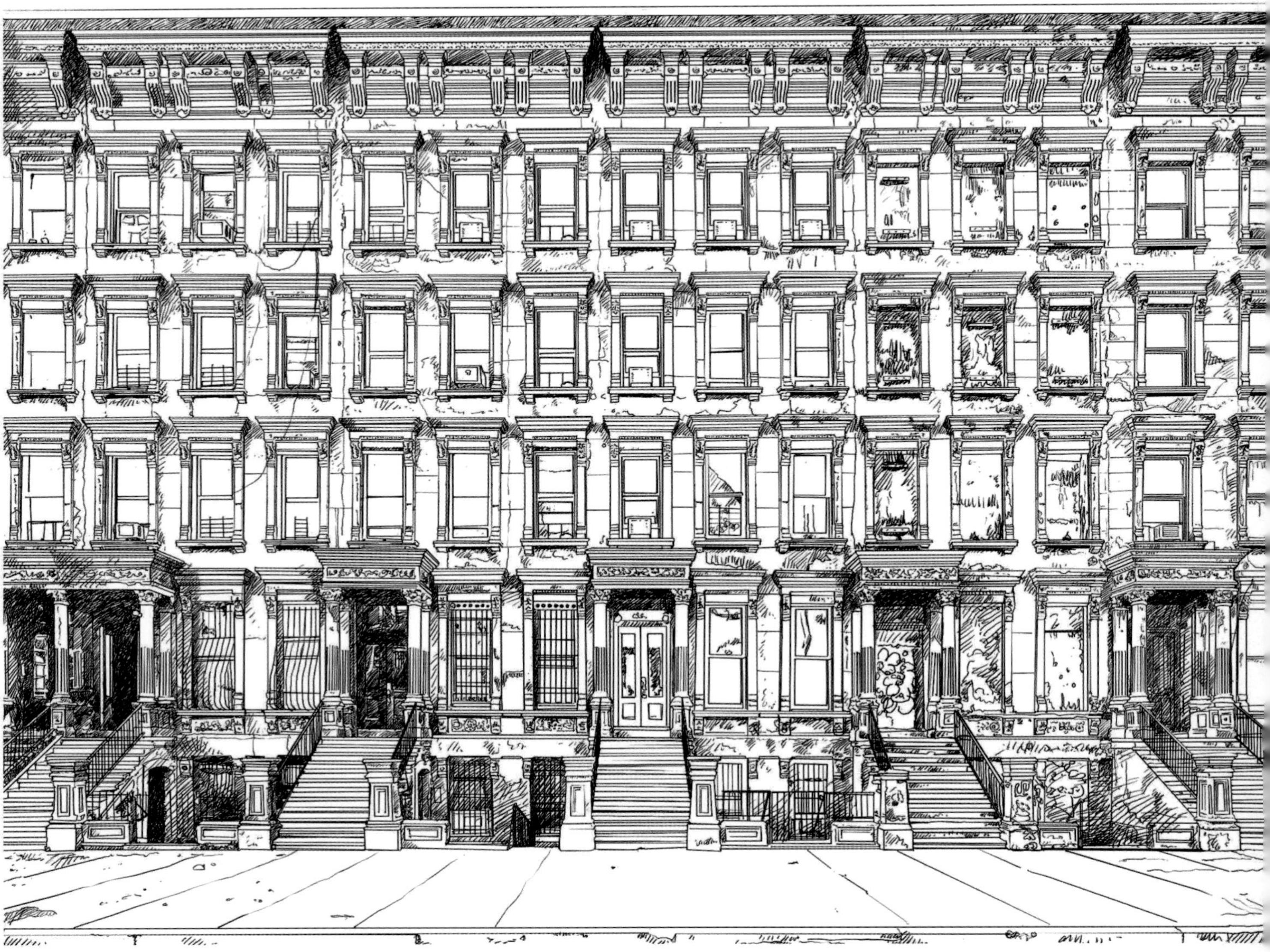

NEW YORK FACADE. DRAWING WITH STYLUS V5 AND V7. THIS IS SURELY THE MOST LABORIOUS DRAWING IN THE COMIC. I WANTED TO CONVEY HOW A FACADE, APPARENTLY BORED B THE REPETITION OF ELEMENTS, BECOMES WITH THE PASSAGE OF TIME IN AN AMAZING SET, WITH INFINITE LAYERS OF INFORMATION. DIRT, CRACKS AND FISSURES, CABLES, AIR CONDITIONERS, GRAFFITI AND ENDLESS NUANCES THAT REQUIRE SPECIAL ATTENTION TO DETAIL WHEN MAKING THE DRAWING.

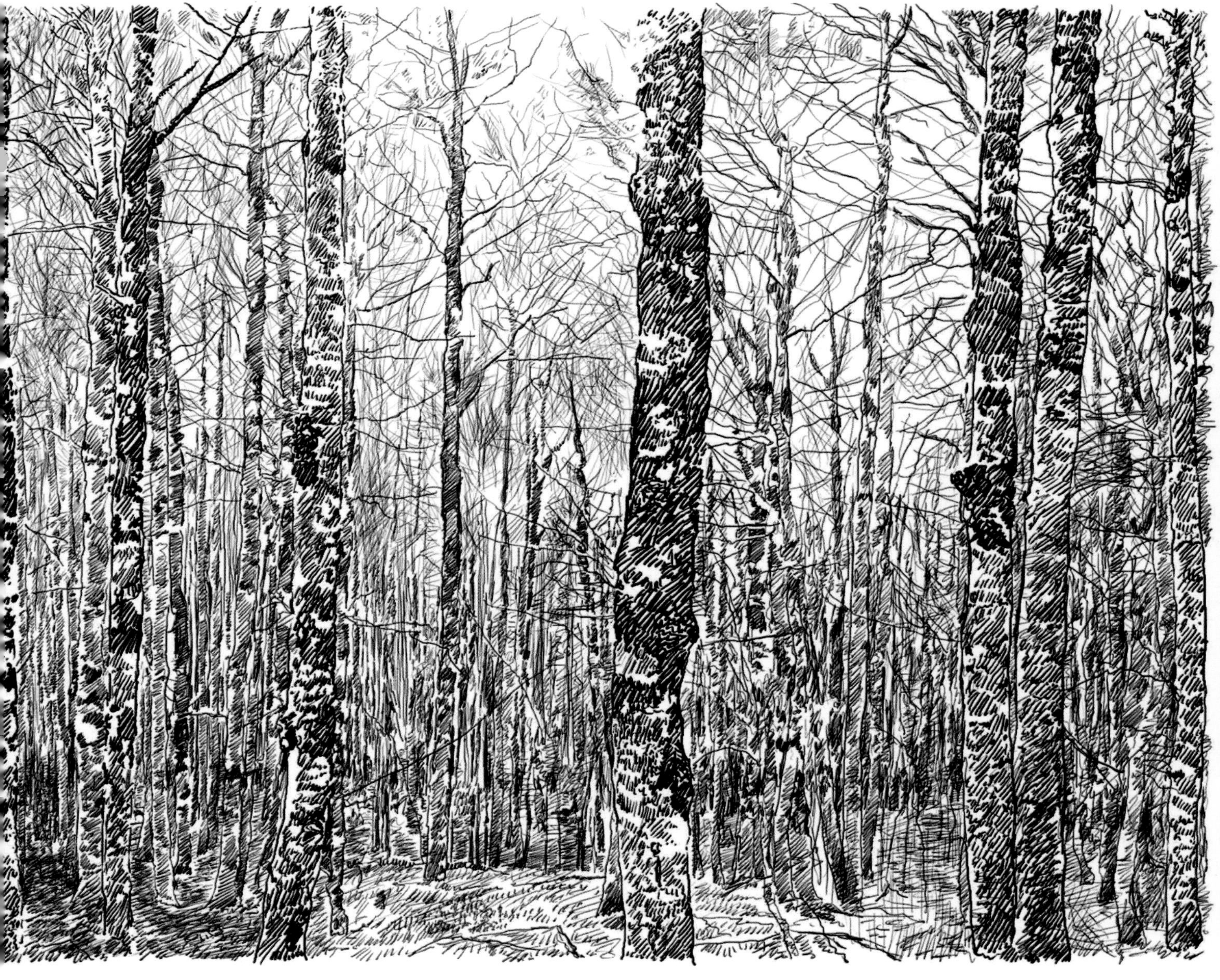

BEECH FOREST. I MADE THE BASE DRAWING ON PAPER, V5 AND V7 STYLUS. I LIKE TO ALTERNATE THESE TWO THICKNESSES, TO DEFINE THE PARTS IN THE FOREGROUND WITH A THICKNESS GREATER THAN THE FARTHEST PARTS. THE STYLUS CAN ALSO CREATE DIFFERENT THICKNESSES DEPENDING ON THE PRESSURE APPLIED ON PAPER. THEN I SCANNED THE DRAWING AND I APPLIED, USING THE DIGITAL PEN, THE STROKES REQUIRED TO GIVE GREATER CONTRAST, VOLUME AND TEXTURE TO THE WHOLE. DESPITE BEING A DRAWING OF AN ORGANIC NATURE, THE COMPOSITION HAS A CLEAR GEOMETRY OF PARALLEL STRAIGHT LINES.

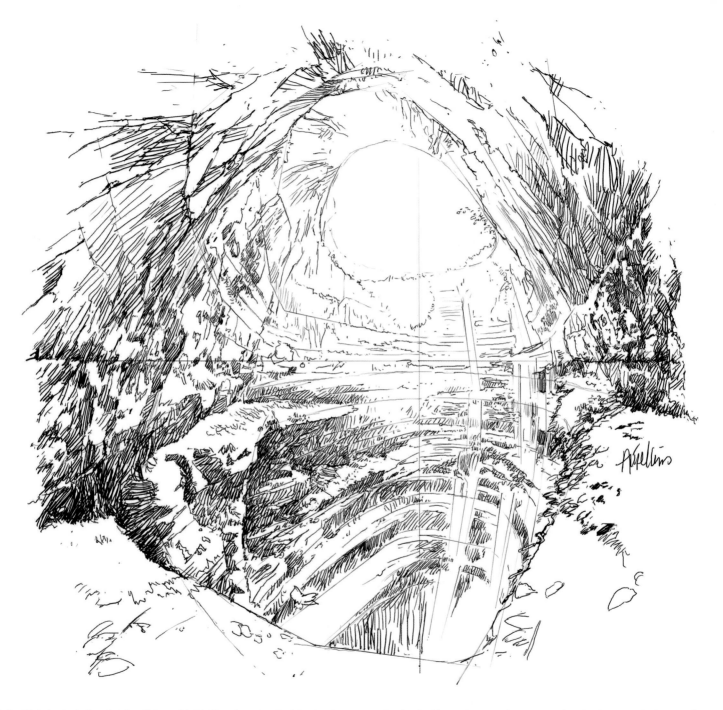

CAVE. DRAWING MADE WITH STYLUS V5 AND V2 PERSPECTIVE IS DEFINED BY THE CIRCLES THAT DEFINE THE VAULT, TRANSFORMED INTO ELLIPSES TO LEAK TO THE VANISHING POINT. IN THE BACKGROUND, THE STROKES ARE EXECUTED BY PRESSING THE STYLUS VERY SLIGHTLY. ON THE OTHER HAND TEXTURES IN THE FOREGROUND APPEAR THICKER AND DEFINED.

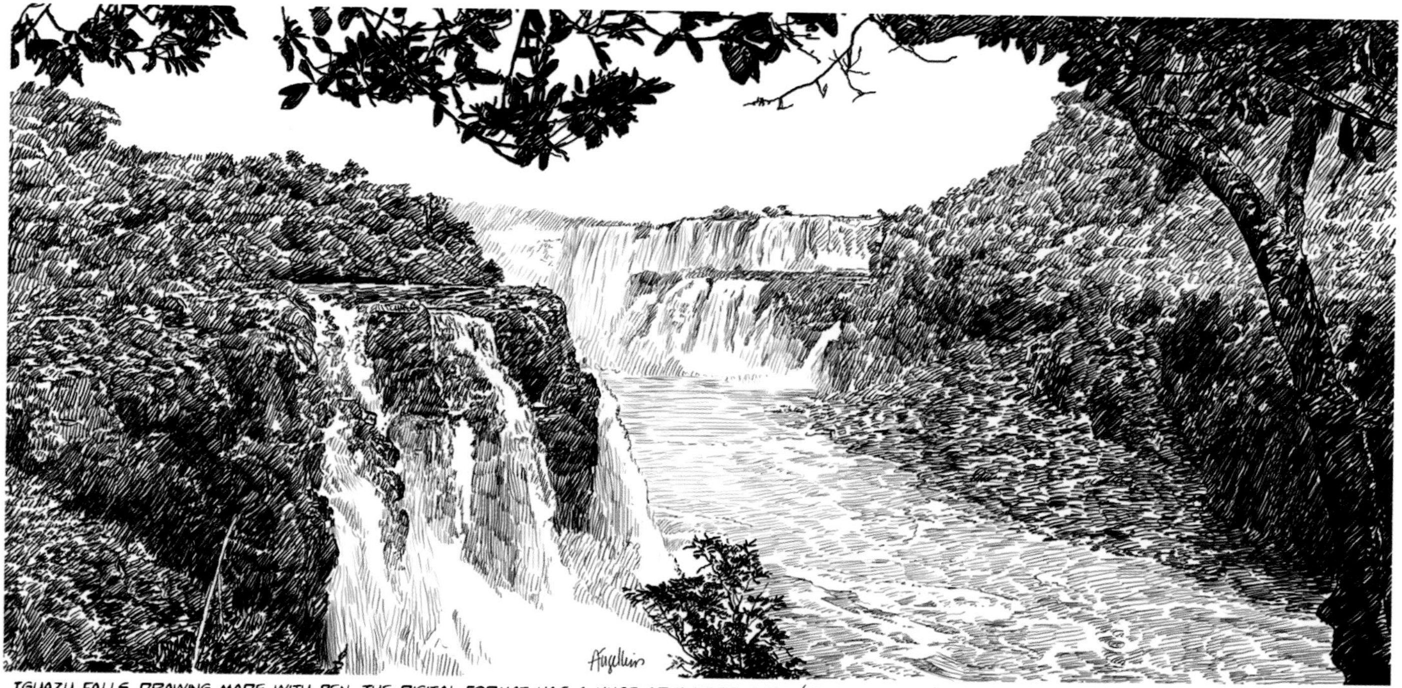

IGUAZU FALLS. DRAWING MADE WITH PEN. THE DIGITAL FORMAT HAS A HUGE ADVANTAGE, AND IT´S THAT ALLOWS A DEGREE OF REALISM, VERY DIFFICULT TO GET ON PAPER. PRINCIPALLY THE ABILITY TO ZOOM WITHOUT LIMITS, THAT ALLOWS US TO WORK WITH GREAT DETAIL IN VERY SMALL PORTIONS OF THE DRAWING.

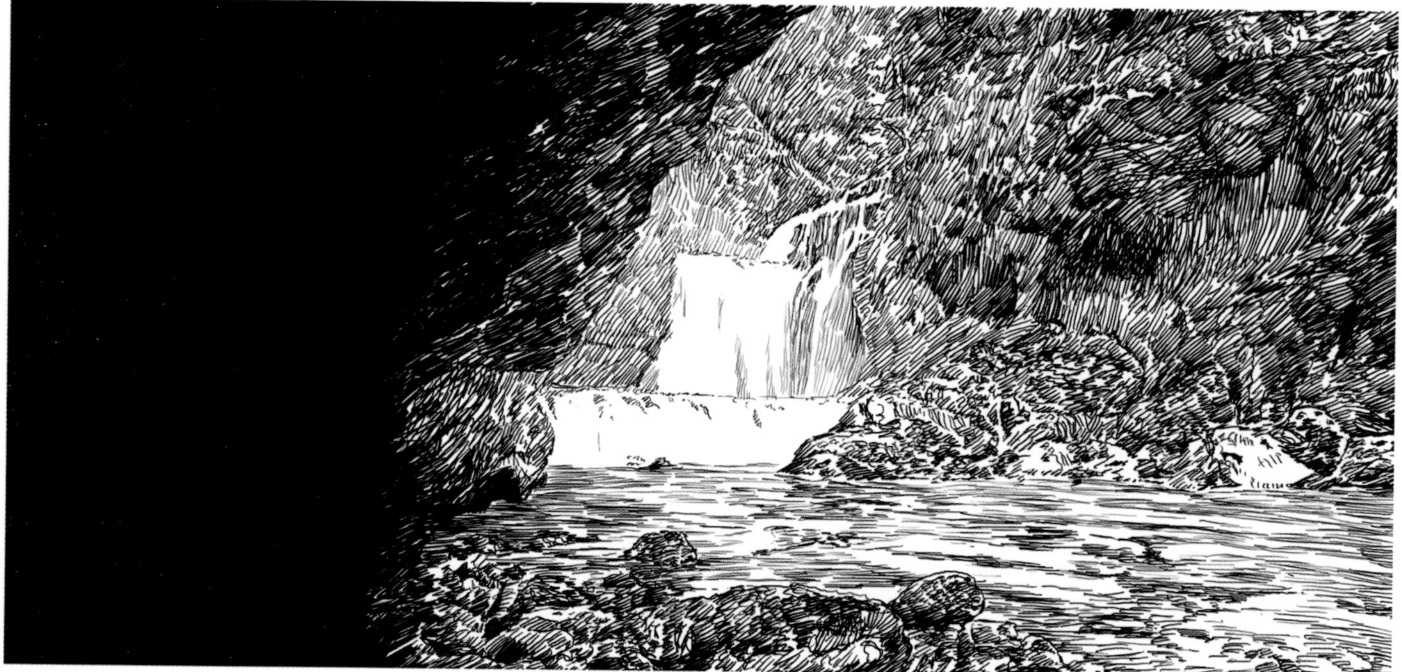

DIGITAL TOOLS ALLOW COUNTLESS NUANCES, AS CALIBRATING WITH THE DIGITAL PEN ANY THICKNESS, COLOR AND DEGREE OF TRANSPARENCY WE WANT. I ALSO NOTE THAT, DESPITE WHAT MANY BELIEVE, DRAWING WITH DIGITAL PEN HAS MUCH MERIT AND DIFFICULTY THAN DOING ON PAPER, BECAUSE WHAT WE EXECUTE WITH THE HAND ON THE DIGITAL TABLET, IS SHOWN ON THE SCREEN AND IT TAKES A LONG ADAPTATION PERIOD.

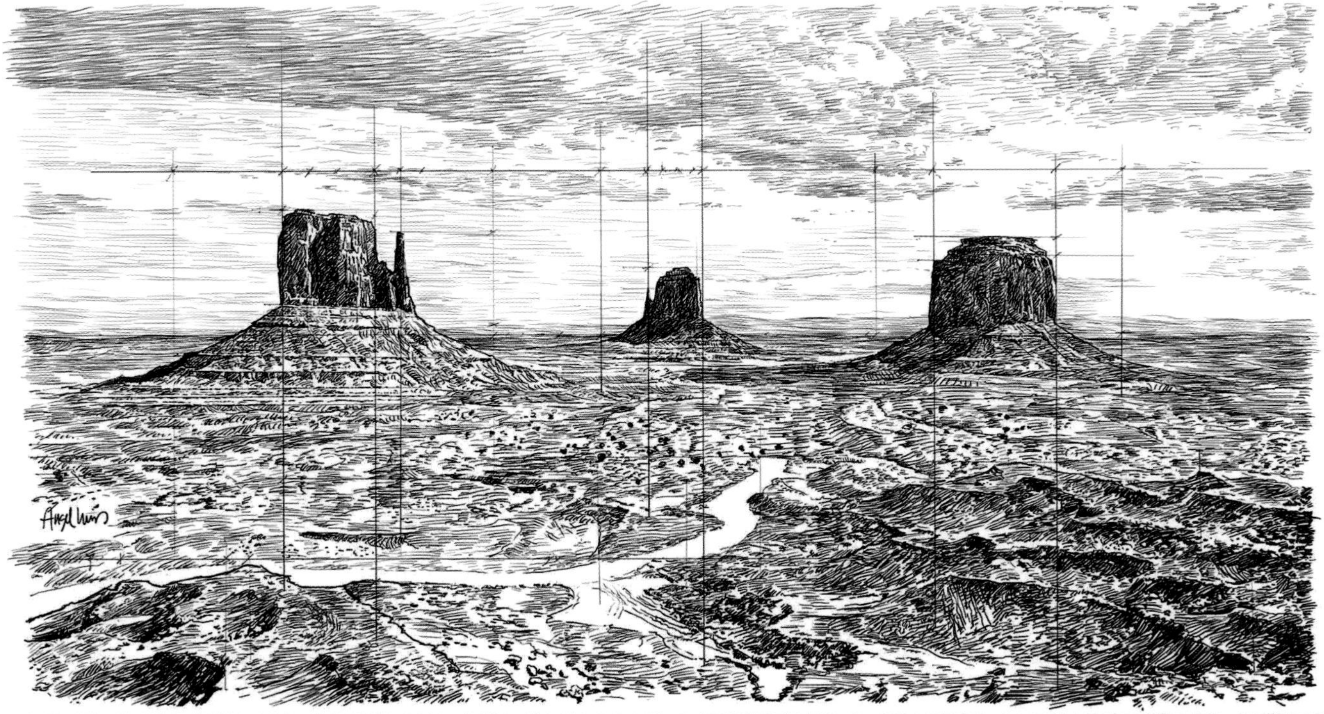

MONUMENT VALLEY. DRAWING MADE WITH STYLUS V5 AND V7. YOU CAN SEE THE CONSTRUCTION LINES OF THE DRAWING, ON WHICH ARE PLACED THE NECESSARY REFERENCES TO MAKE THE RIGHT PROPORTION. THOROUGHNESS OF THE STROKE ALLOWS TO PERCEIVE THE ENORMOUS DEPTH OF THE SCENE.

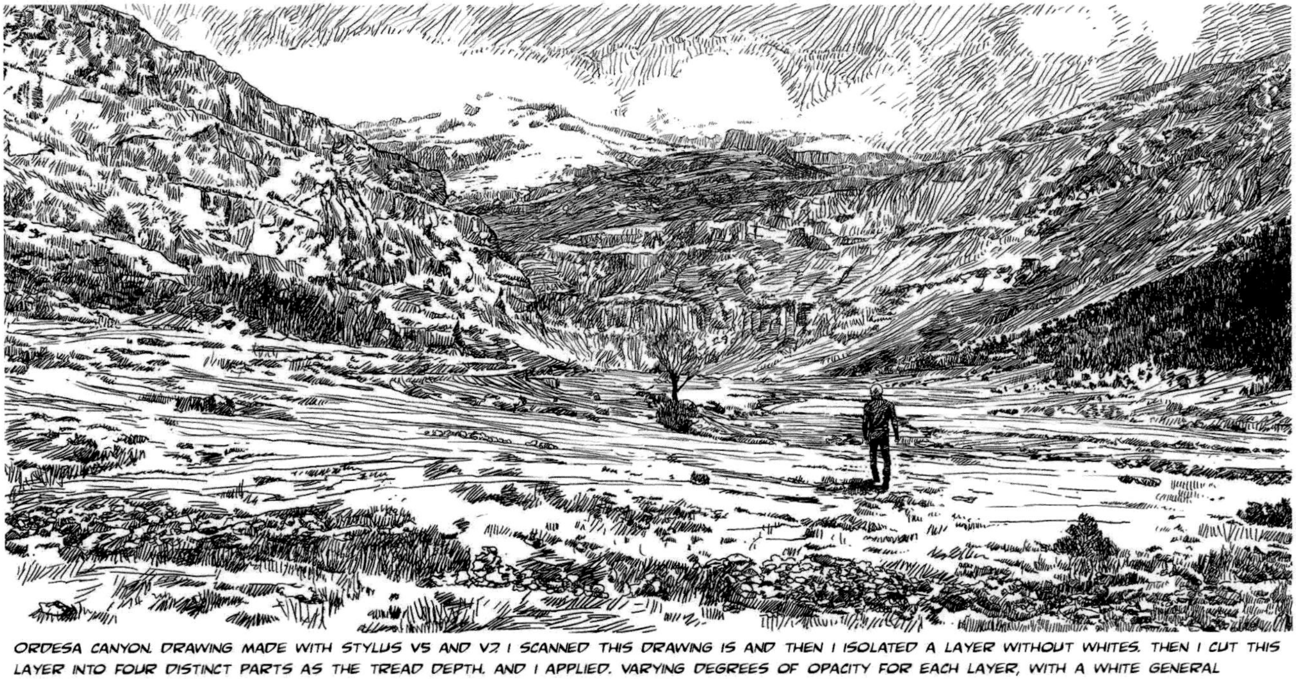

ORDESA CANYON. DRAWING MADE WITH STYLUS V5 AND V7. I SCANNED THIS DRAWING IS AND THEN I ISOLATED A LAYER WITHOUT WHITES. THEN I CUT THIS LAYER INTO FOUR DISTINCT PARTS AS THE TREAD DEPTH. AND I APPLIED. VARYING DEGREES OF OPACITY FOR EACH LAYER, WITH A WHITE GENERAL BACKGROUND. LAYERS HAVE A DEGREE OF OPACITY INVERSELY PROPORTIONAL TO THE DISTANCE OF WHAT APPEARS IN EACH LAYER.

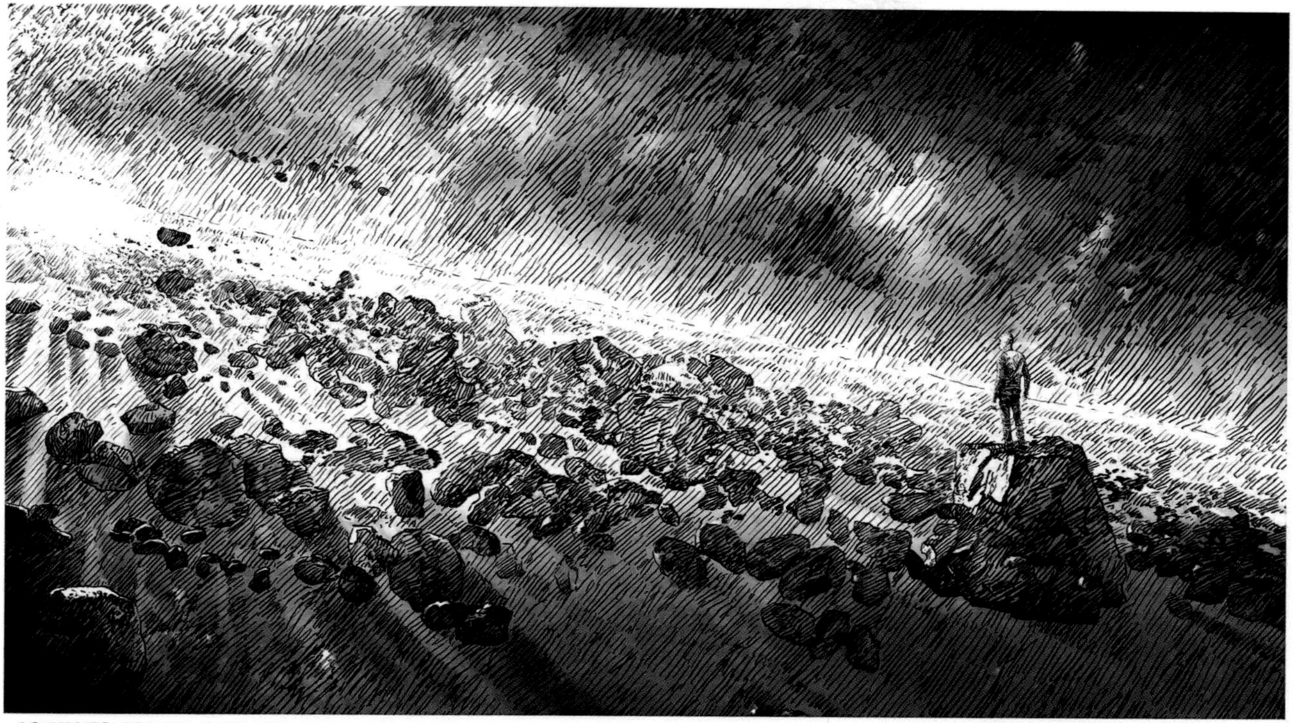

ASTEROIDS. DRAWING MADE WITH DIGITAL PEN. BEHIND THE DRAWING LAYER I APPLIED BLACK AND WHITE STAINS, TO CREATE THE EFFECT OF LIGHT FROM THE STAR. THEN I APPLIED A GAUSSIAN BLUR AND USE THE TOOLS OF OVEREXPOSURE AND UNDEREXPOSURE FOR NUANCES.

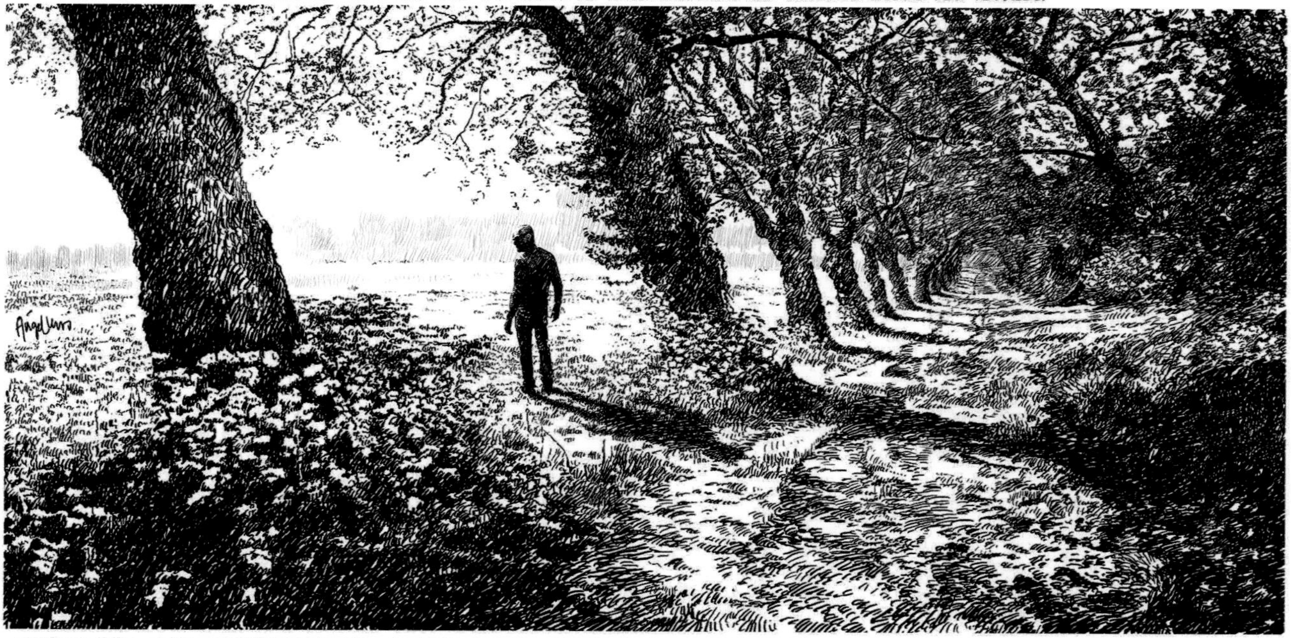

ORGANIC VAULT. MIXED TECHNIQUE DRAWING. THE BASE IS A DRAWING DONE WITH STYLUS V5 AND V7, WHICH I COMPLETED WITH THE DIGITAL PEN. I WANT TO HIGHLIGHT THE VOLUME THAT SOMETIMES WE GET WITH A GOOD USE OF TEXTURES, LIKE THE FLOWERS THAT GROW UNDER THE TREE IN THE FOREGROUND ON THE LEFT. OR THE DEPTH GOT IN THE BACKGROUND, AT THE END OF THE VAULT.

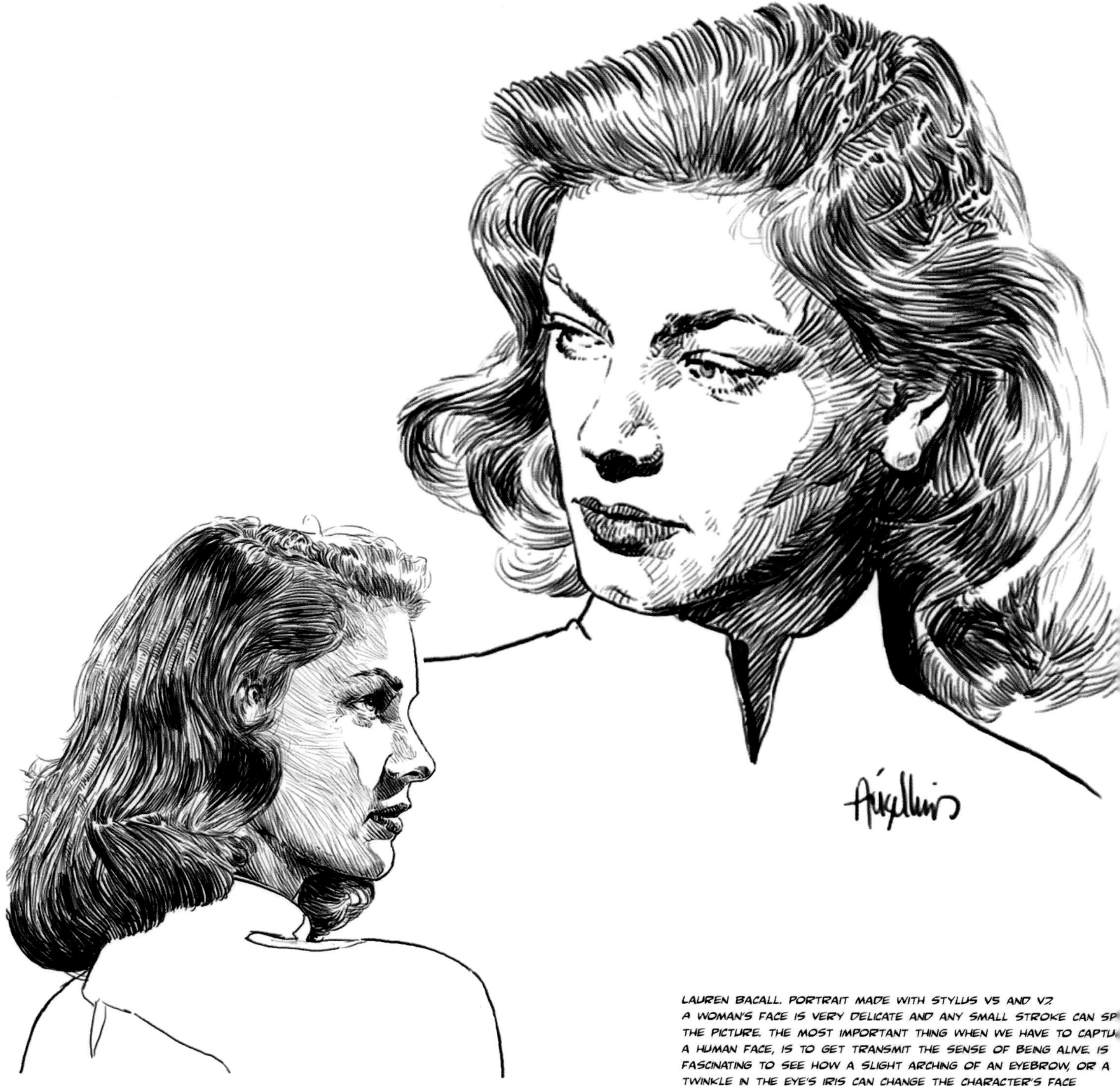

LAUREN BACALL. PORTRAIT MADE WITH STYLUS V5 AND V7.
A WOMAN'S FACE IS VERY DELICATE AND ANY SMALL STROKE CAN SP
THE PICTURE. THE MOST IMPORTANT THING WHEN WE HAVE TO CAPTU
A HUMAN FACE, IS TO GET TRANSMIT THE SENSE OF BEING ALIVE. IS
FASCINATING TO SEE HOW A SLIGHT ARCHING OF AN EYEBROW, OR A
TWINKLE IN THE EYE'S IRIS CAN CHANGE THE CHARACTER'S FACE
ABSOLUTELY.

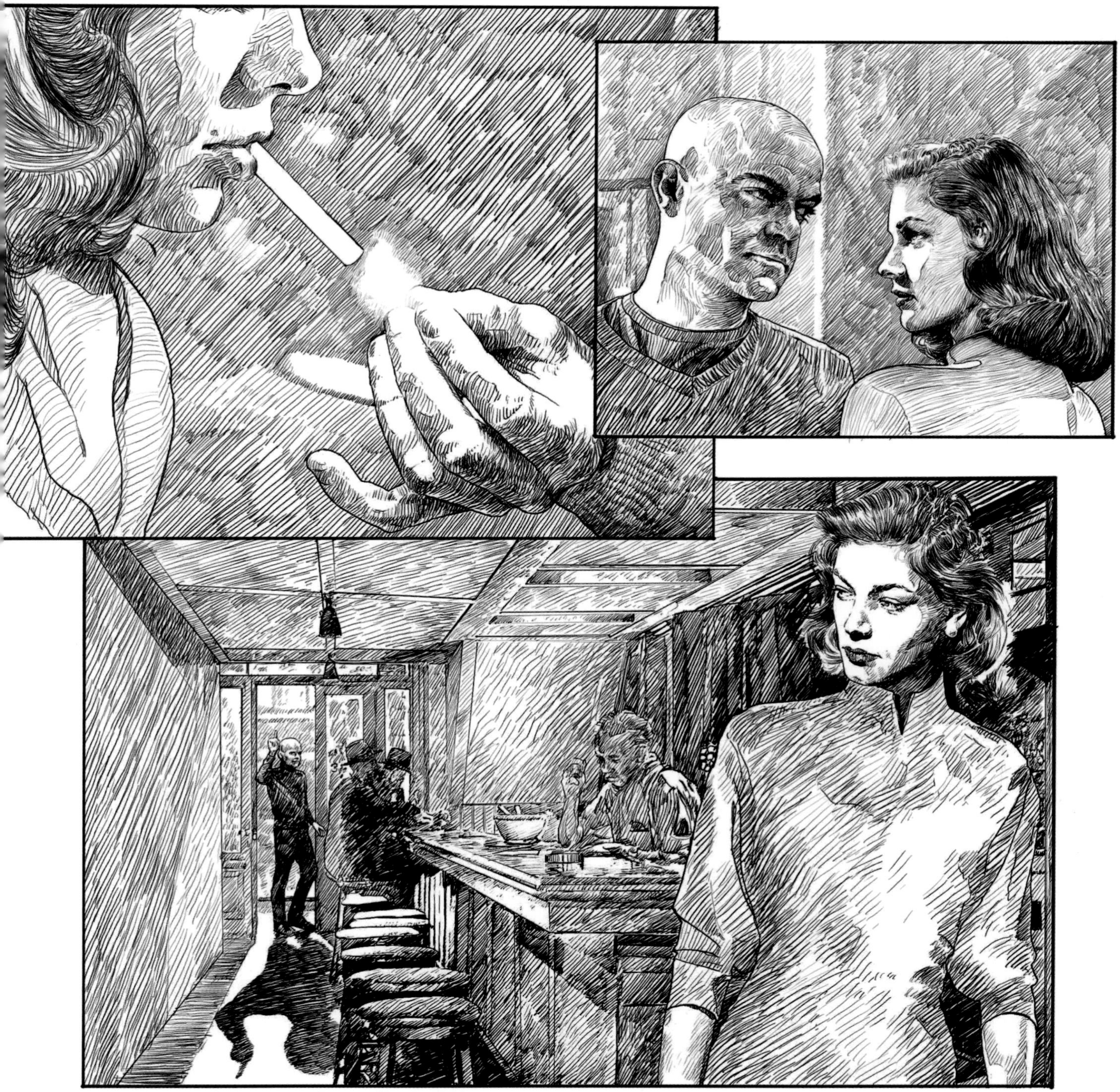

LAUREN BACALL. THIS IS A PAGE TRIBUTE TO BLACK AMERICAN CINEMA AND LAUREN BACALL. DRAWINGS WERE MADE WITH PILOT V5-7, INDEPENDENTLY, AND I PUT ALL TOGETHER ON THIS PAGE AFTER SCANNING THEM, THEN I APPLIED A LIGHT COAT OF BLACK AND WHITE.

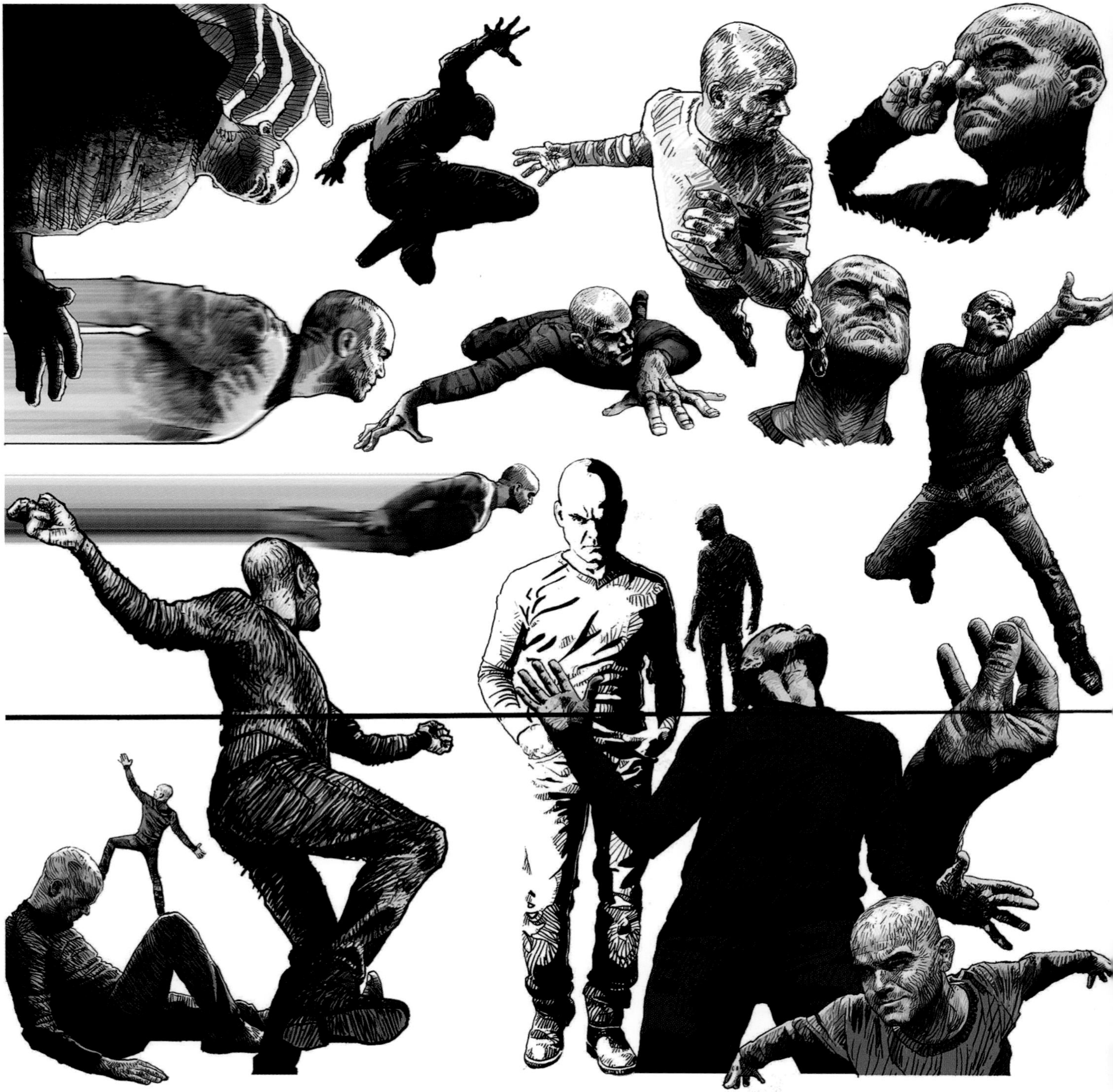

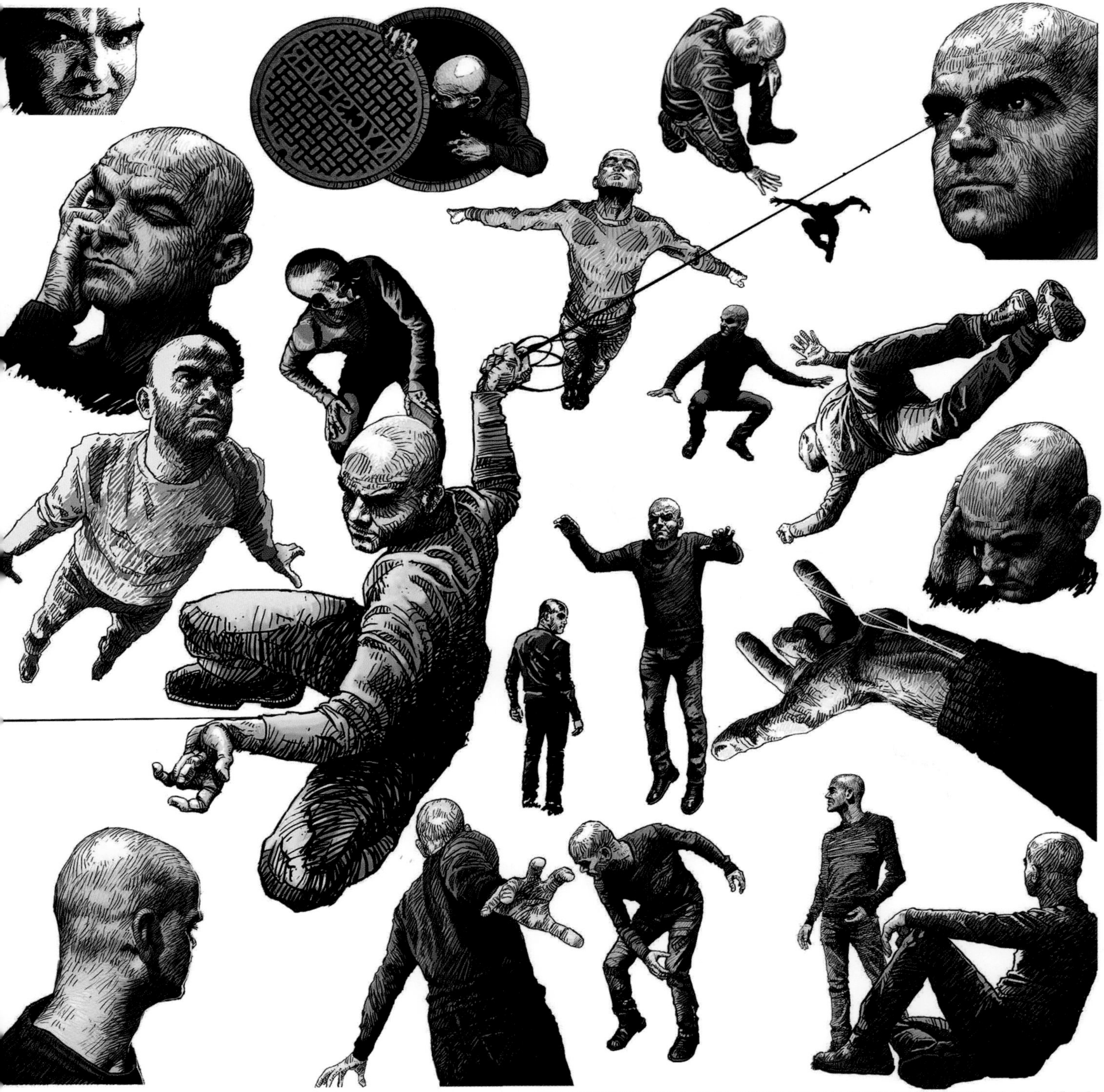

ALTS. DOUBLE PAGE WITH SOME HUMAN FIGURES PRESENT IN THE COMIC

ALT. DRAWINGS OF THE HUMAN FACE. I DID A PRELIMINARY SKETCH WITH PENCIL 2H, AND SUBSEQUENTLY I SCANNED IT AND ISOLATED IT IN A LAYER, ELIMINATING WHITES.
AS I WANTED TO PLACE IT ON A BLACK BACKGROUND, I DID NOT DELIMIT THE DARKER PARTS. THE DEFINITIVE STROKES WERE IMPLEMENTED WITH DIGITAL PEN.

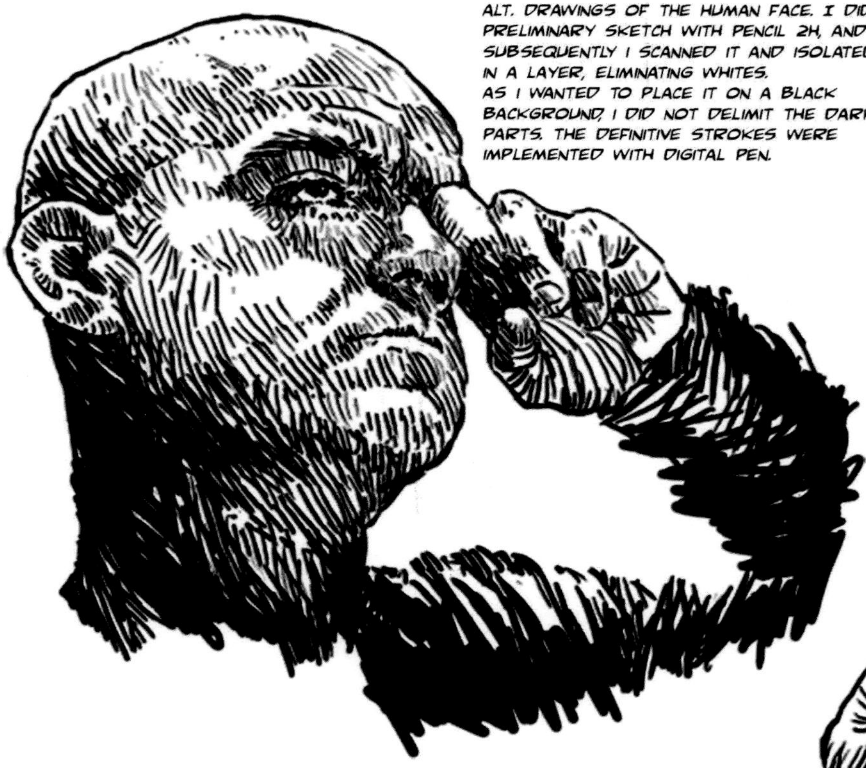

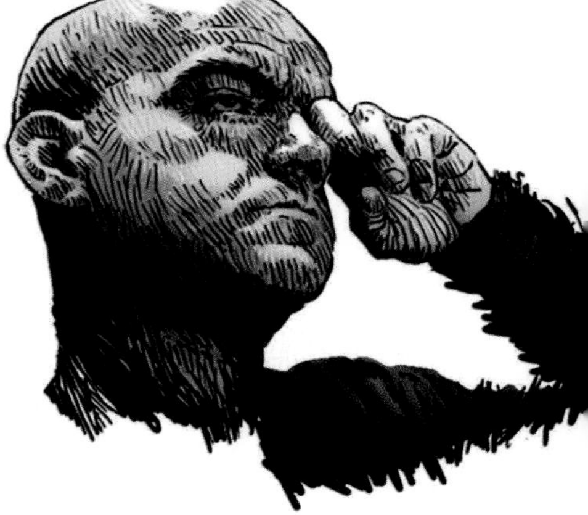

I APPLIED THE COLOR IN A BACK LAYER USING THE BRUSH TOOL AND ONLY FOUR OR FIVE FLESH TONES. THE COLOR IS APPLIED USING A TECHNIQUE OF SCRATCHING, EQUAL AS USED IN BLACK AND WHITE DRAWING.
I WANT TO EMPHASIZE THAT IT IS REALLY DIFFICULT TO CAPTURE THE MOOD OF THE PERSON, BECAUSE ANY LITTLE NUANCE CHANGES THE CHARACTER COMPLETELY.

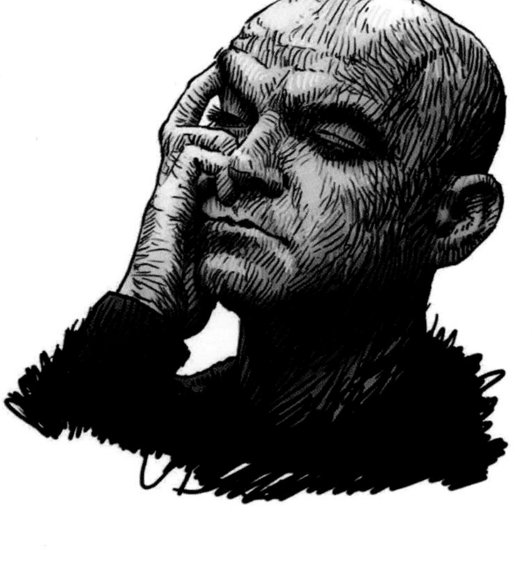

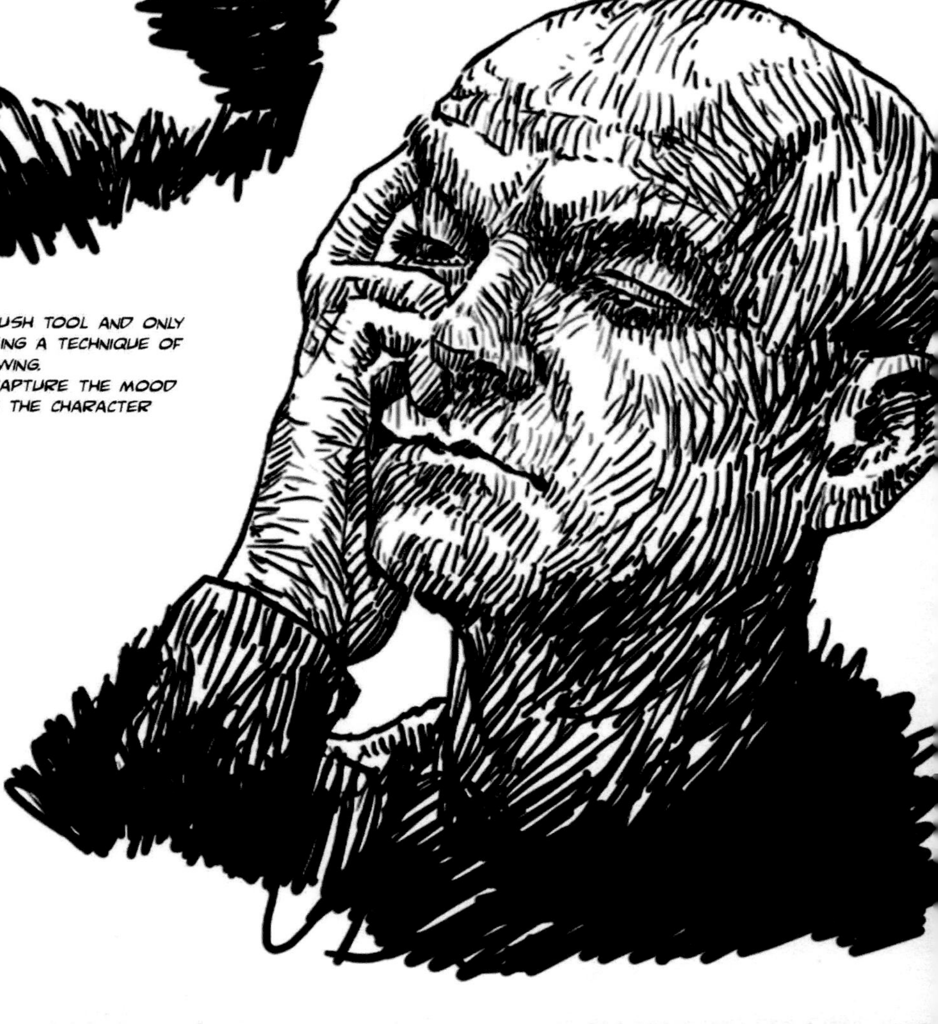

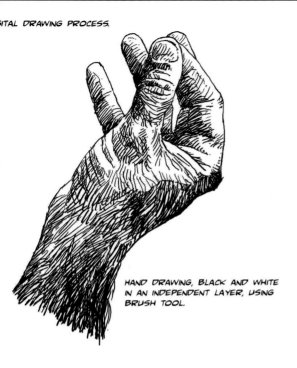

HAND DRAWING, BLACK AND WHITE
IN AN INDEPENDENT LAYER, USING
BRUSH TOOL.

COLOR APPLIED WITH BRUSH TOOL
AT A BACK LAYER. HERE WE SEE
ONLY THE COLOR LAYER, BUT IN
DOING SO, THE LAYER OF BLACKS
MUST BE VISIBLE.

RESULT OF THE UNION OF LAYERS
OF BLACK AND COLOR.

FINAL RESULT, WITH BLACK
BACKGROUND LAYER.

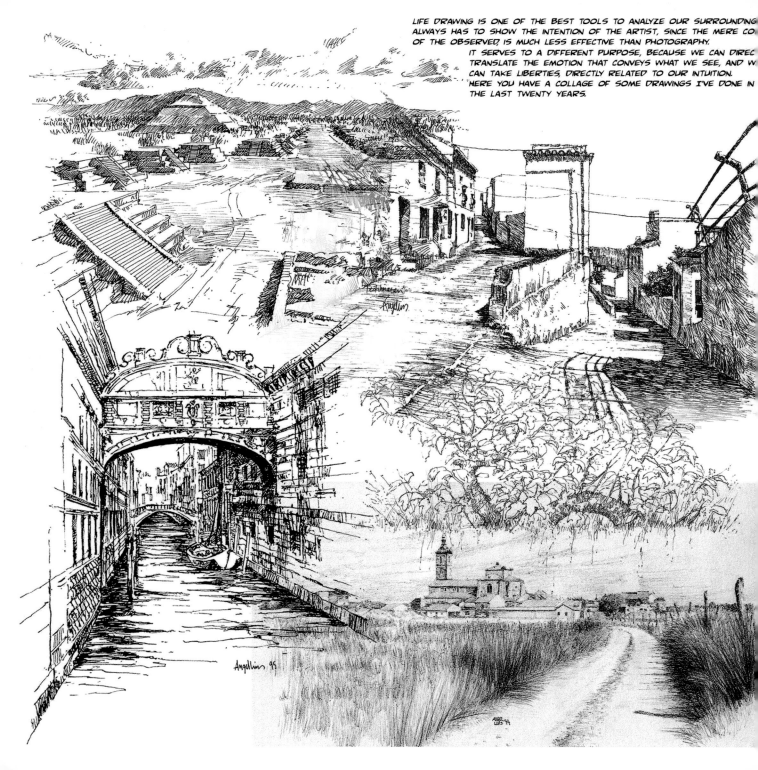

LIFE DRAWING IS ONE OF THE BEST TOOLS TO ANALYZE OUR SURROUNDING
ALWAYS HAS TO SHOW THE INTENTION OF THE ARTIST, SINCE THE MERE CO
OF THE OBSERVED, IS MUCH LESS EFFECTIVE THAN PHOTOGRAPHY.
IT SERVES TO A DIFFERENT PURPOSE, BECAUSE WE CAN DIREC
TRANSLATE THE EMOTION THAT CONVEYS WHAT WE SEE, AND W
CAN TAKE LIBERTIES, DIRECTLY RELATED TO OUR INTUITION.
HERE YOU HAVE A COLLAGE OF SOME DRAWINGS I'VE DONE IN
THE LAST TWENTY YEARS.

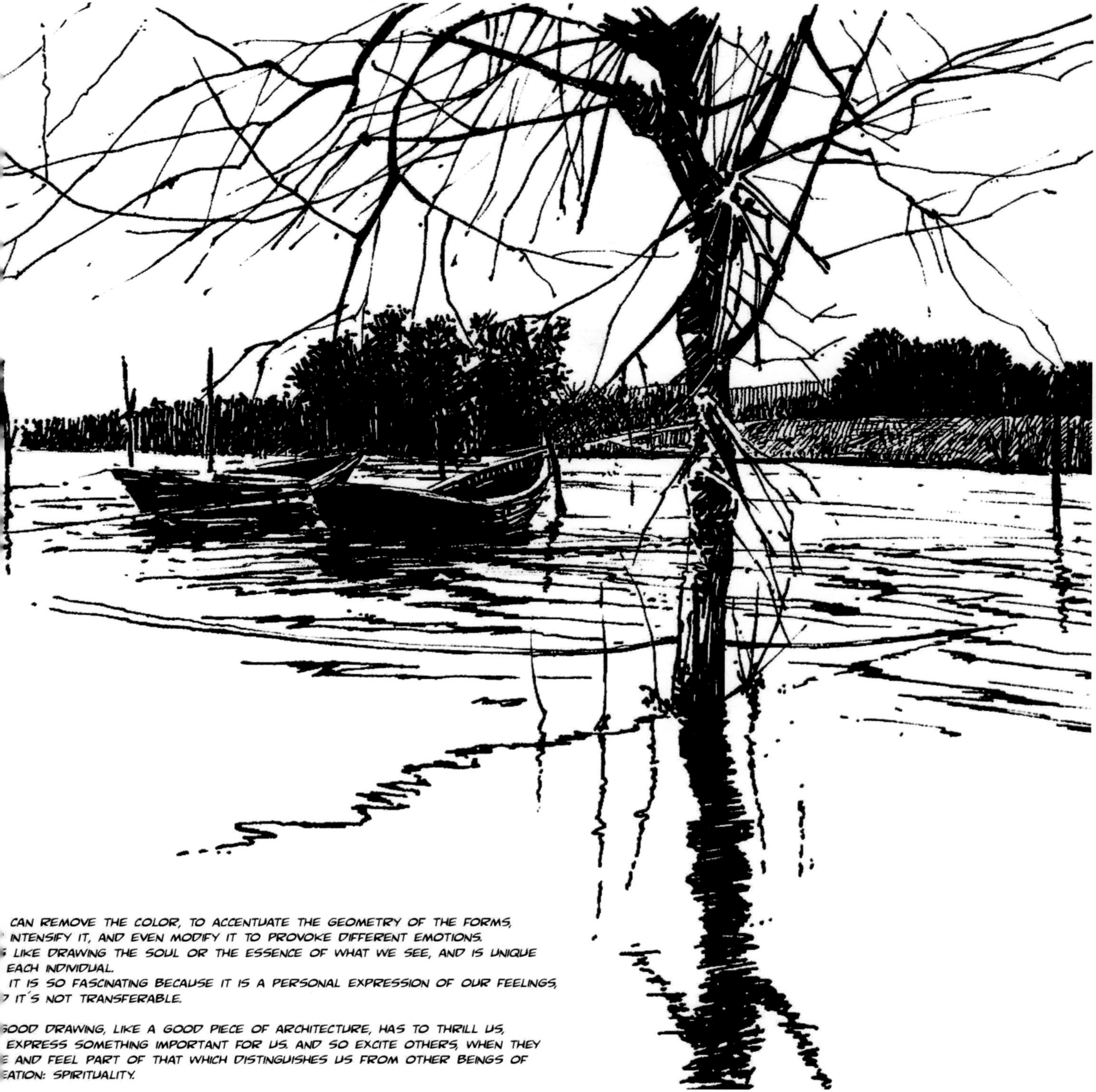

CAN REMOVE THE COLOR, TO ACCENTUATE THE GEOMETRY OF THE FORMS,
INTENSIFY IT, AND EVEN MODIFY IT TO PROVOKE DIFFERENT EMOTIONS.
LIKE DRAWING THE SOUL OR THE ESSENCE OF WHAT WE SEE, AND IS UNIQUE
EACH INDIVIDUAL.
IT IS SO FASCINATING BECAUSE IT IS A PERSONAL EXPRESSION OF OUR FEELINGS,
IT'S NOT TRANSFERABLE.

GOOD DRAWING, LIKE A GOOD PIECE OF ARCHITECTURE, HAS TO THRILL US,
EXPRESS SOMETHING IMPORTANT FOR US. AND SO EXCITE OTHERS, WHEN THEY
E AND FEEL PART OF THAT WHICH DISTINGUISHES US FROM OTHER BEINGS OF
EATION: SPIRITUALITY.

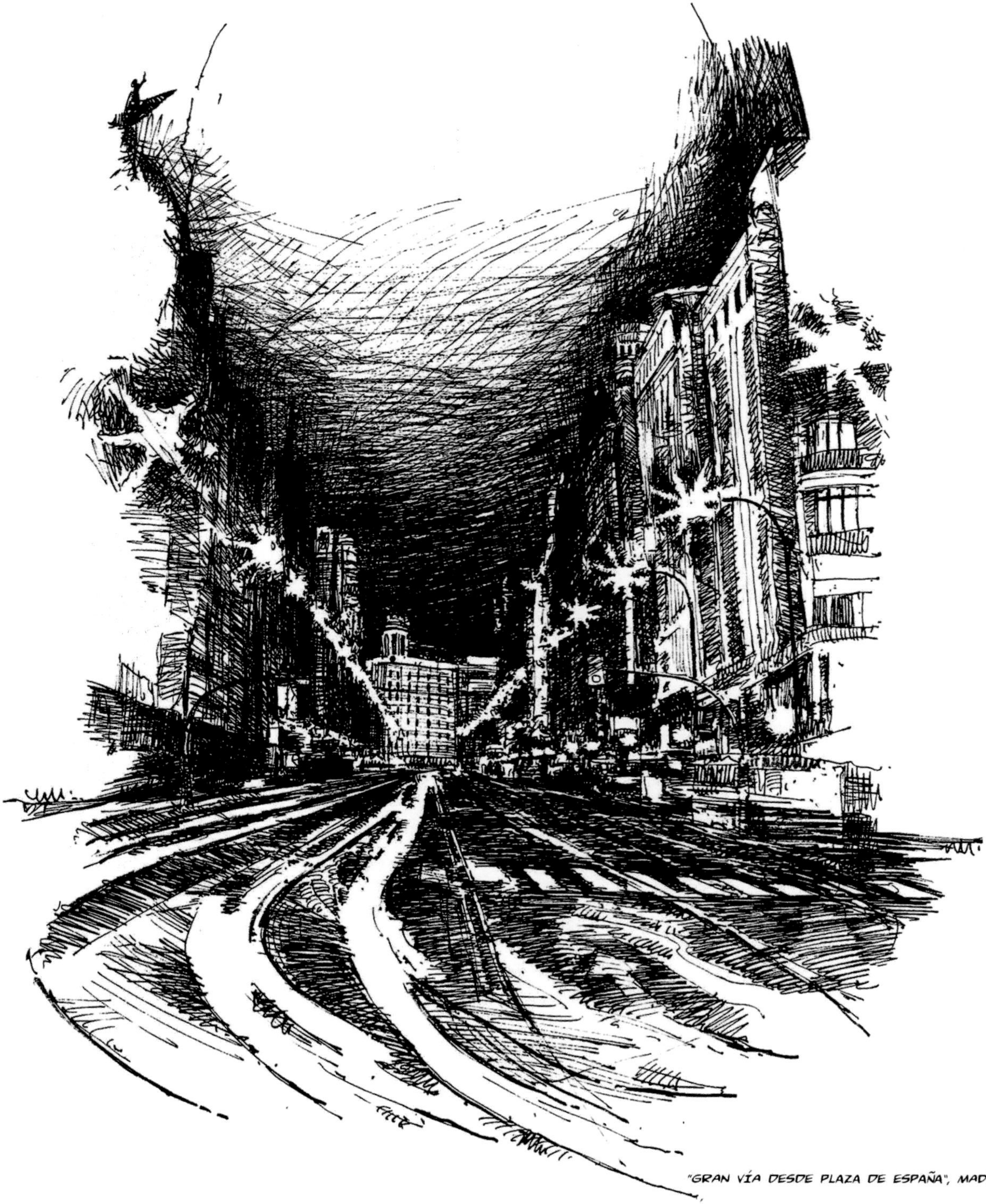

"GRAN VÍA DESDE PLAZA DE ESPAÑA", MADRID, PILOT V5

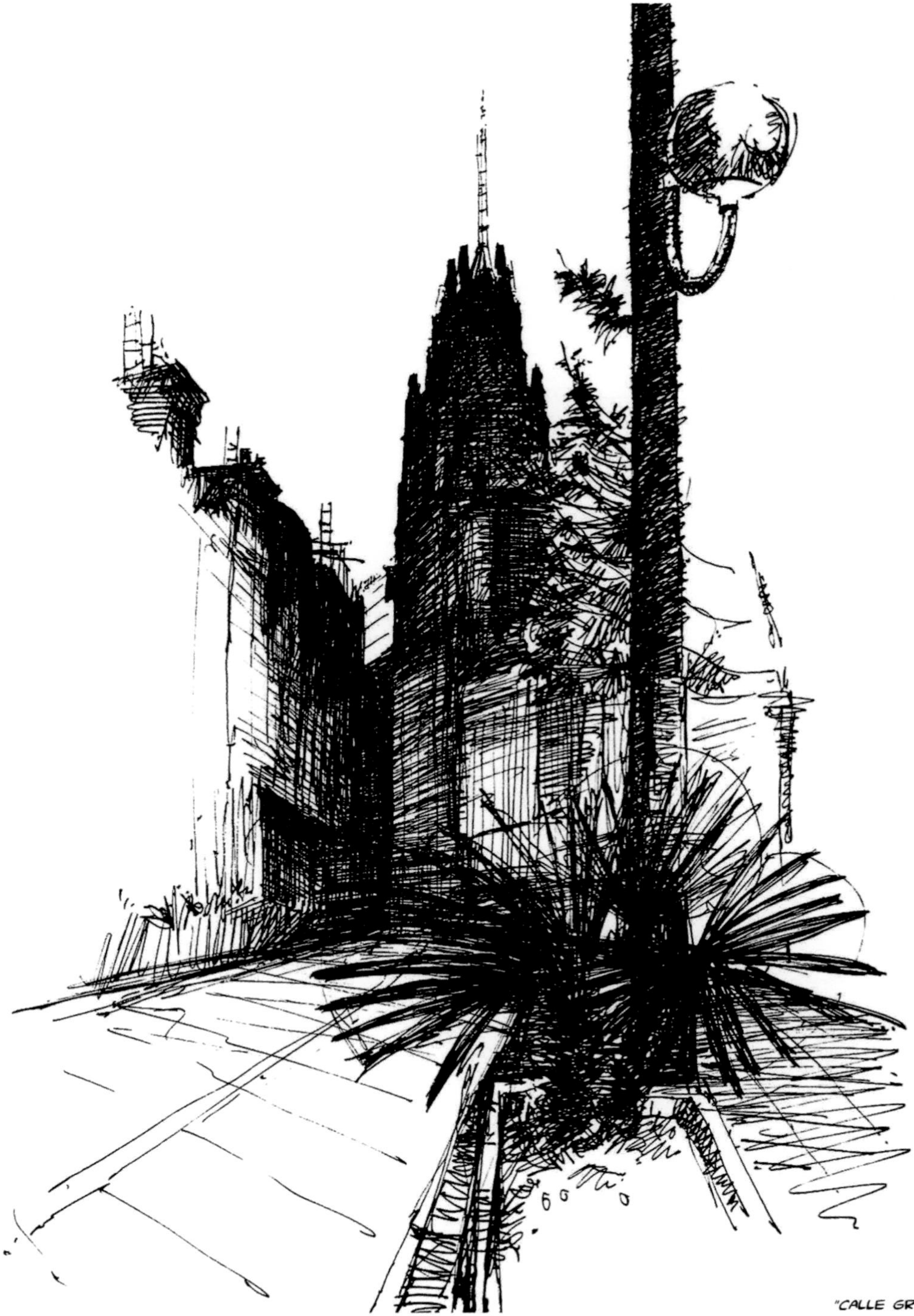

"CALLE GRAN VÍA", MADRID, PILOT V5.

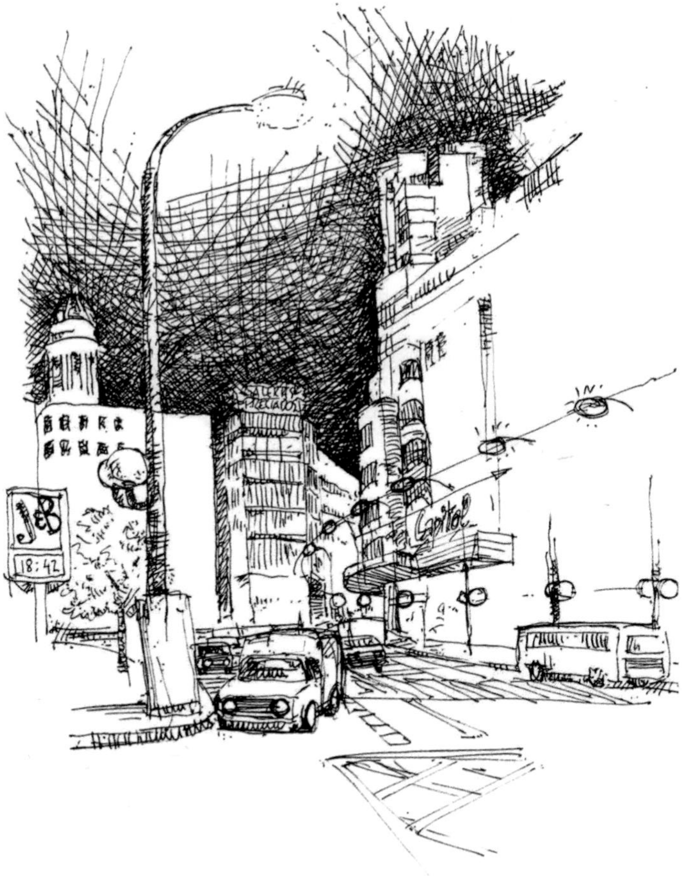
J&B
18:42
Capitol

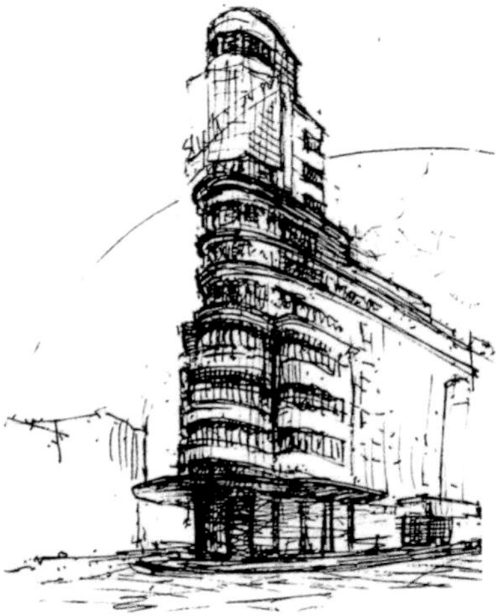

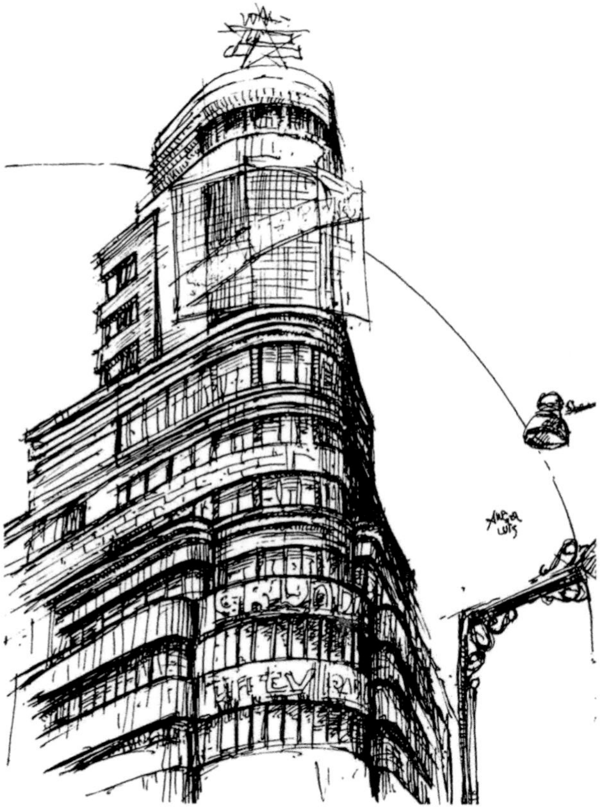

"CAPITOL", MADRID, PILOT V5.

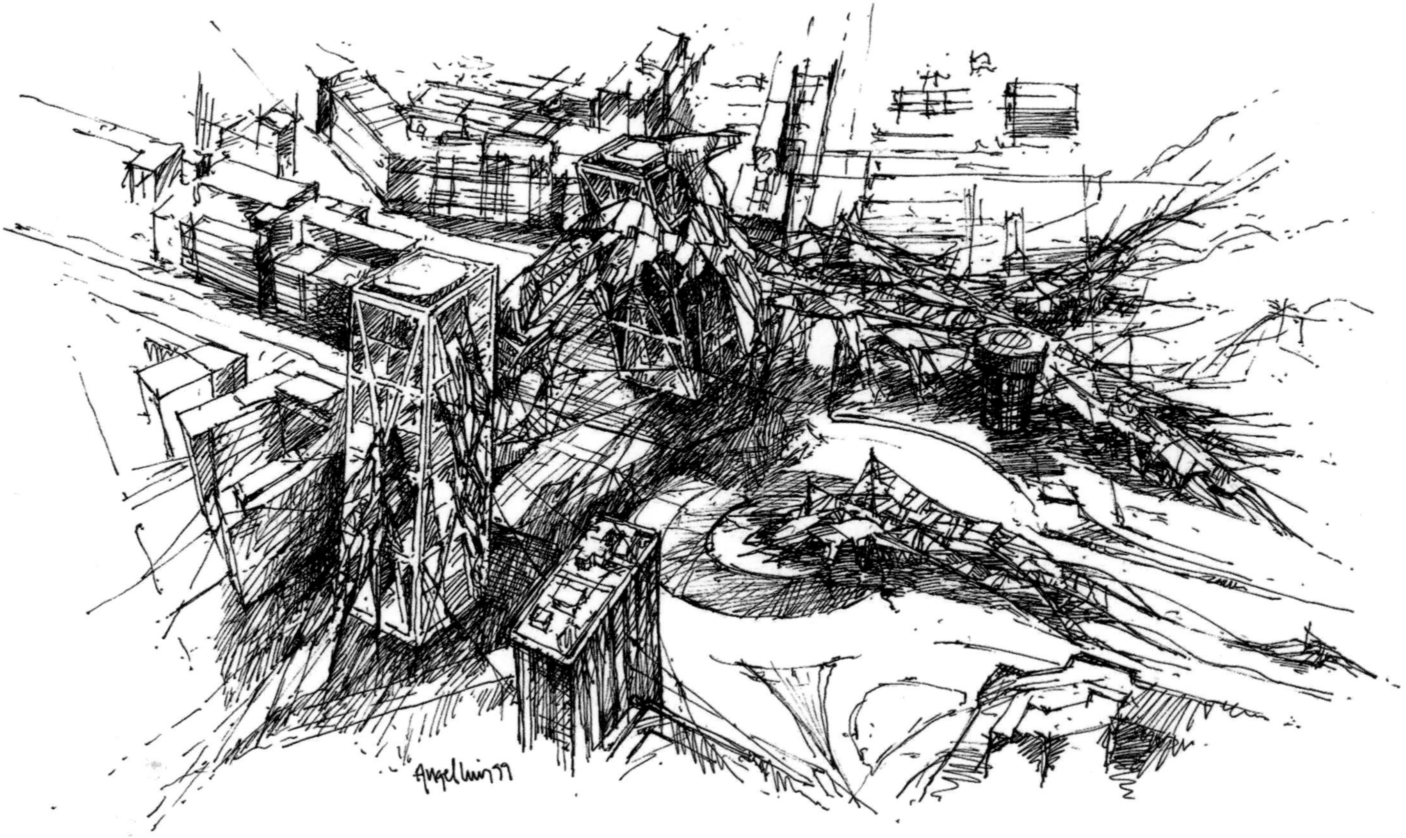

"ATAQUE ORGÁNICO A LAS TORRES KIO", MADRID, PILOT V5.

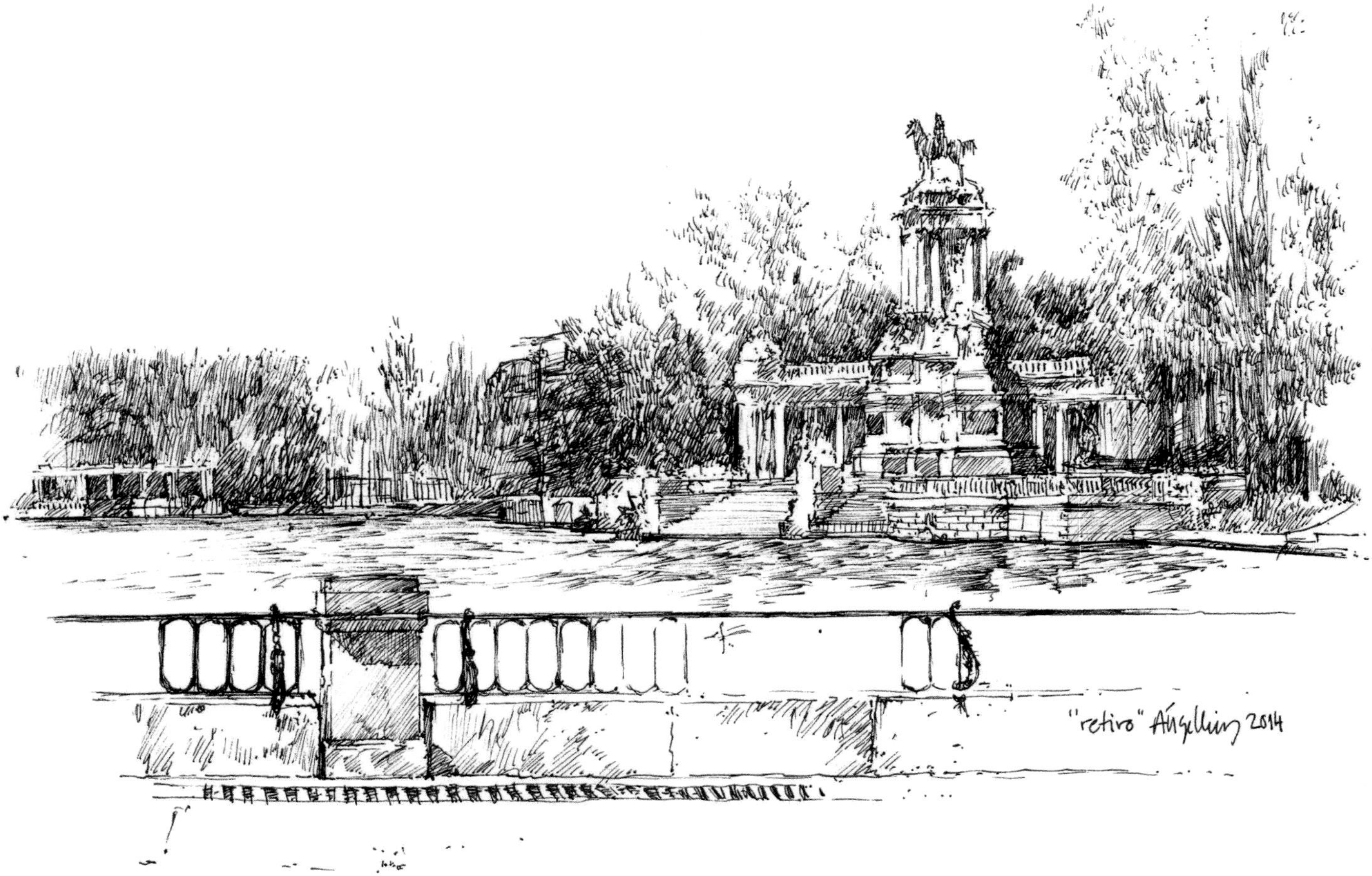
"retiro" Ángel Luis 2014

"LAGO DEL PARQUE DEL RETIRO", MADRID, PILOT V5.

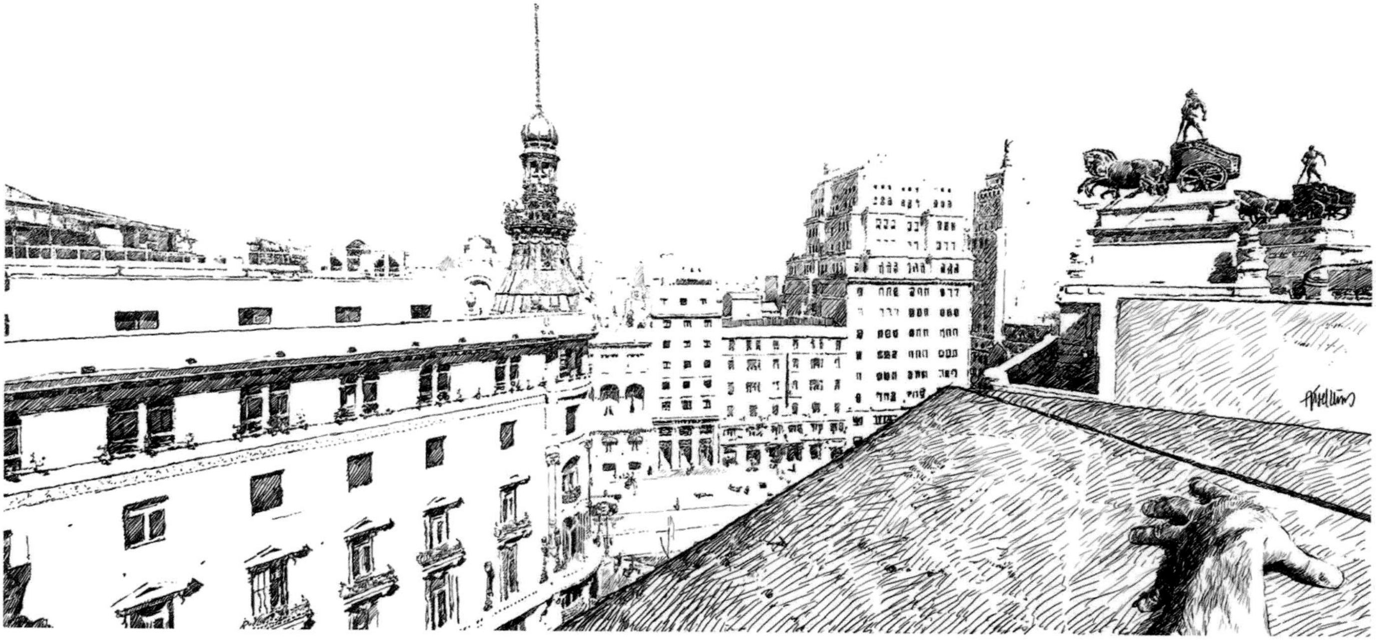

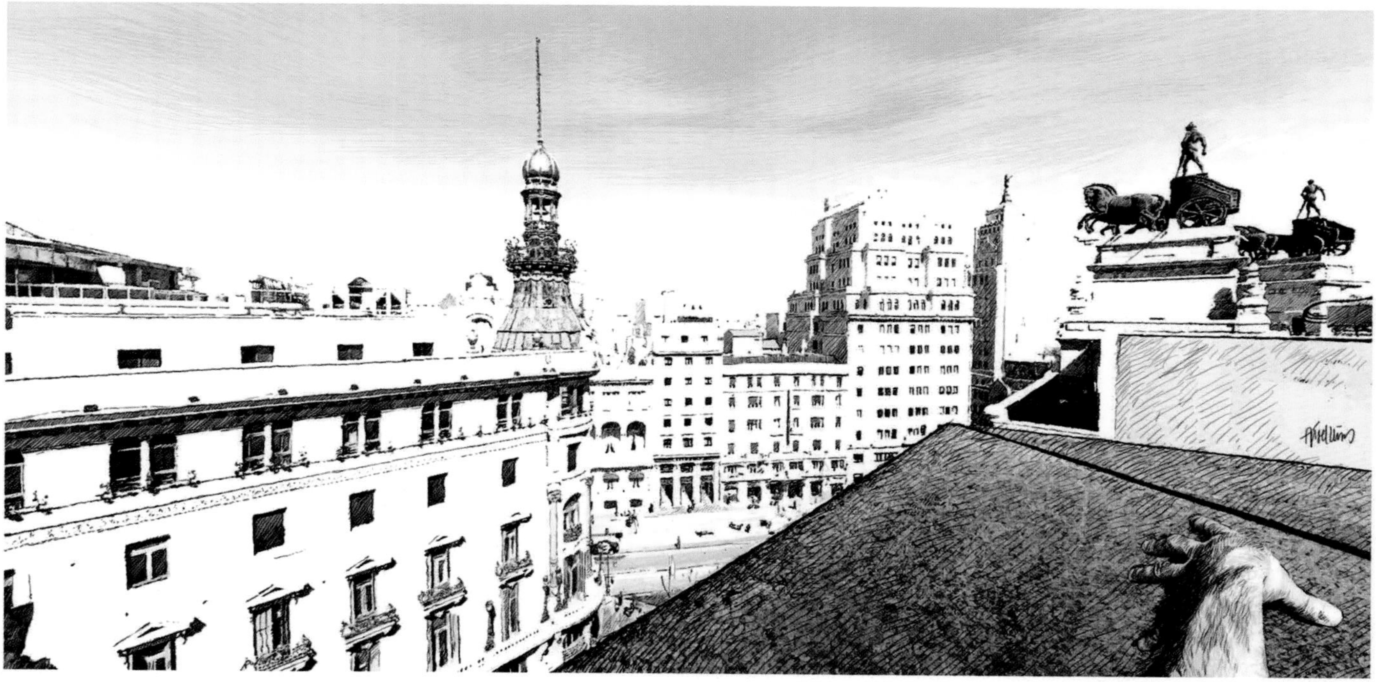

"CALLE DE ALCALÁ / CALLE SEVILLA", MADRID, PILOT V5, COLOR DIGITAL.

"AUDITORIO ALFREDO KRAUS", MAJADAHONDA, MADRID, PILOT V5.

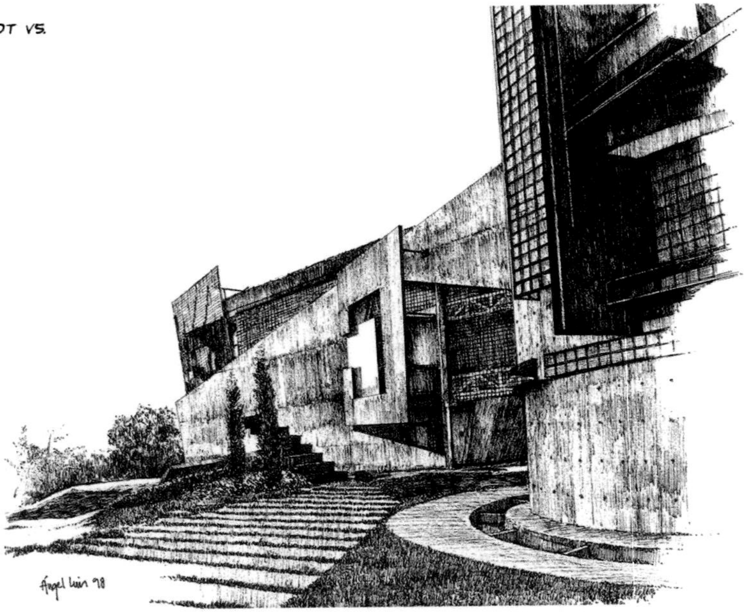

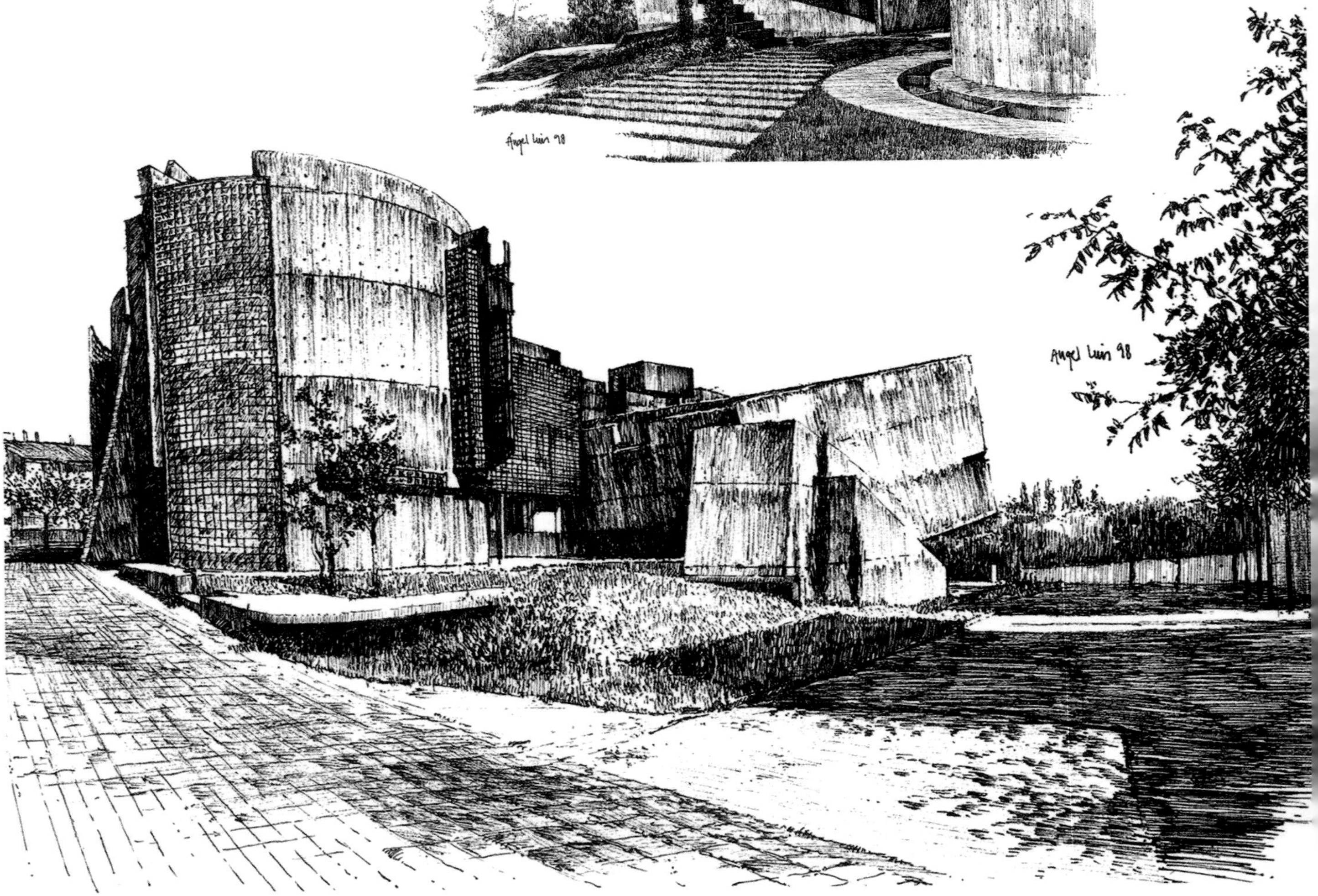

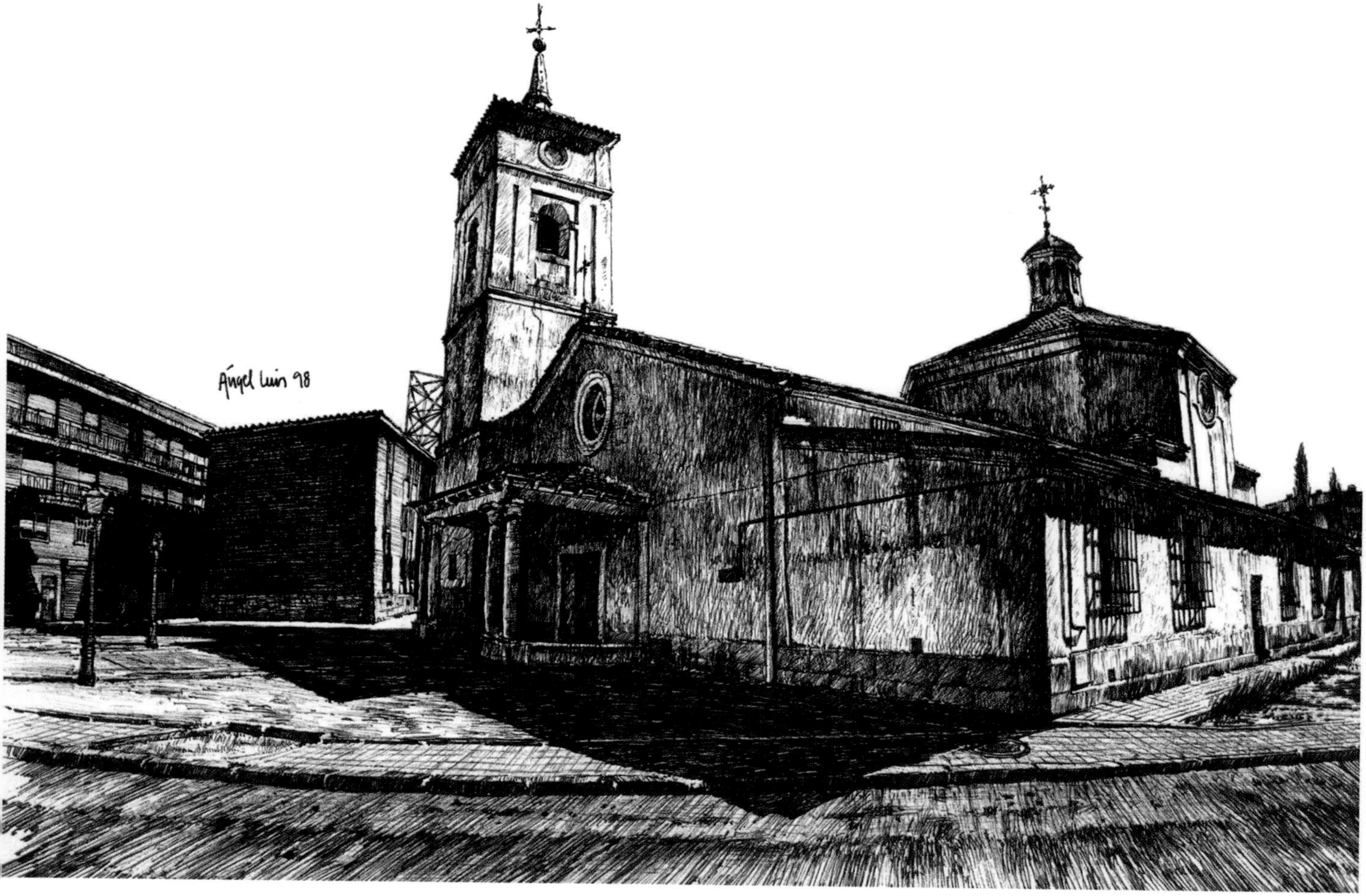
Ángel Luis 98

"IGLESIA DE SANTA CATALINA", MAJADAHONDA, MADRID, BOLÍGRAFO.

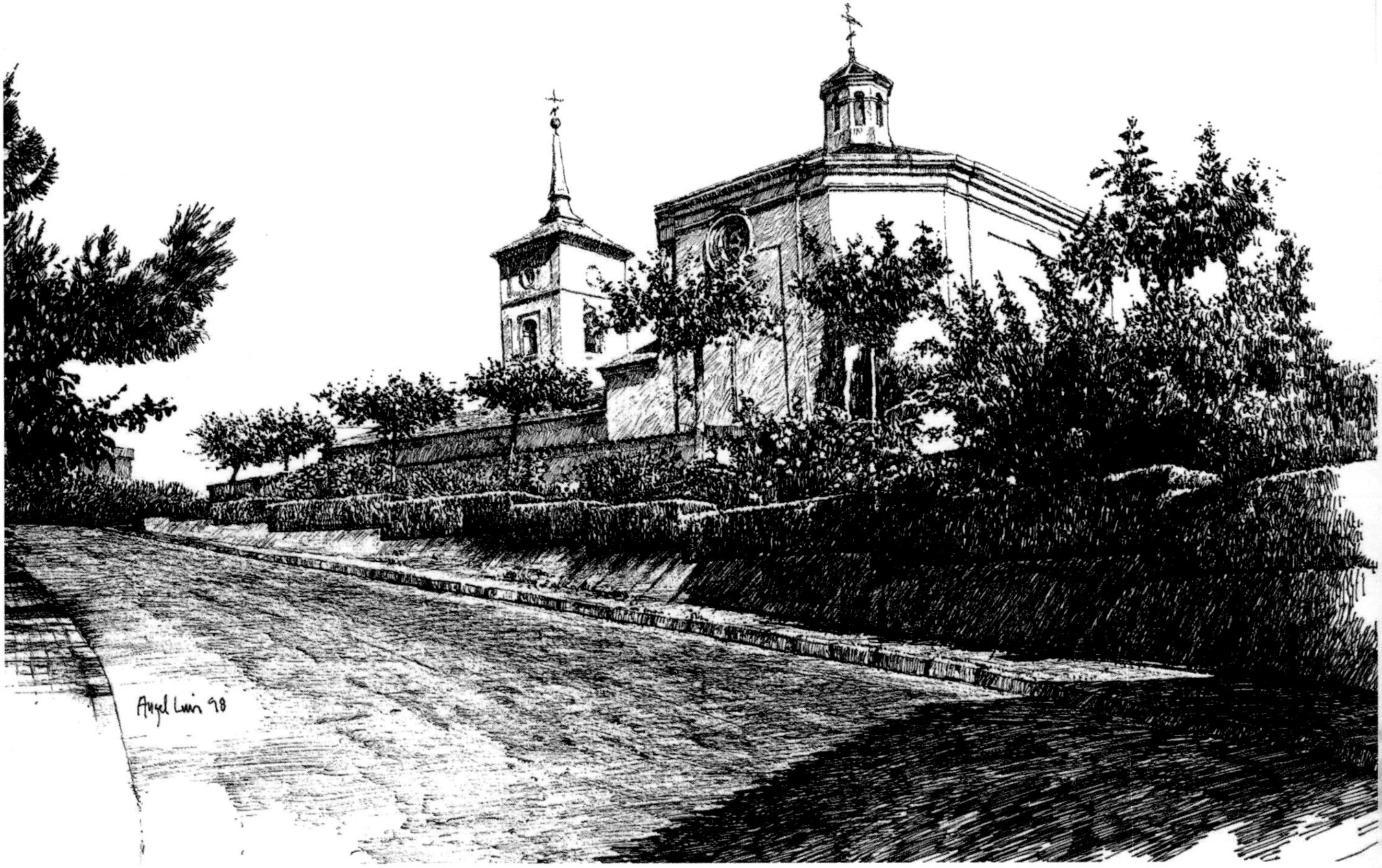
Angel Luis 98

"IGLESIA DE SANTA CATALINA", MAJADAHONDA, MADRID, BOLÍGRAFO

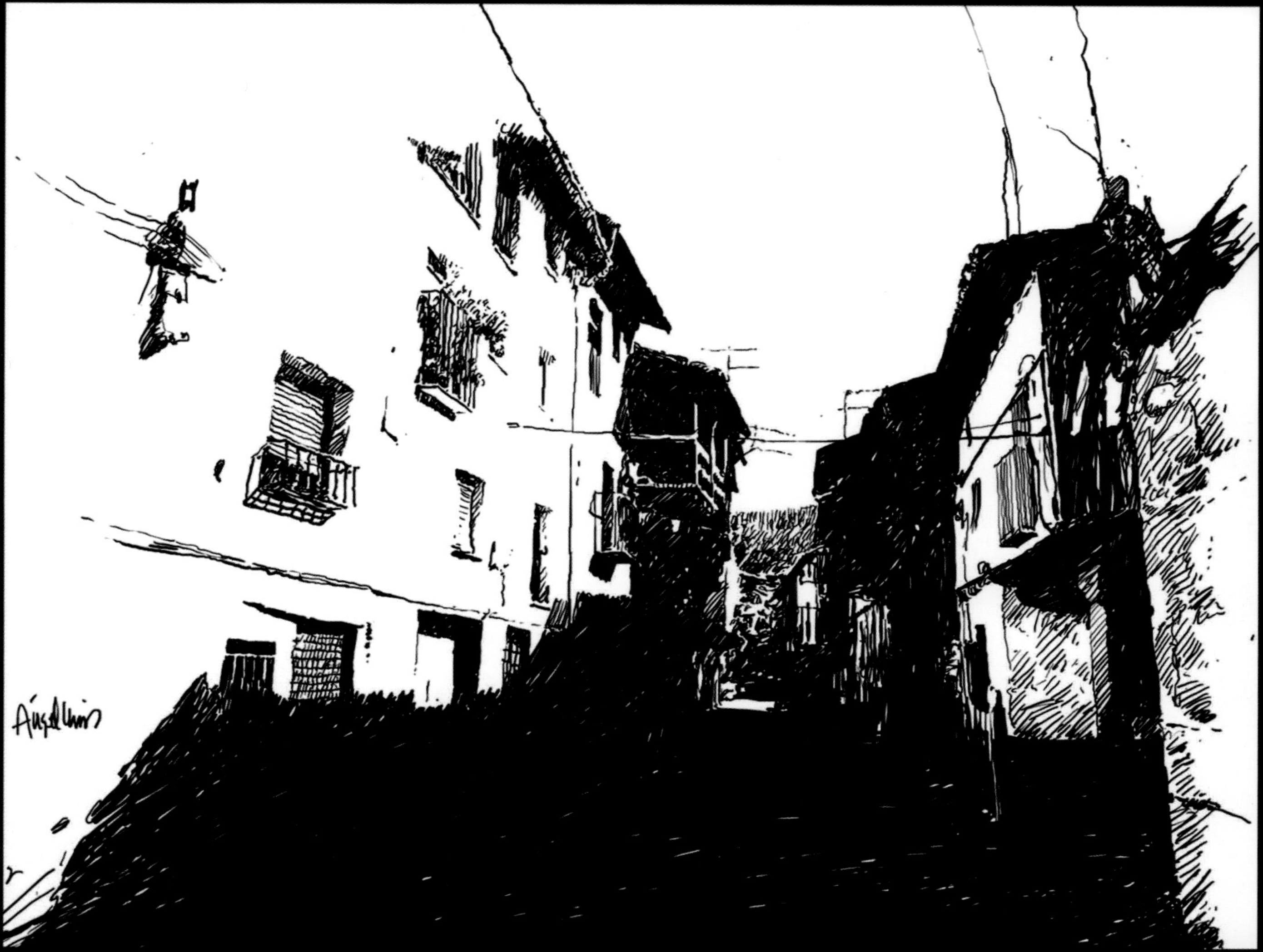
Ángel Luis

"GARGANTA DE LA OLLA", PILOT V5

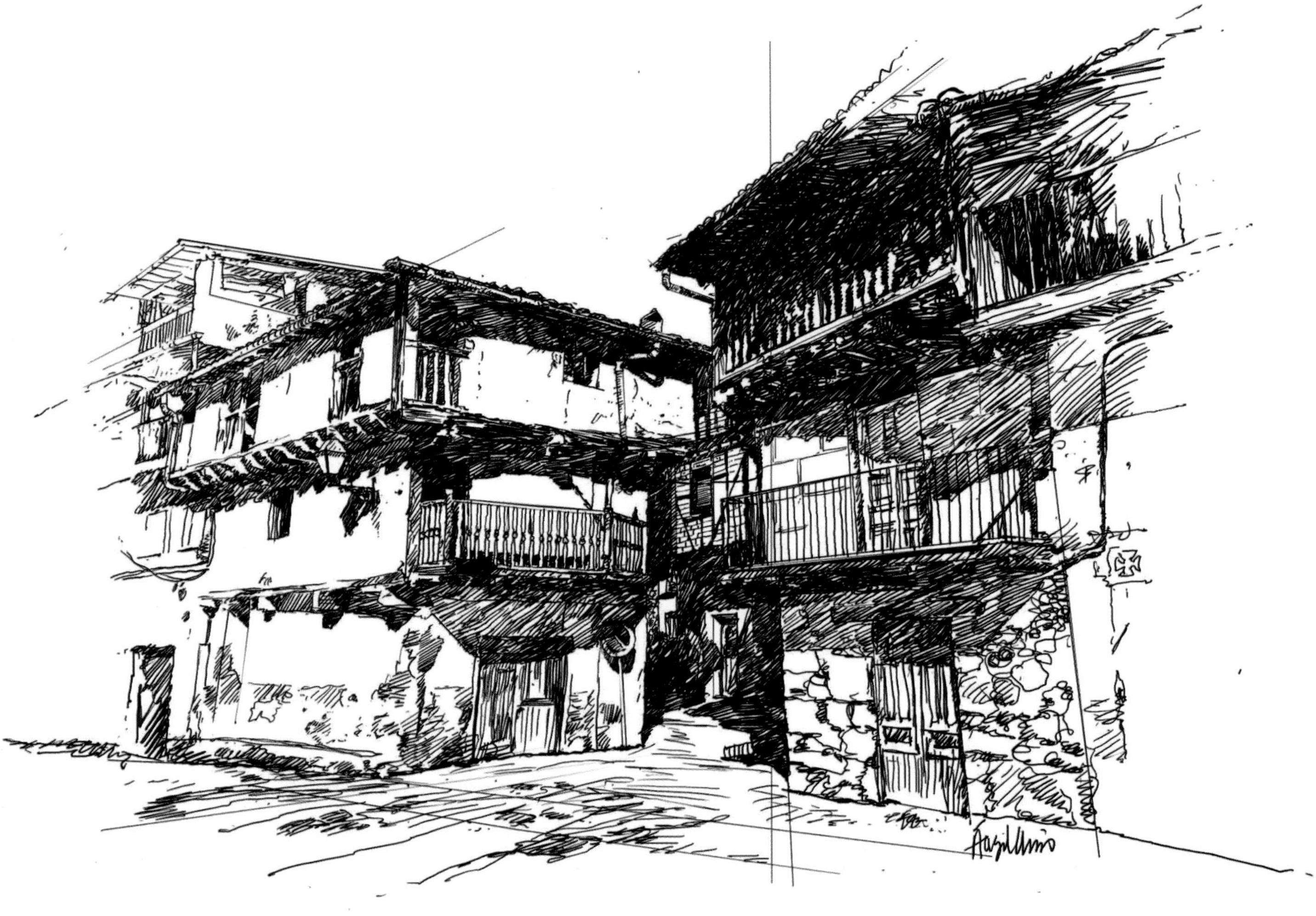

"GARGANTA DE LA OLLA", PILOT V

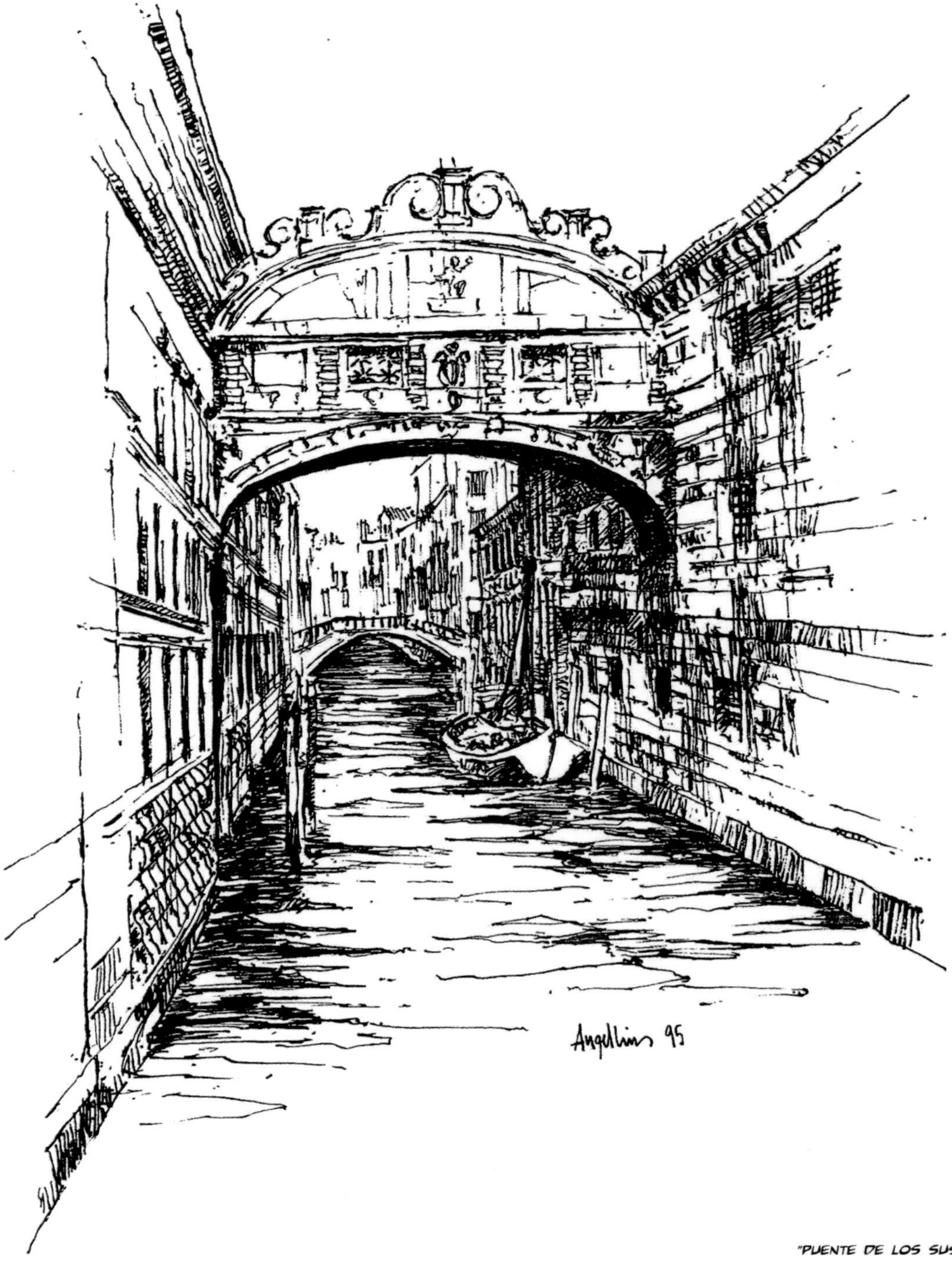
Angelliers 95

"PUENTE DE LOS SUSPIROS", VENECIA, PILOT V5.

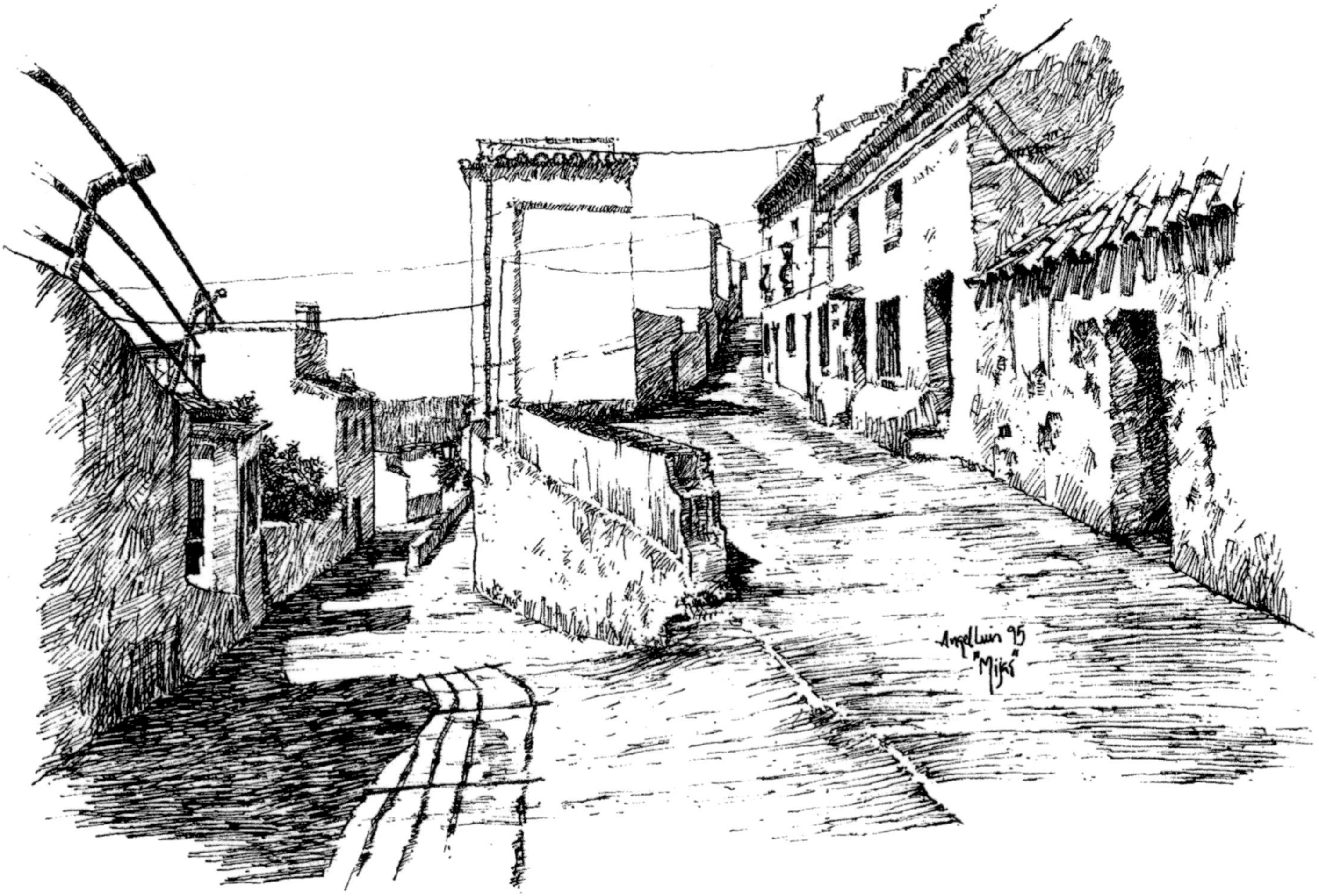
AngelLuis 95
"Mijas"

"MIJAS", MÁLAGA, PILOT V

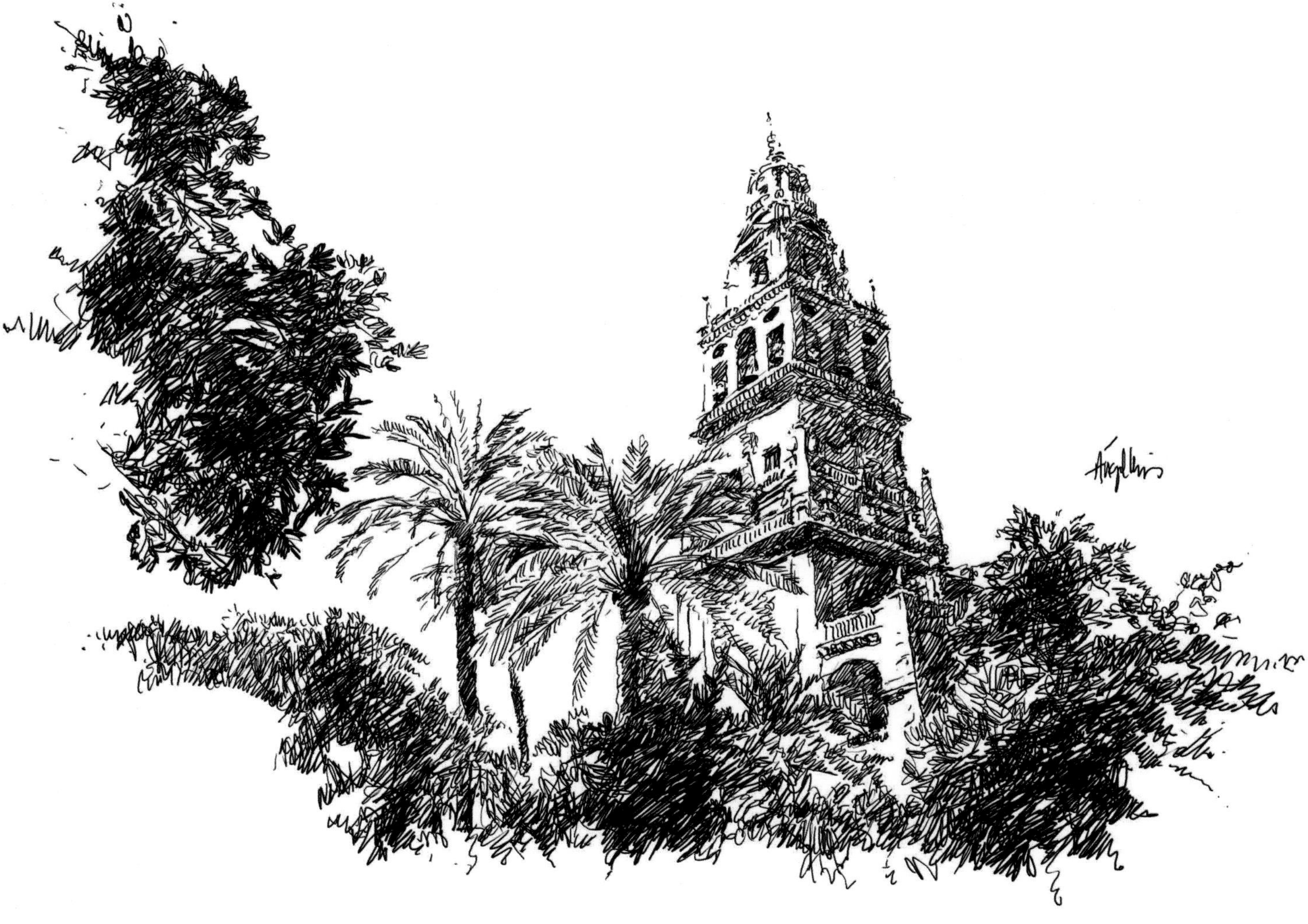

"ALMINAR MEZQUITA DE CÓRDOBA", PILOT V5.

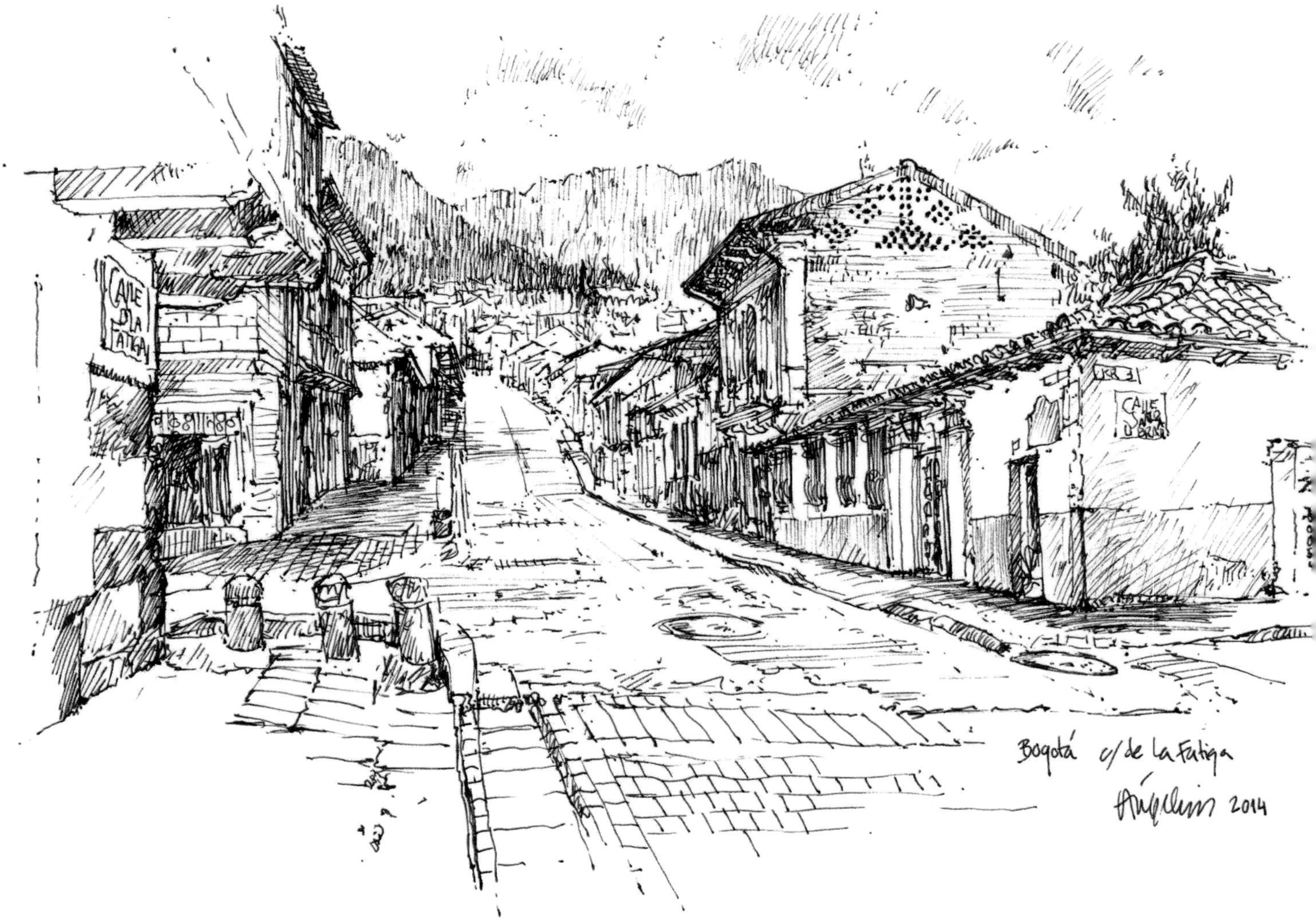
CALLE DE LA FATIGA
Bogotá c/ de la Fatiga
2014

"CALLE DE LA FATIGA", BOGOTÁ, PILOT V5

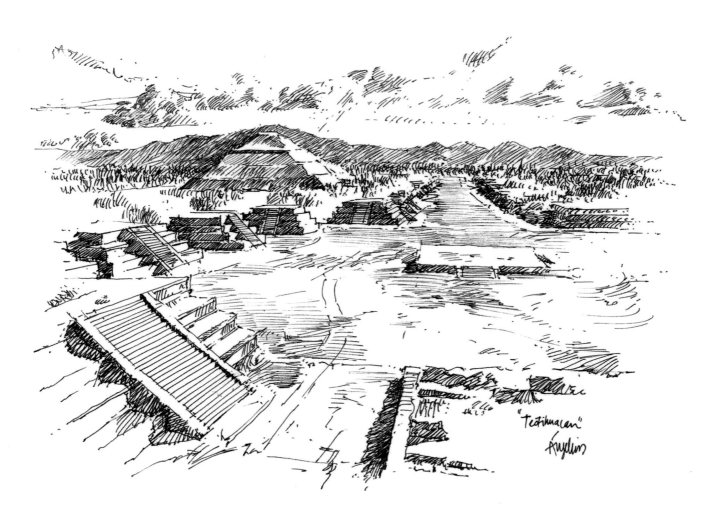

"Teotihuacan"
Anselm

"TEOTIHUACAN", MÉXICO. PILOT V5.

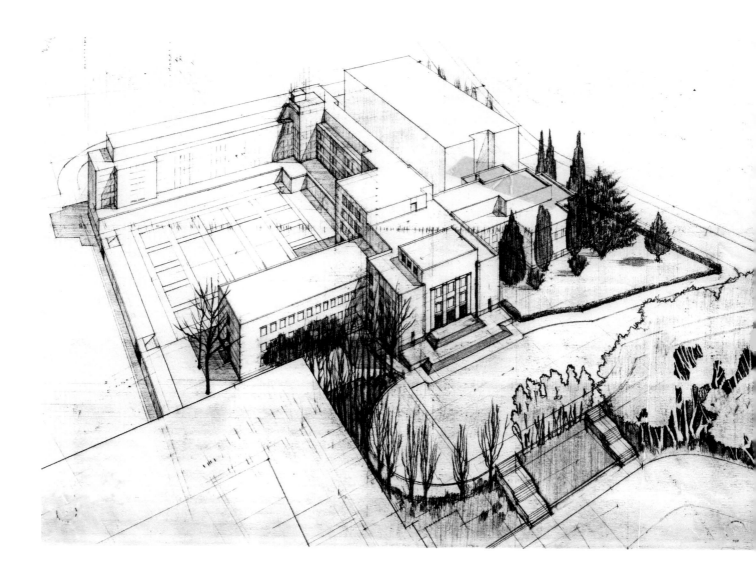

"ESCUELA TÉCNICA SUPERIOR DE ARQUITECTURA DE MADRID", PORTAMNAS DUREZA 3H

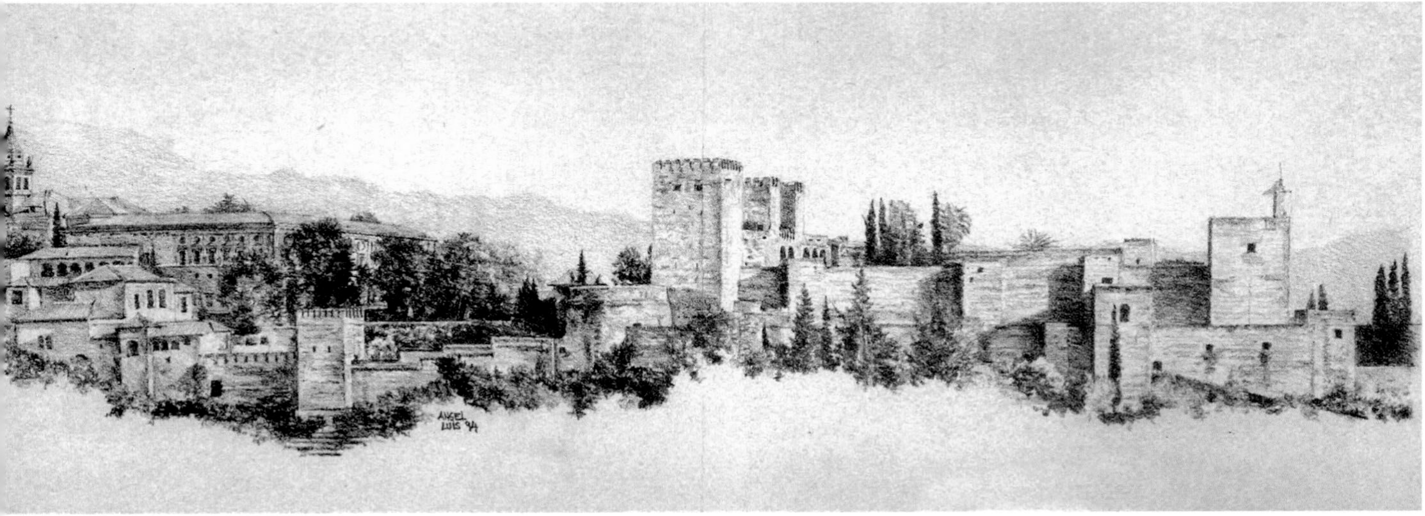
ANGEL
LUIS '94

"ALHAMBRA", GRANADA, LÁPIZ DUREZA 2B.

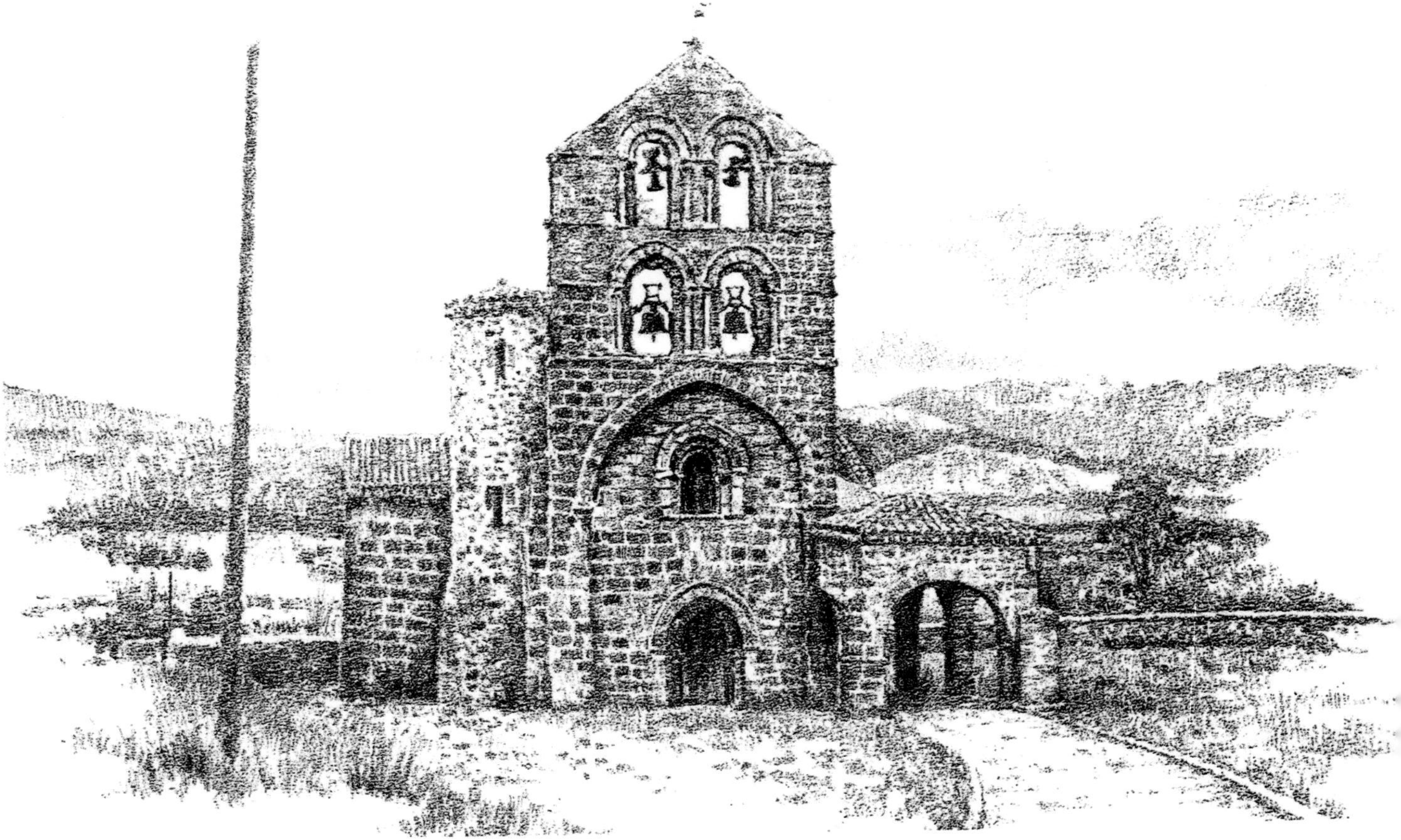

"ERMITA DE SAN SALVADOR DE CANTAMUDA", PALENCIA, LÁPIZ DUREZA 2B

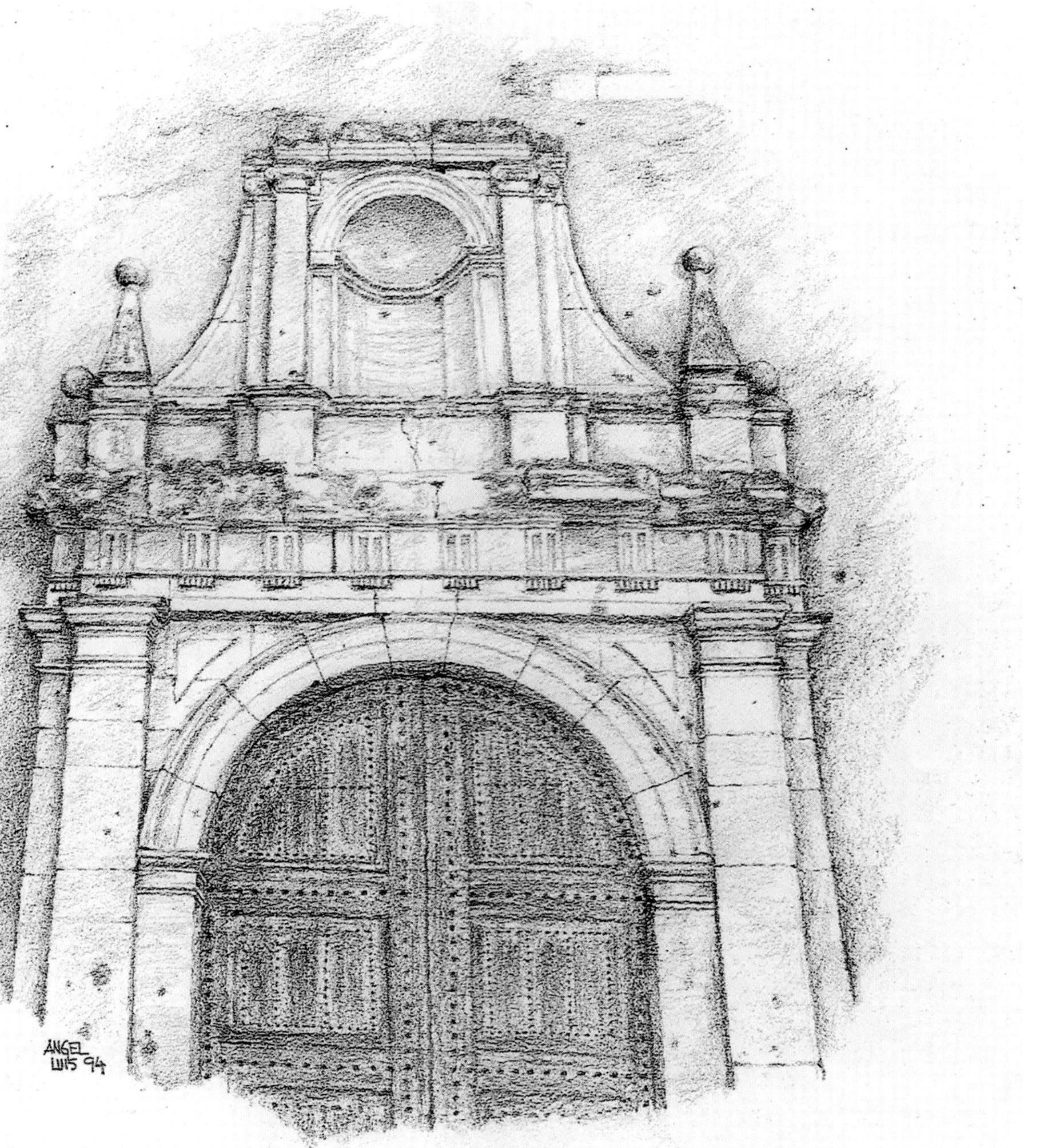
ANGEL
LUIS 94

"PORTADA IGLESIA SAN PEDRO APÓSTOL", FUENTE EL SAZ DEL JARAMA, MADRID, LÁPIZ DUREZA 2B.

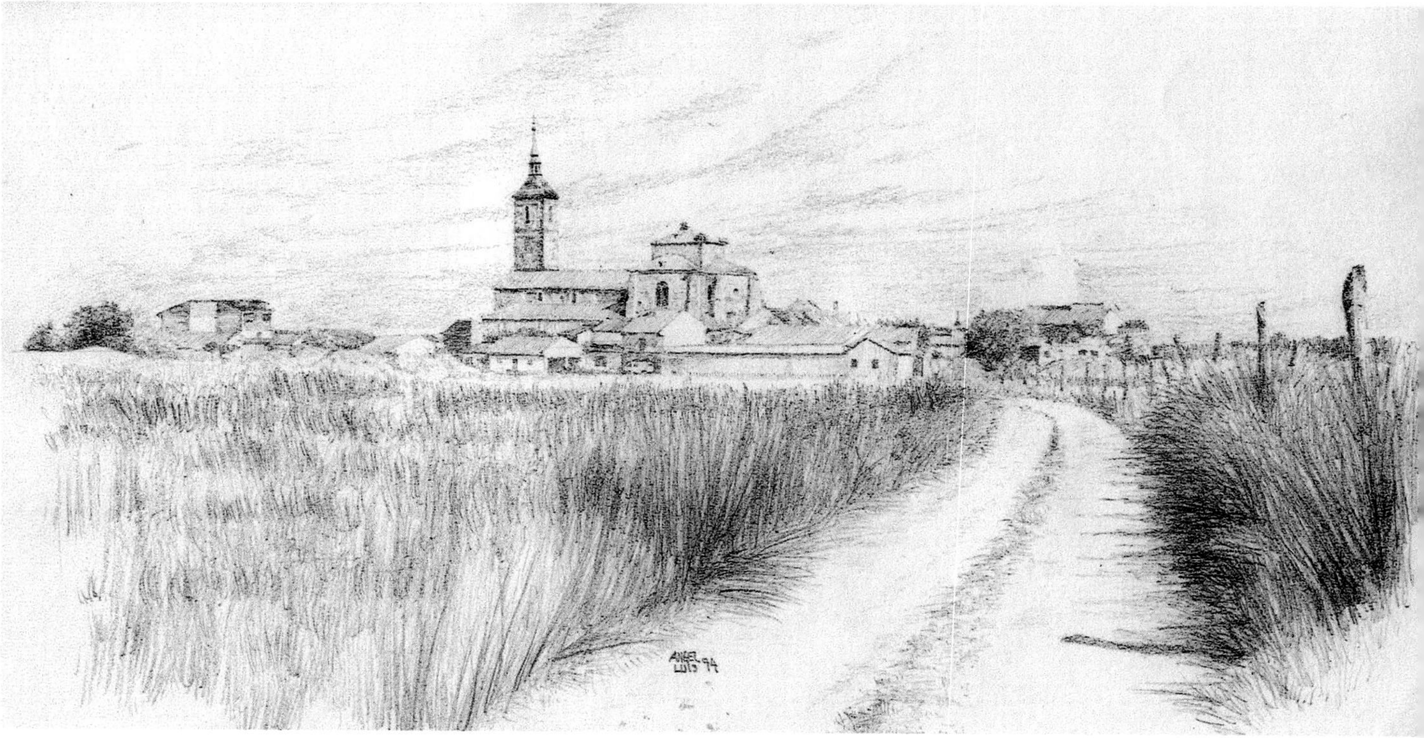
ANGEL
LUIS 94

"FUENTE EL SAZ DEL JARAMA", MADRID, LÁPIZ DUREZA 2

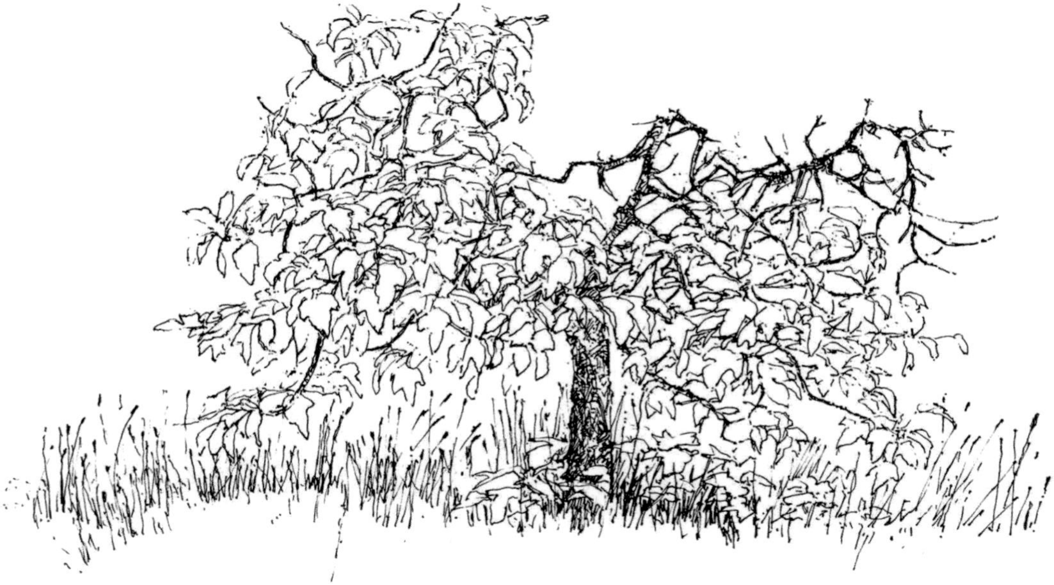

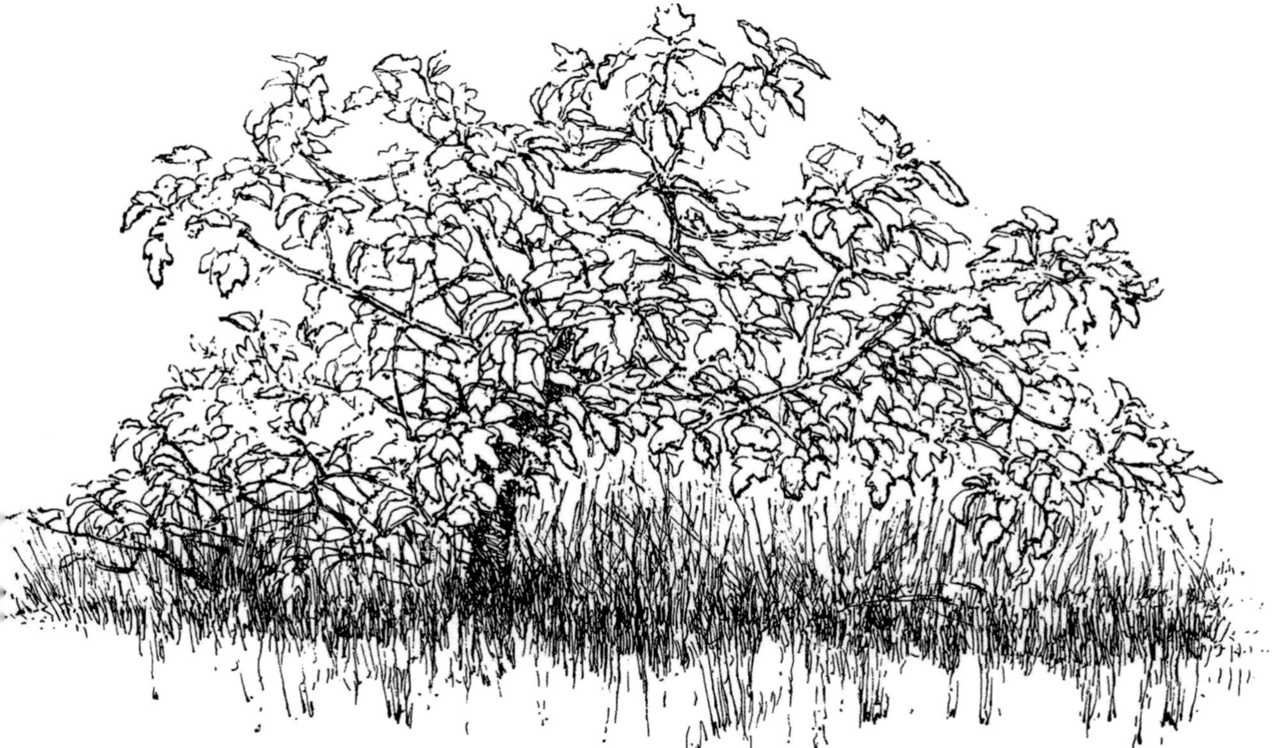

"HIGUERAS", MAJADAHONDA, MADRID. PILOT V5.

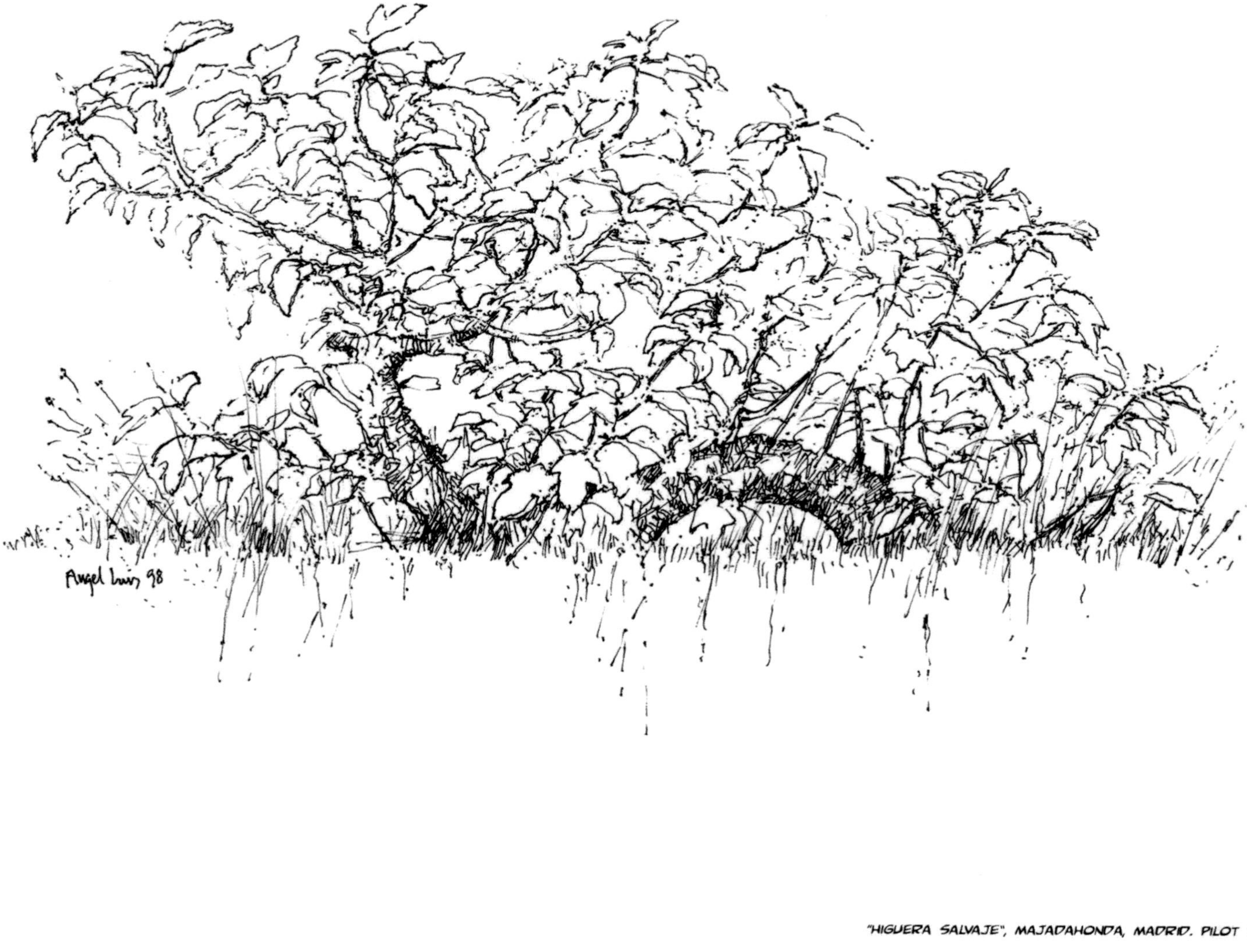
Angel Luis 98

"HIGUERA SALVAJE", MAJADAHONDA, MADRID. PILOT V

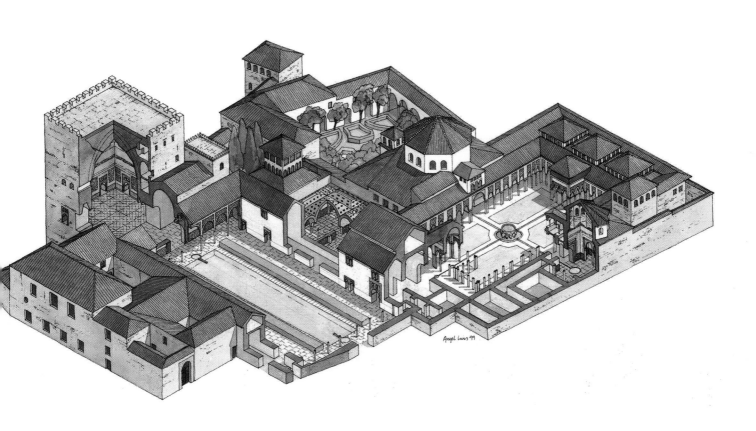

"ALHAMBRA", GRANADA. PORTAMINAS DUREZA 3H, ROTRING 0.1 Y 0.3, ACUARELA. ISOMÉTRICA.

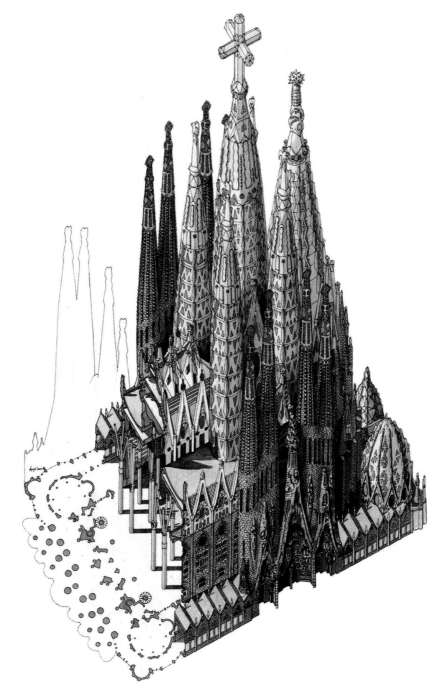

"LA SAGRADA FAMILIA", BARCELONA. PORTAMINAS DUREZA 3H, ROTRING 0.1 Y 0.3, ACUARELA. AXONOMÉTRIC

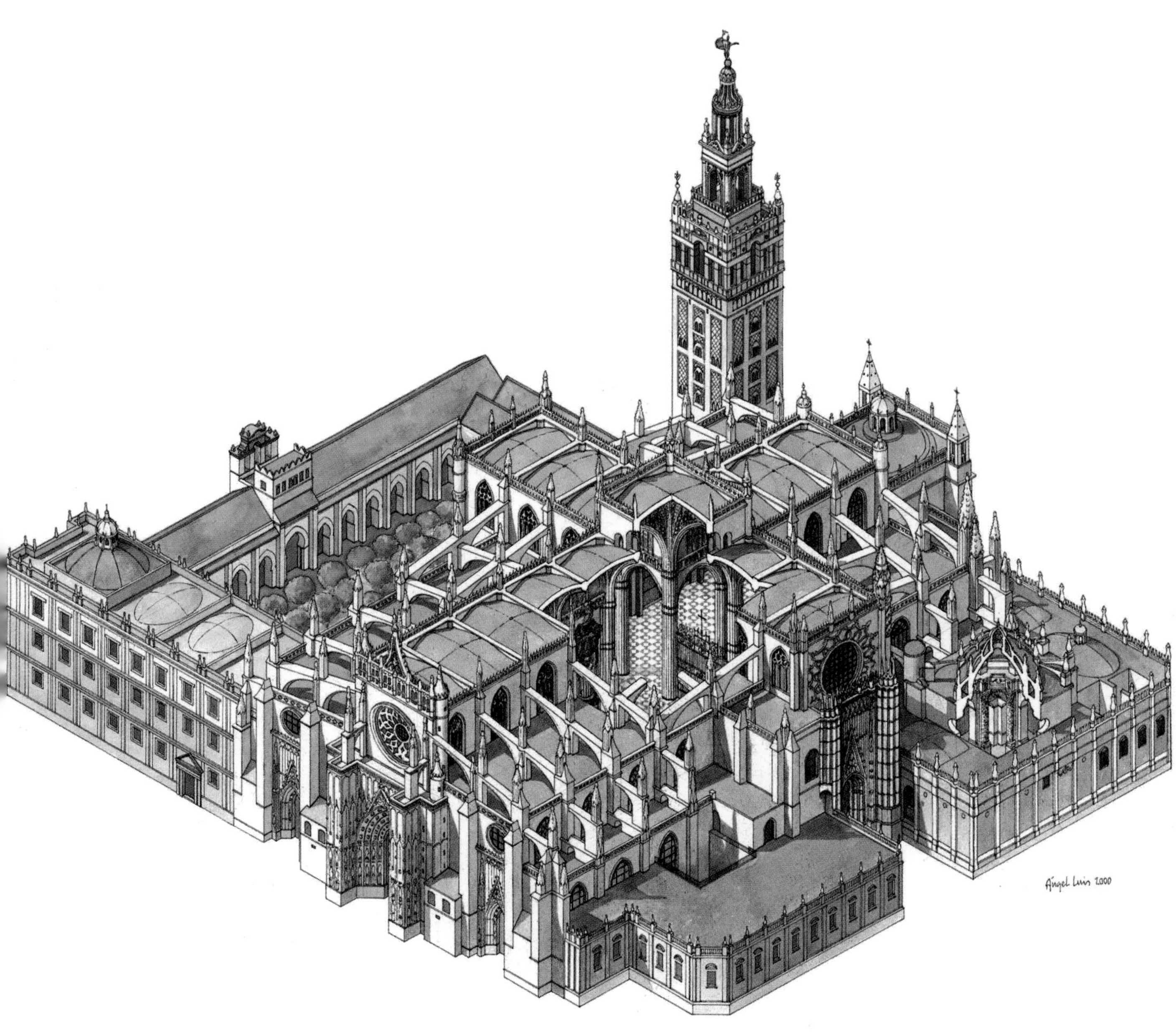
Ángel Luis 2000

"LA CATEDRAL DE SEVILLA". PORTAMINAS DUREZA 3H, ROTRING 0.1 Y 0.3, ACUARELA. ISOMÉTRICA.

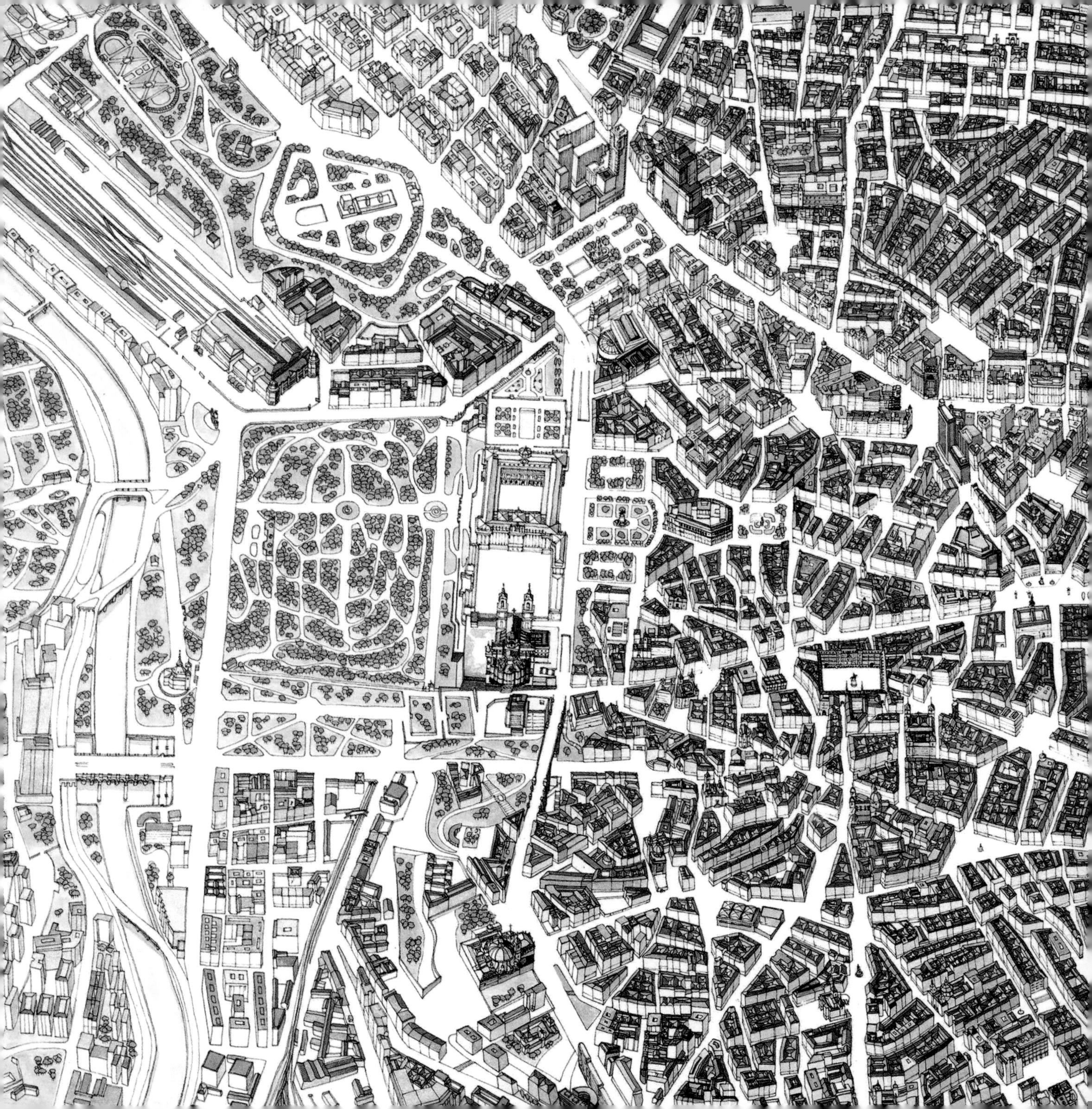

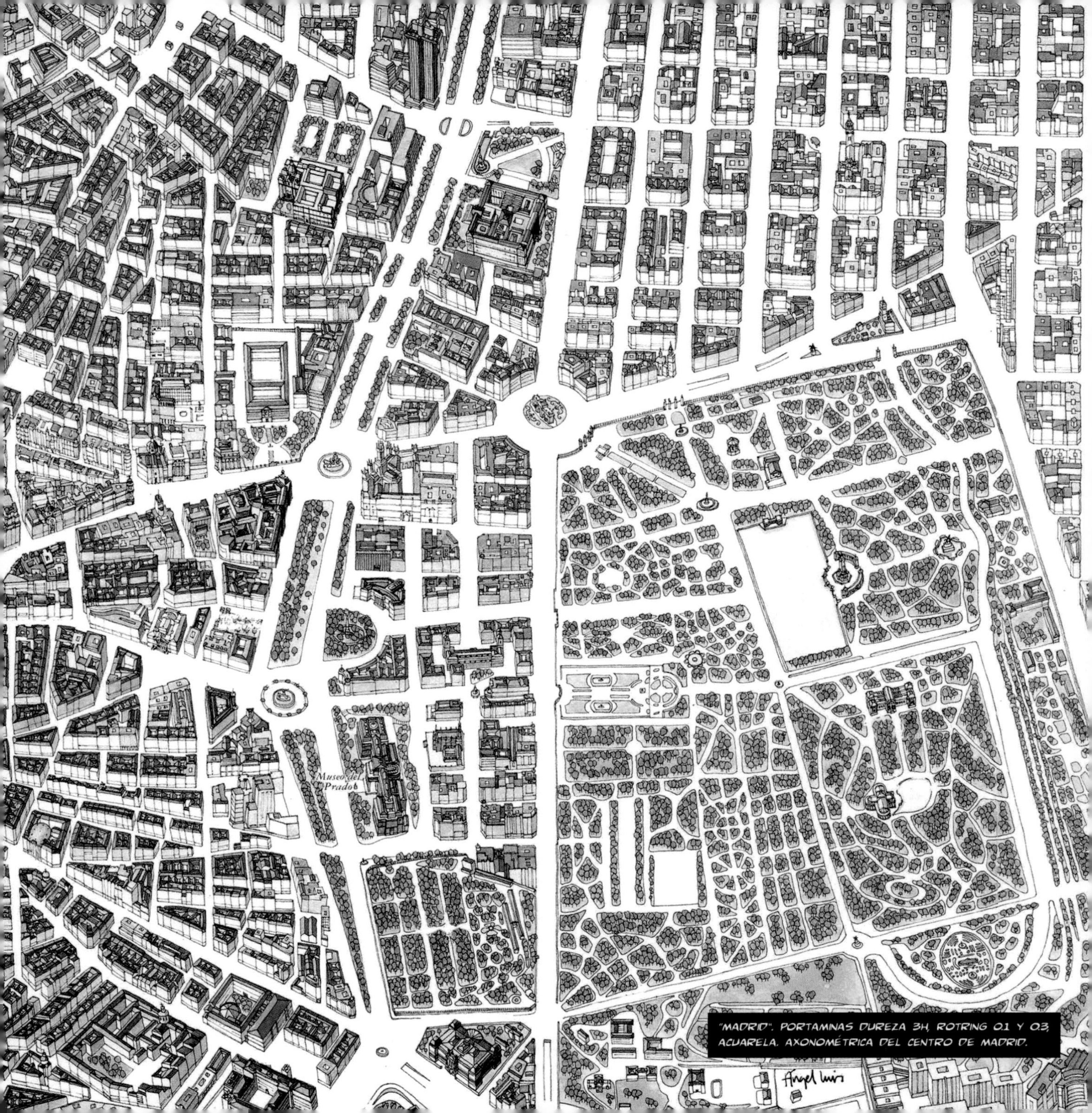
Museo del Prado

"MADRID". PORTAMINAS DUREZA 3H, ROTRING 0.1 Y 0.3, ACUARELA. AXONOMÉTRICA DEL CENTRO DE MADRID.

ARCHITECTURE ALSO HAS TO PROVOKE EMOTION, SO THE DRAWING IS AN ESSENTIAL T IN THE MOMENT OF CREATION. IT HELPS US TO HIGHLIGHT, WITH LITTLE GESTURES, THE CHARACTER THAT WE WANT TO PRINT TO OUR PROJECTS, AND ALLOWS US TO INVESTIG MANY ALTERNATIVES IN VERY LITTLE TIME.

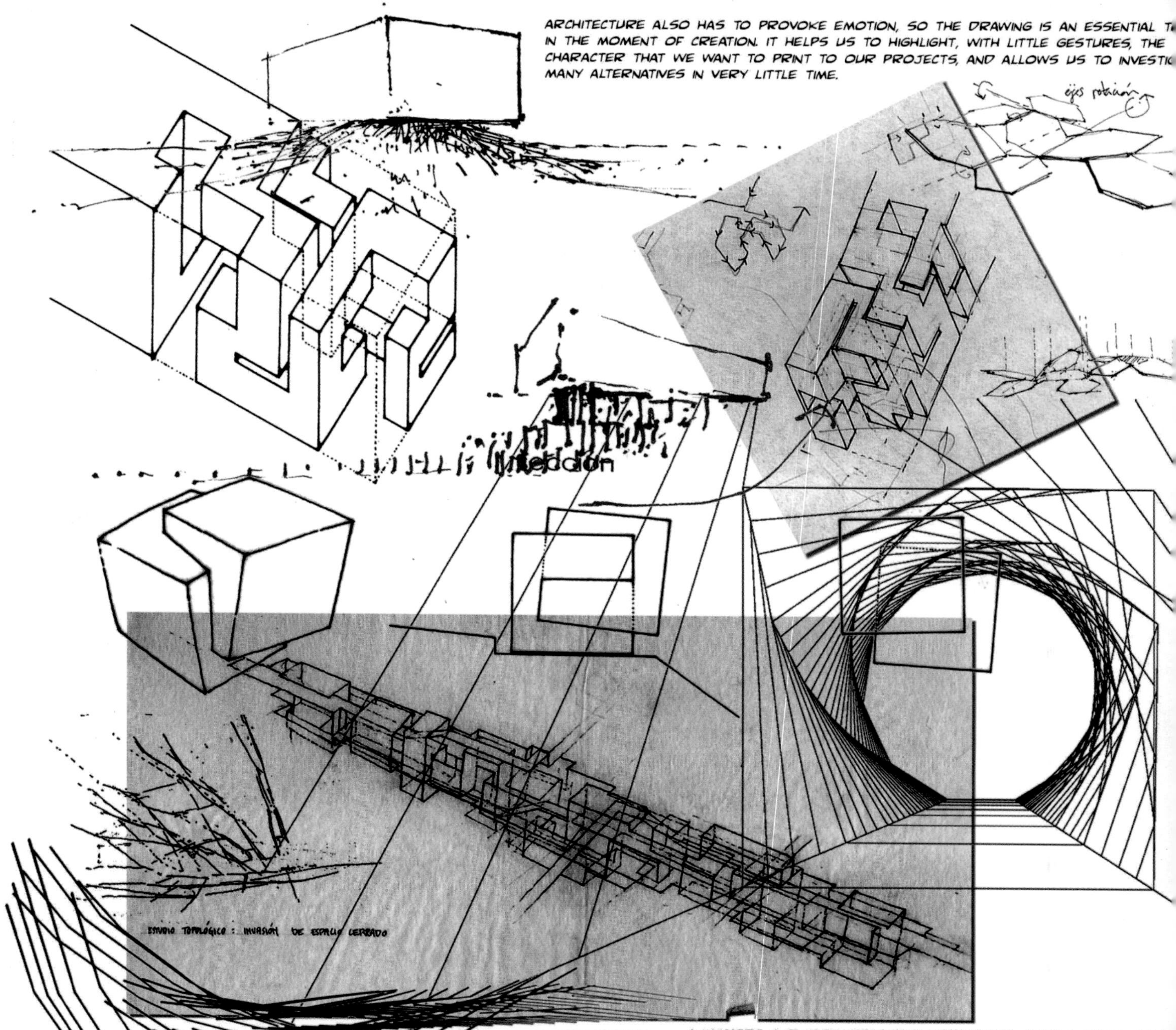
ESTUDIO TOPOLÓGICO : INVASIÓN DE ESPACIO CERRADO

ANYWHERE AND WITH VERY FEW RESOURCES. JUST A PENCIL AND A PAPER NAPKIN RIGHT?. THE DRAWING IS A MATTER OF JUDGMENT AND APPROPRIATE CHOICE, AND NOT OF VIRTUOSITY. YOU CAN HAVE EXCELLENT TECHNIQUE AND DO NOT TRANSMIT ANYTHING, OR HAVE N TECHNICAL AT ALL AND WITH TWO STROKES CONVEY A LOT. COMPUTER ASSISTED DRAWING IS AS VALID AS DRAWING BY HAND, AND ARE COMPLEMENTARY. THE PROPER USE OF THEM IS A GUARANTEE OF SUCCESS WHEN PROJECTING. HERE YOU CAN SEE SOME DRAWINGS, SOME HANDMADE AND OTHER DIGI WHICH WERE INSTRUMENTAL IN THE GENESIS OF SOME OF MY PROJECTS.

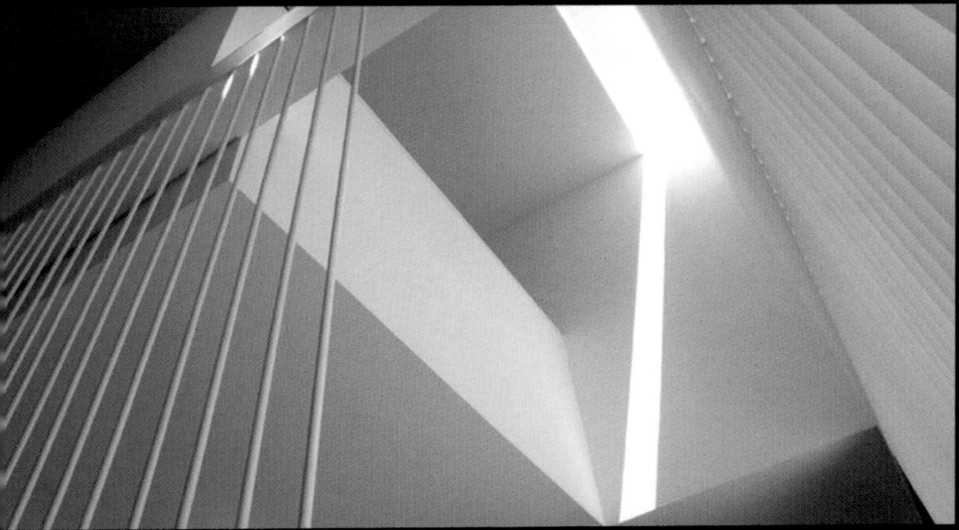

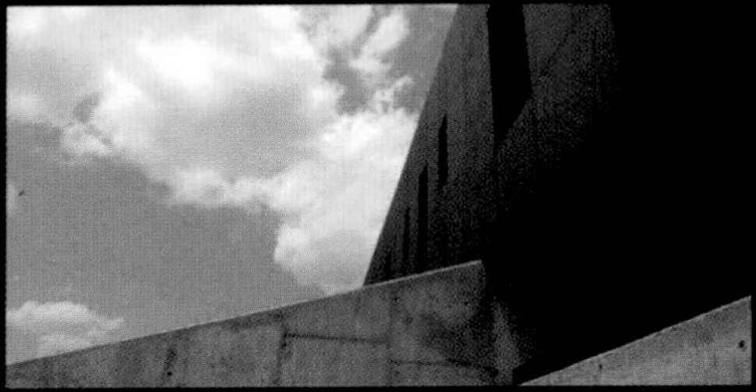

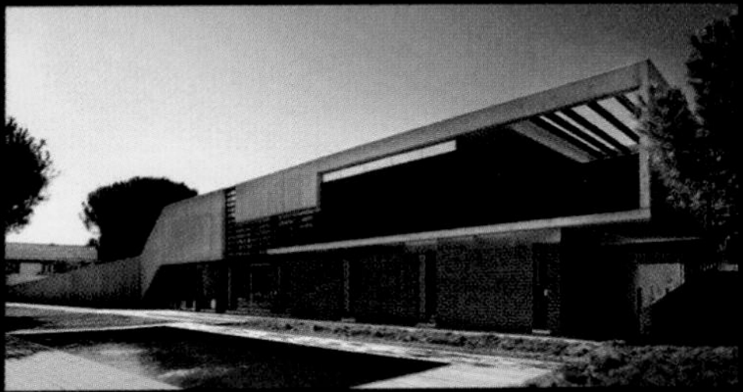

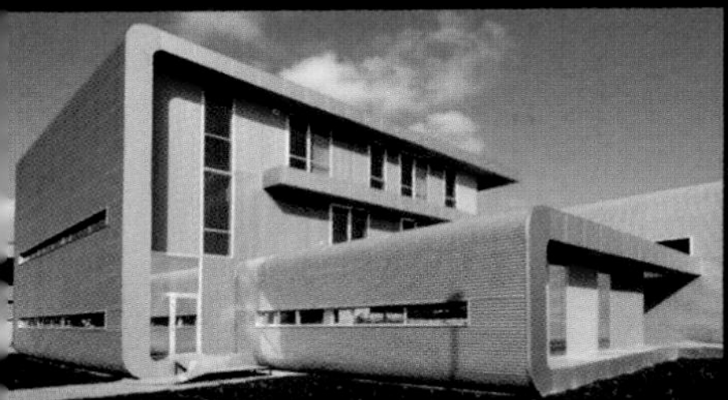

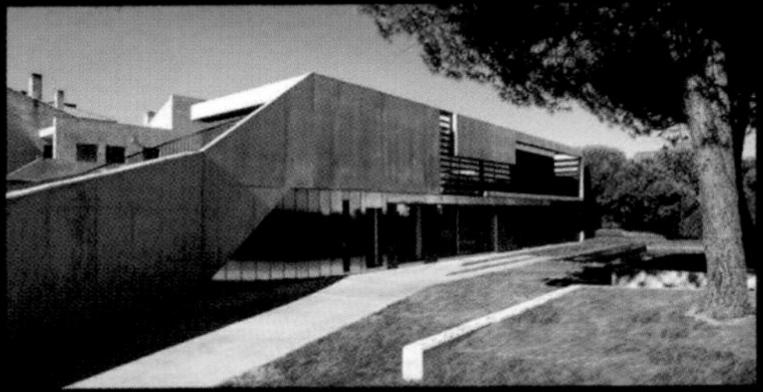

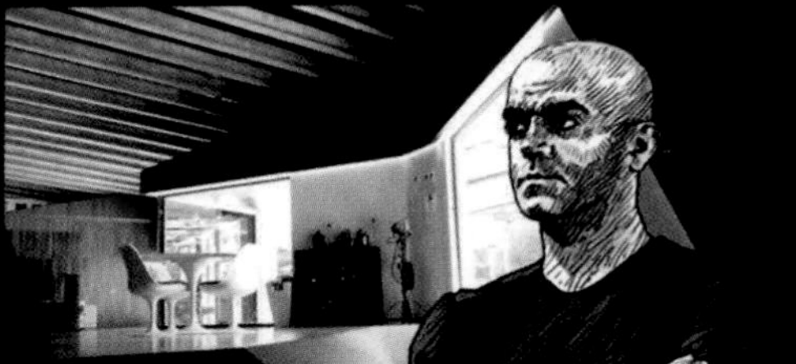

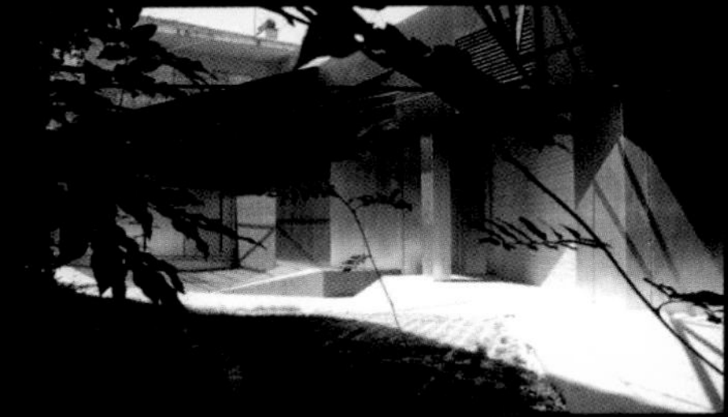

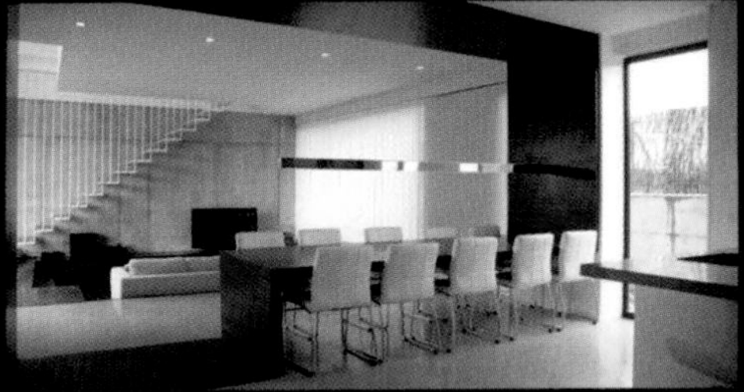

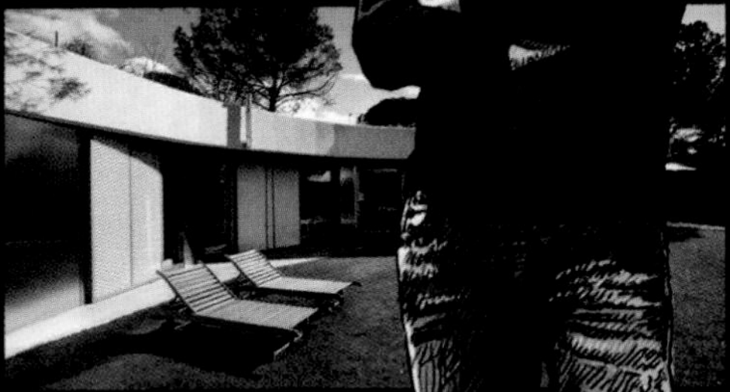

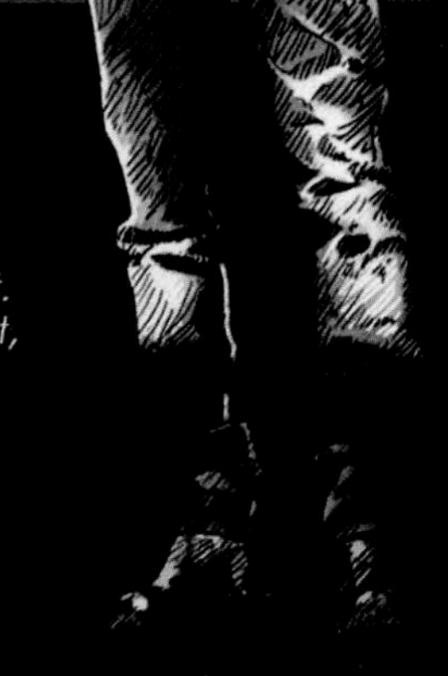

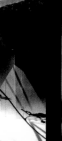

Alt arquitectura + obra

ou want to know about our work, you can do it
visiting our fan page on **facebook**:

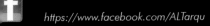

https://www.facebook.com/ALTarqu

The purpose of all artistic creation is thrilling, and we have seen how analyzing our environment we can find endless excitements caused by the form and space.

In **Alt** *arquitectura try to convey this emotion through our architecture, looking for the right tools for developing each project. We always try to integrate our work and dialogue with environment, using what we call pure materials.*
Stone (concrete understood as a malleable stone), steel, wood and glass.

Here you can see some of the work performed by our study.

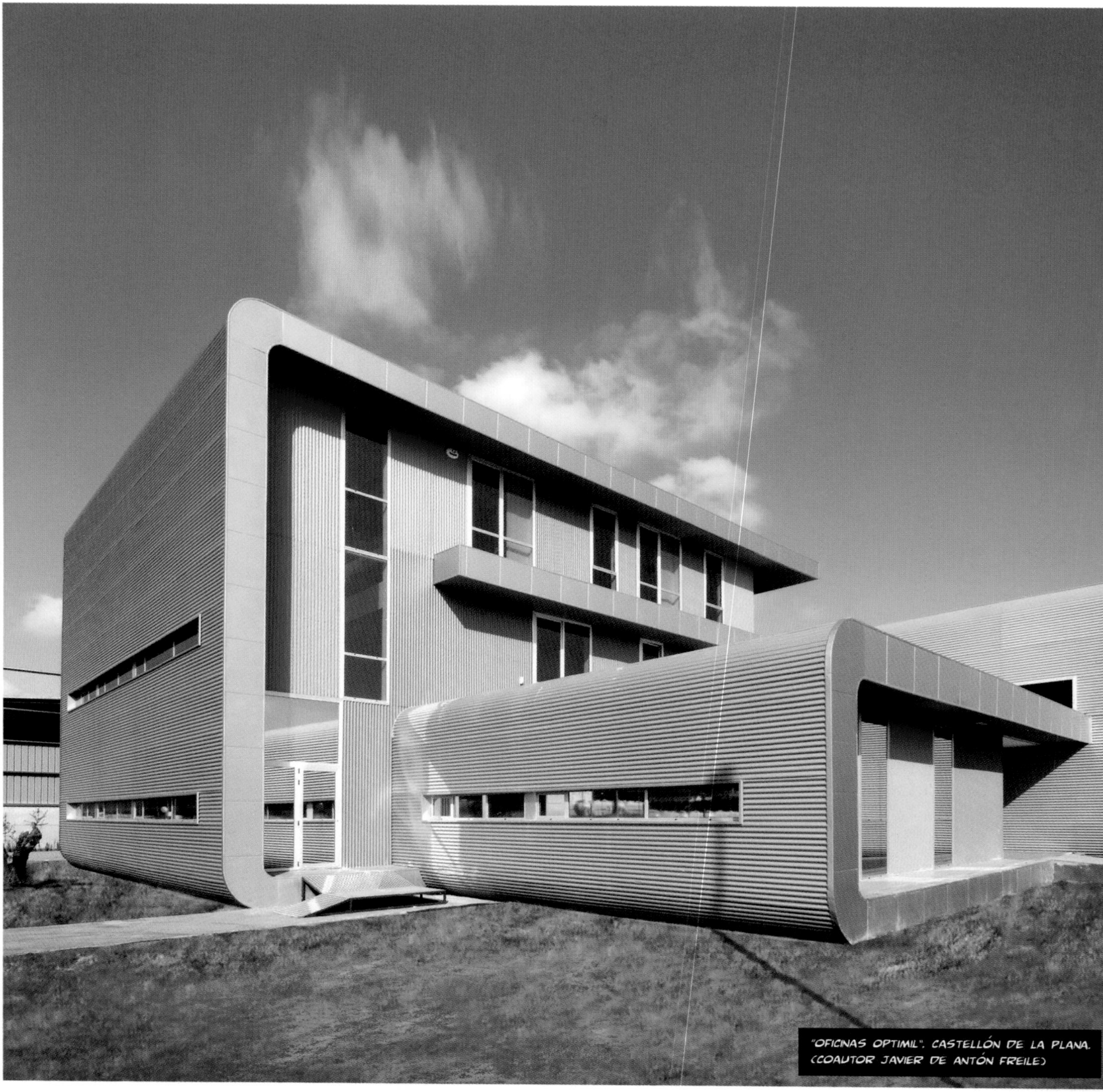
"OFICINAS OPTIMIL". CASTELLÓN DE LA PLANA.
(COAUTOR JAVIER DE ANTÓN FREILE)

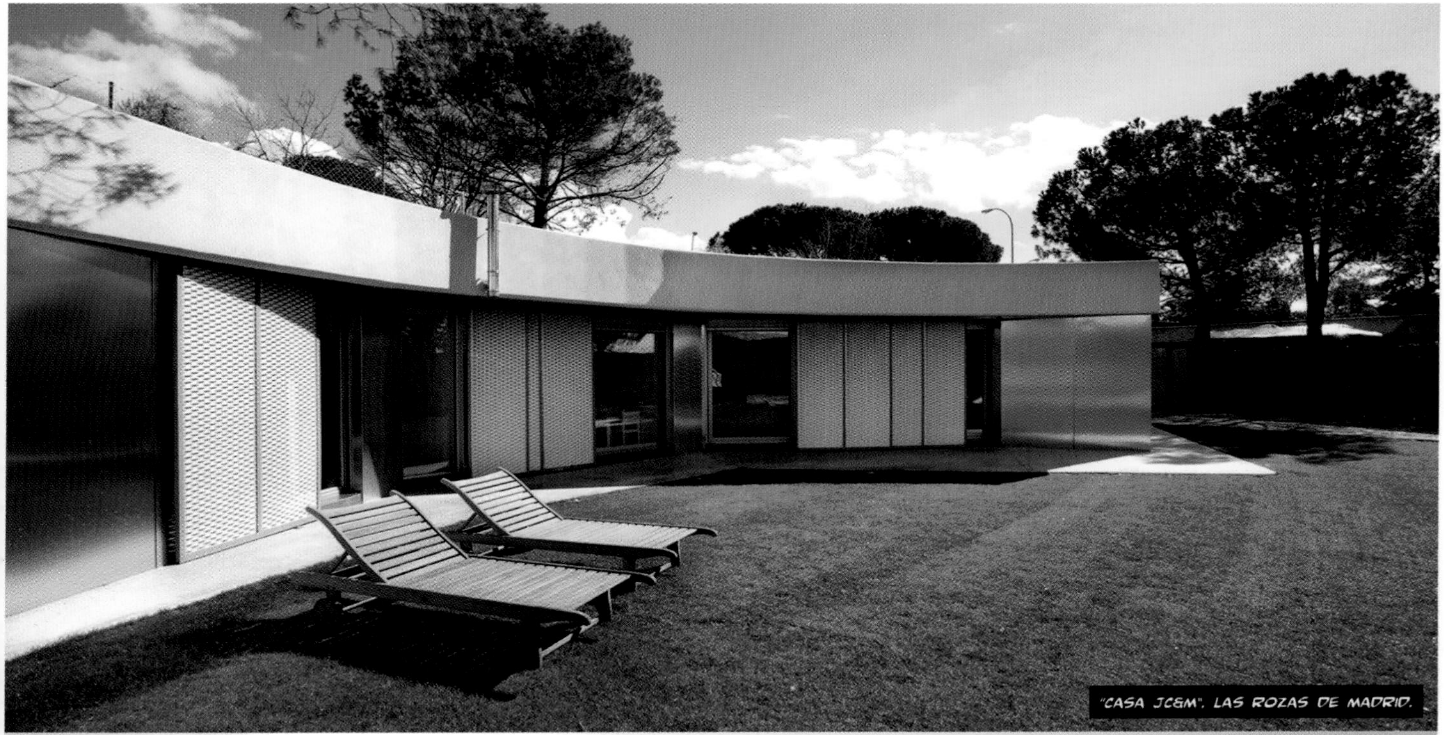
"CASA JC&M". LAS ROZAS DE MADRID.

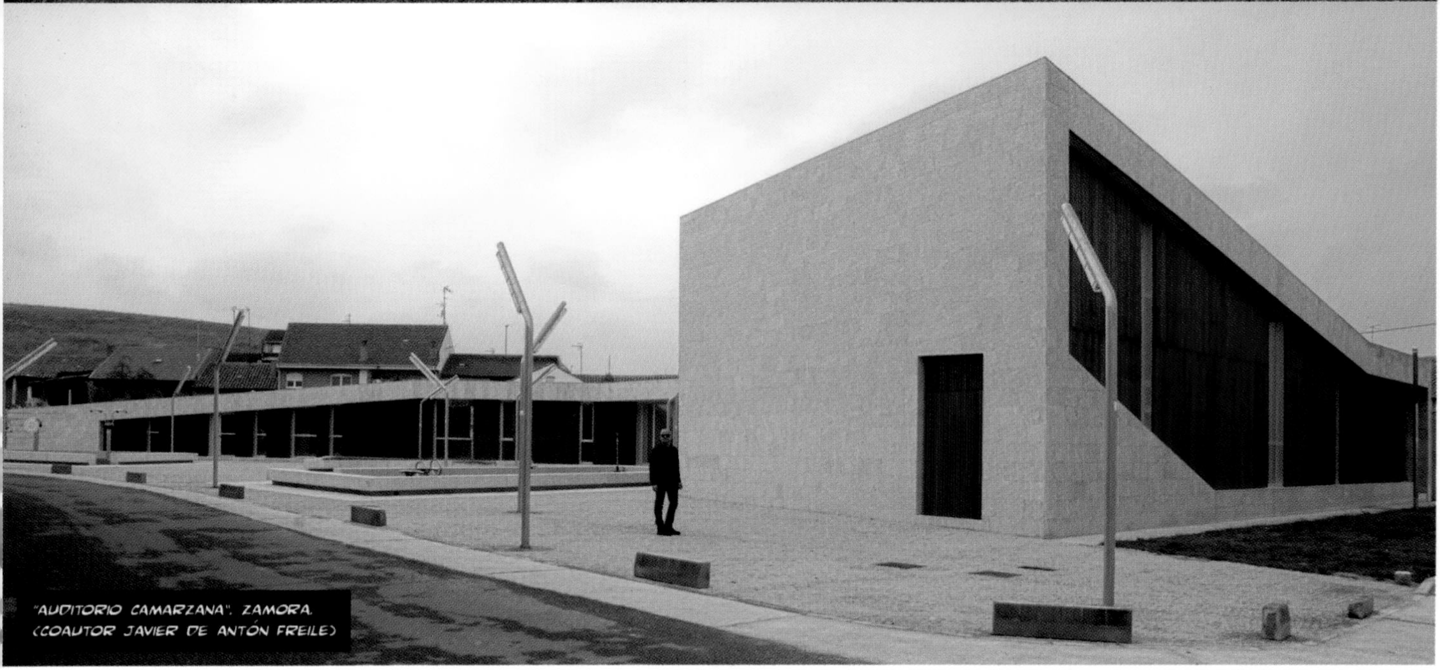
"AUDITORIO CAMARZANA". ZAMORA.
(COAUTOR JAVIER DE ANTÓN FREILE)

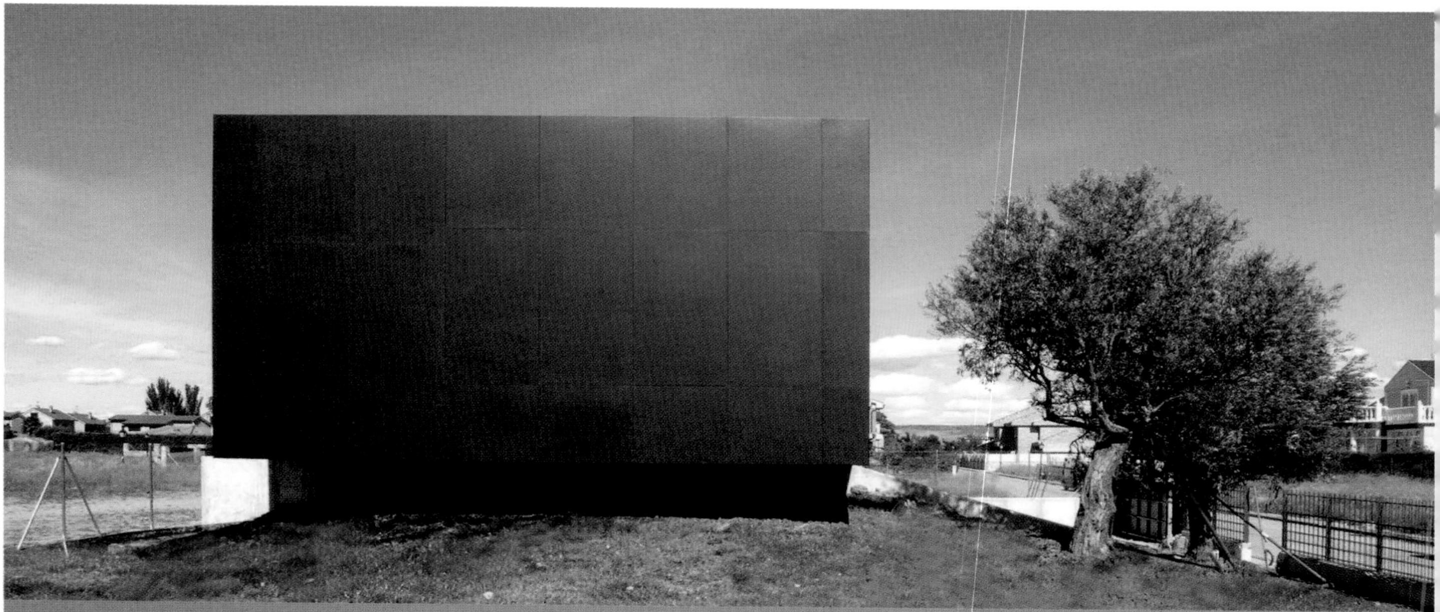

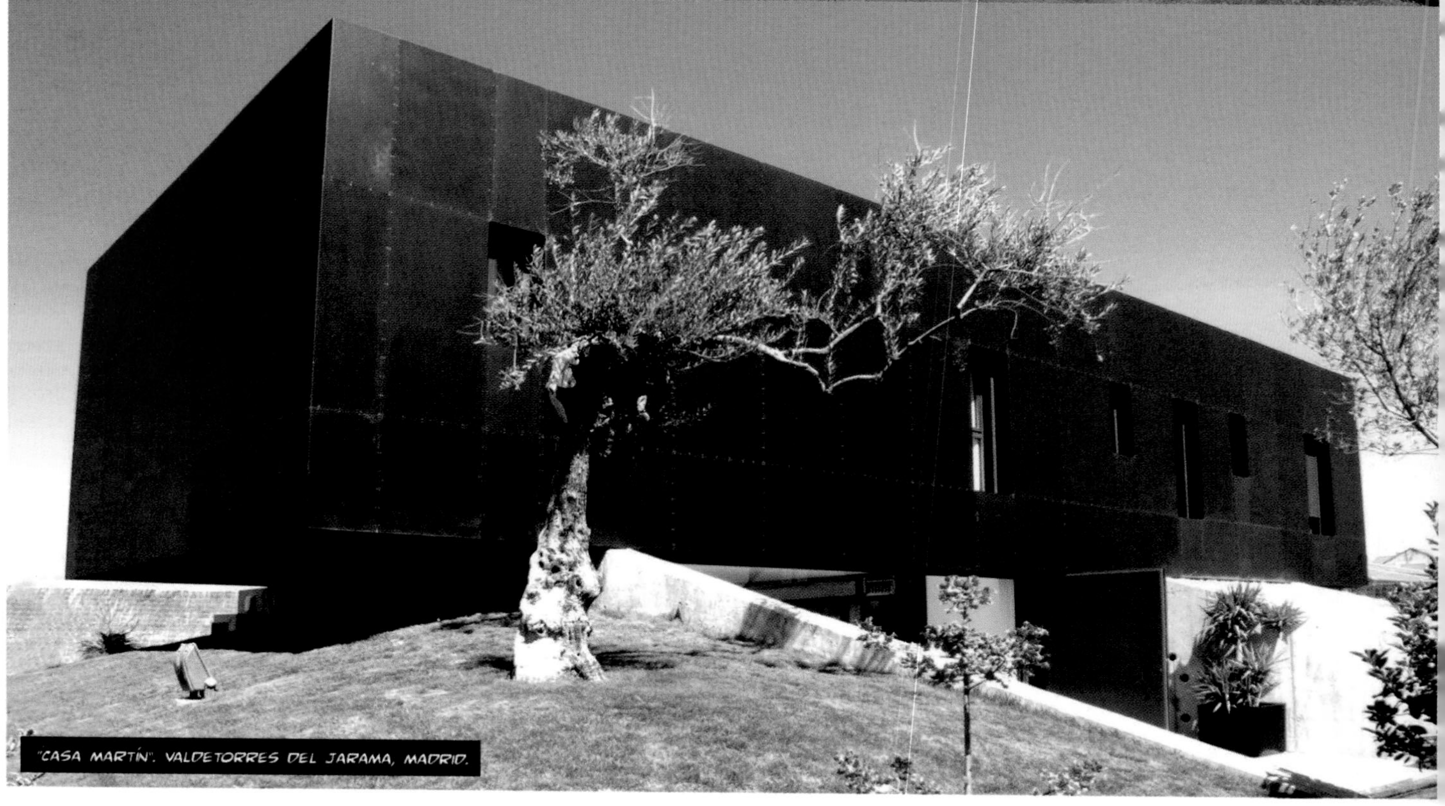

"CASA MARTÍN". VALDETORRES DEL JARAMA, MADRID.

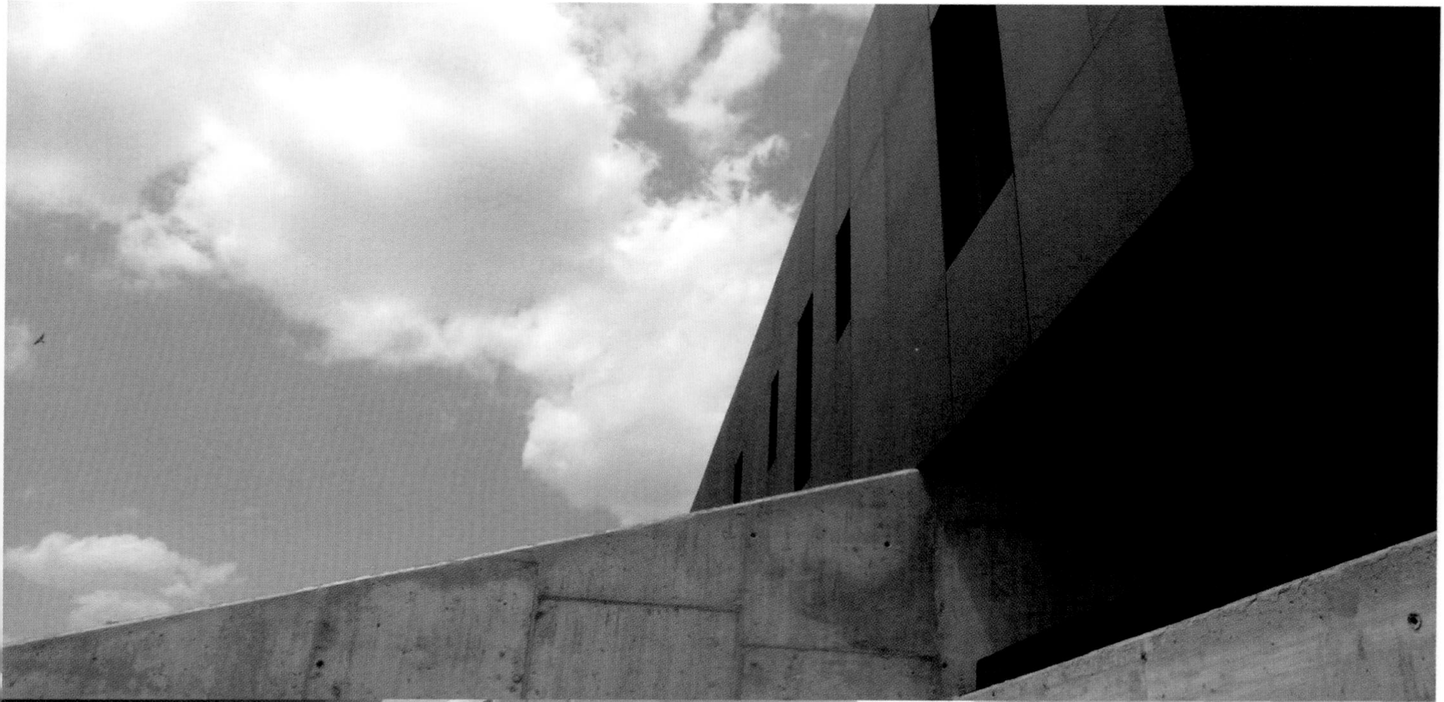

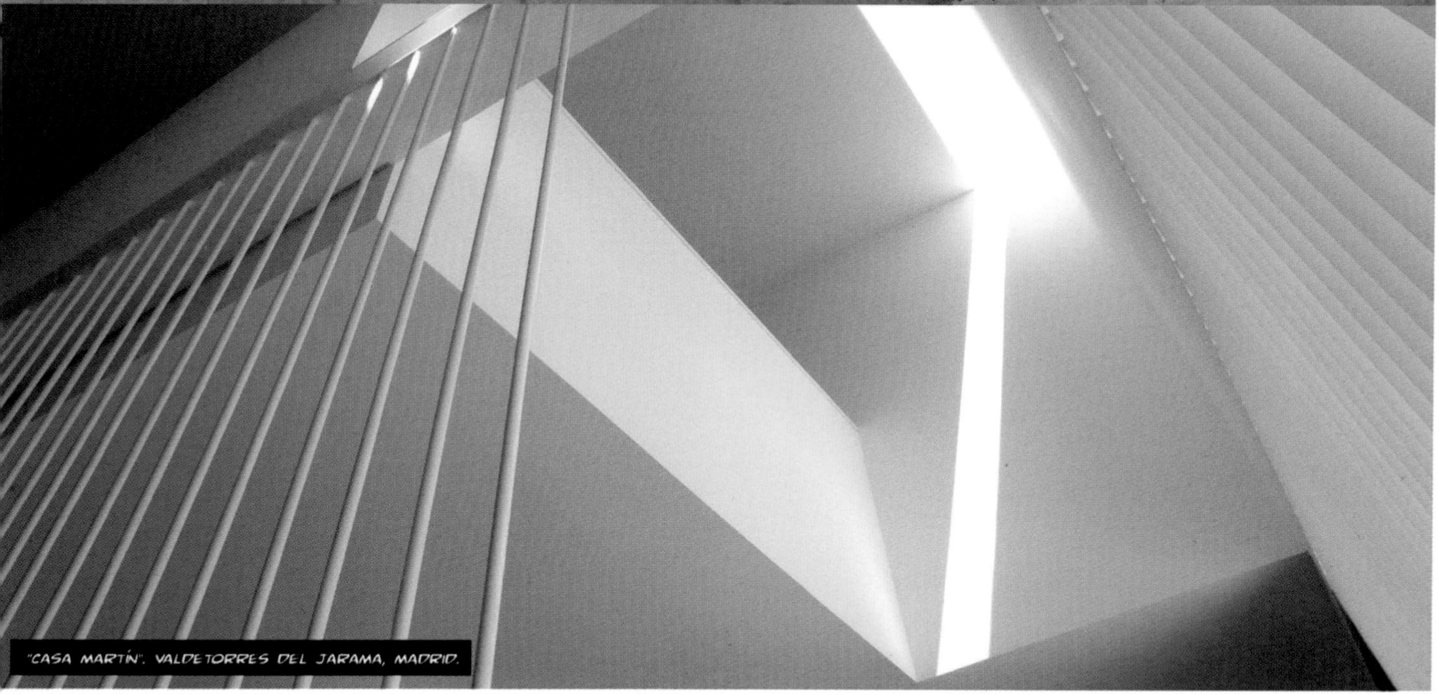

"CASA MARTÍN". VALDETORRES DEL JARAMA, MADRID.

"CASA RONCERO". SAN SEBASTIÁN DE LOS REYES, MADRID.

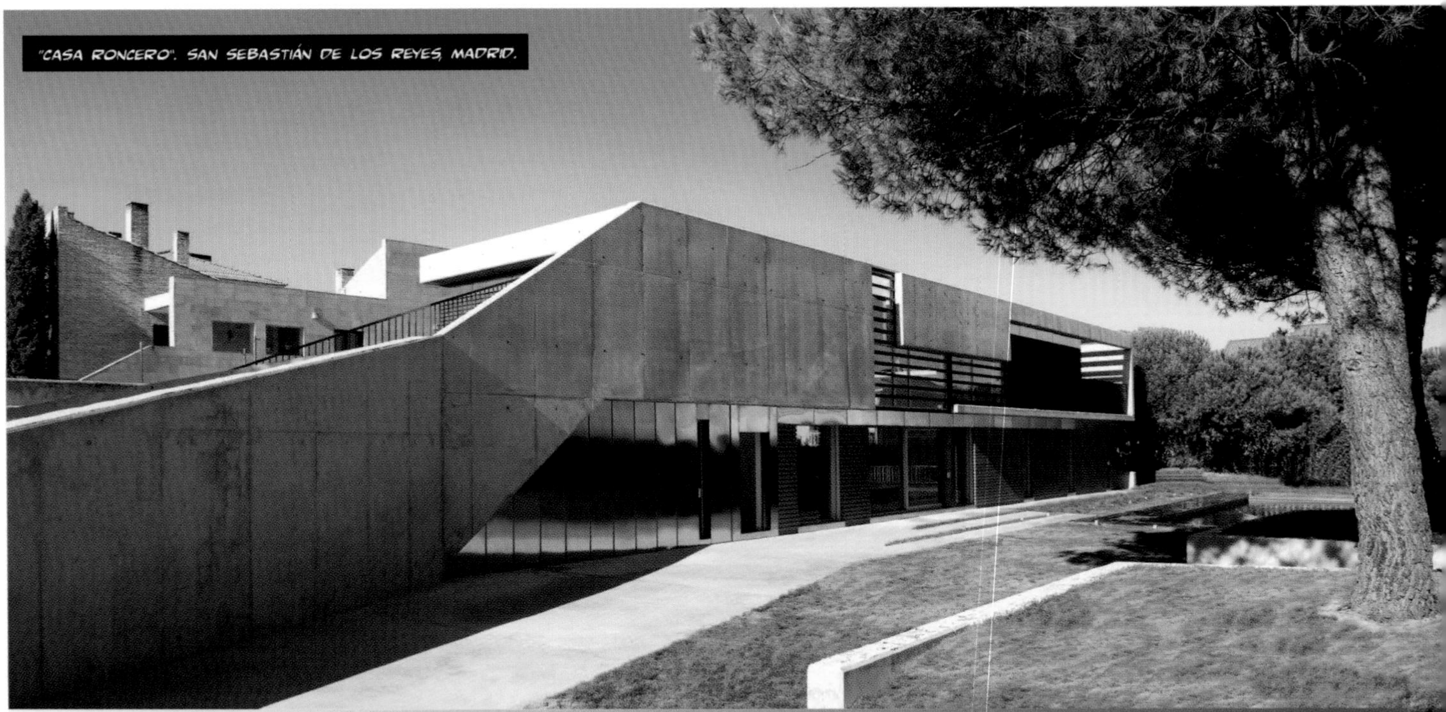

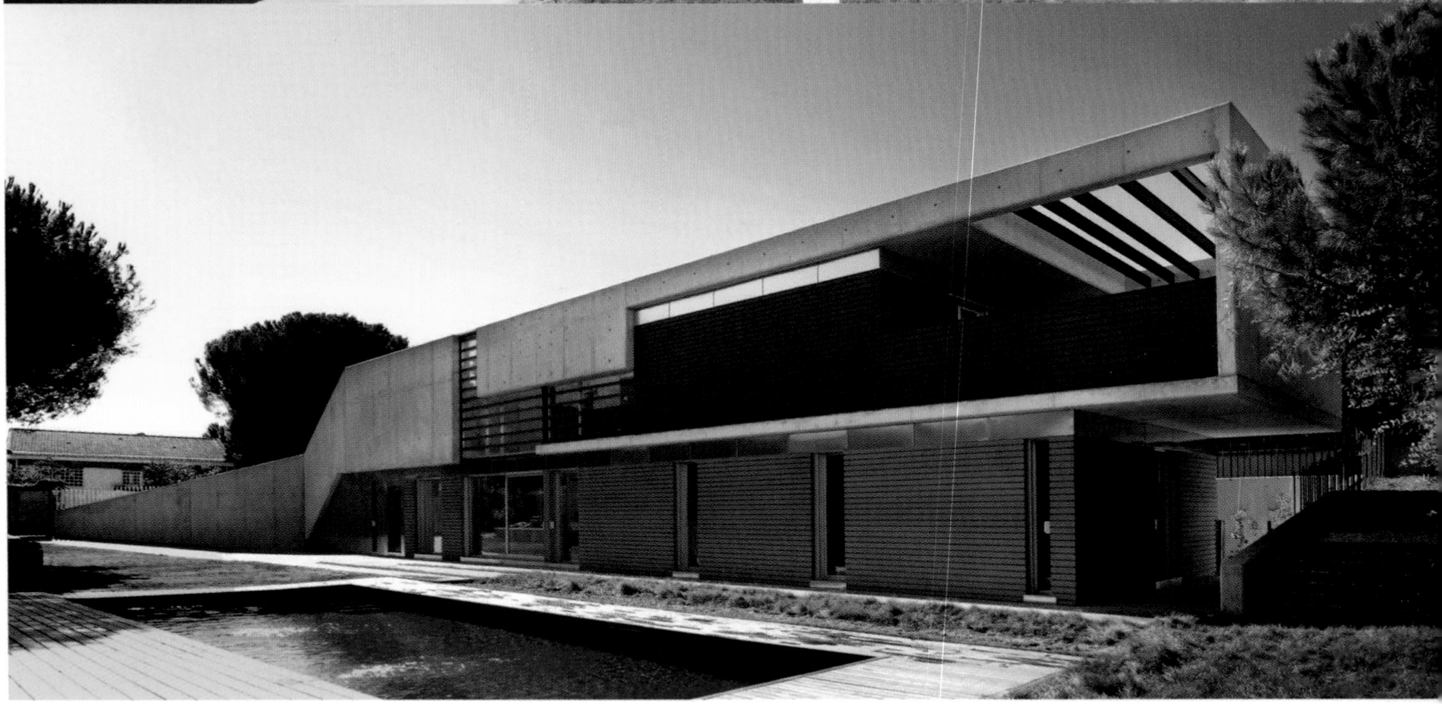

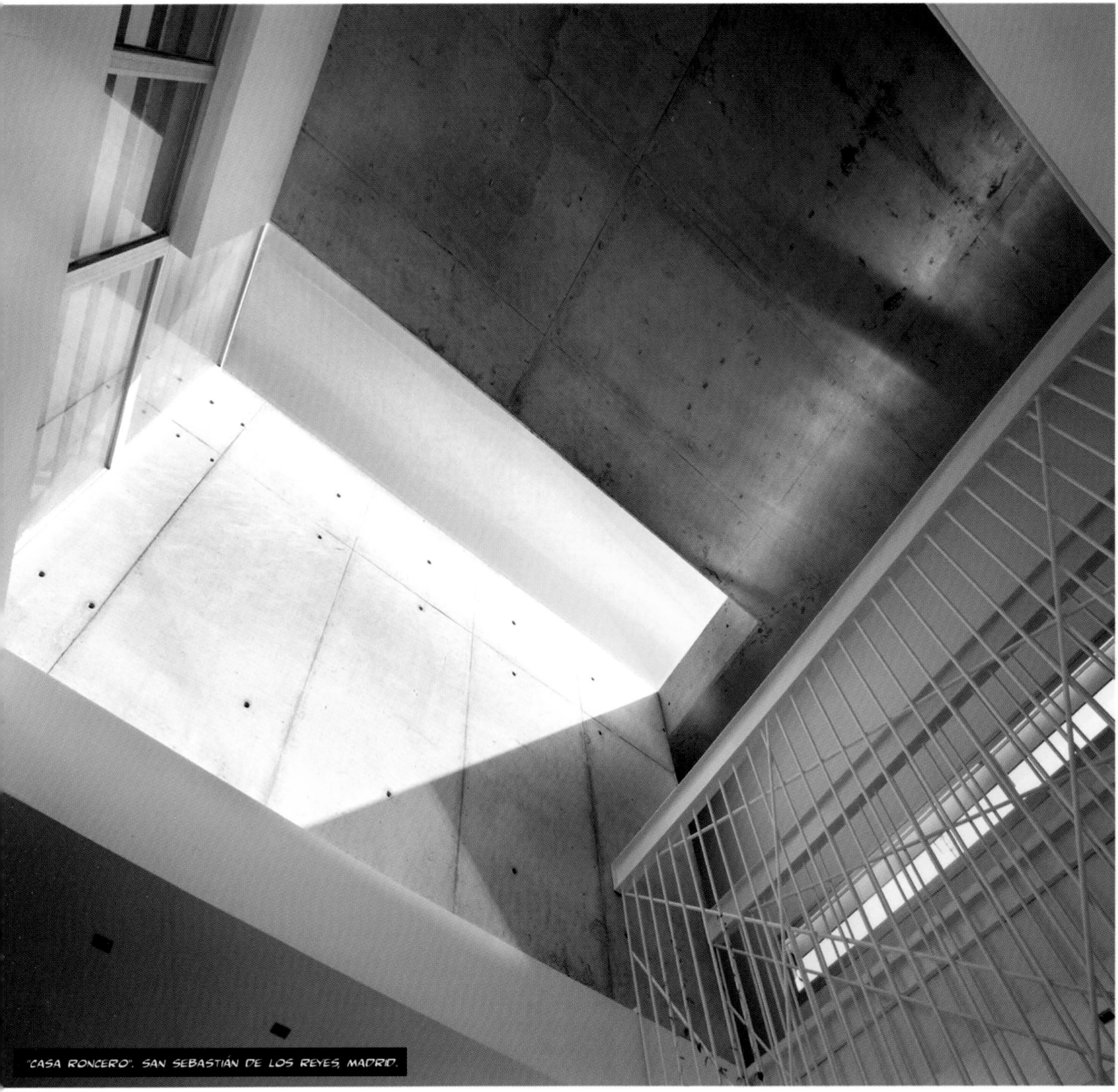

"CASA RONCERO". SAN SEBASTIÁN DE LOS REYES, MADRID.

"CASA ALVENAT". MADRID.

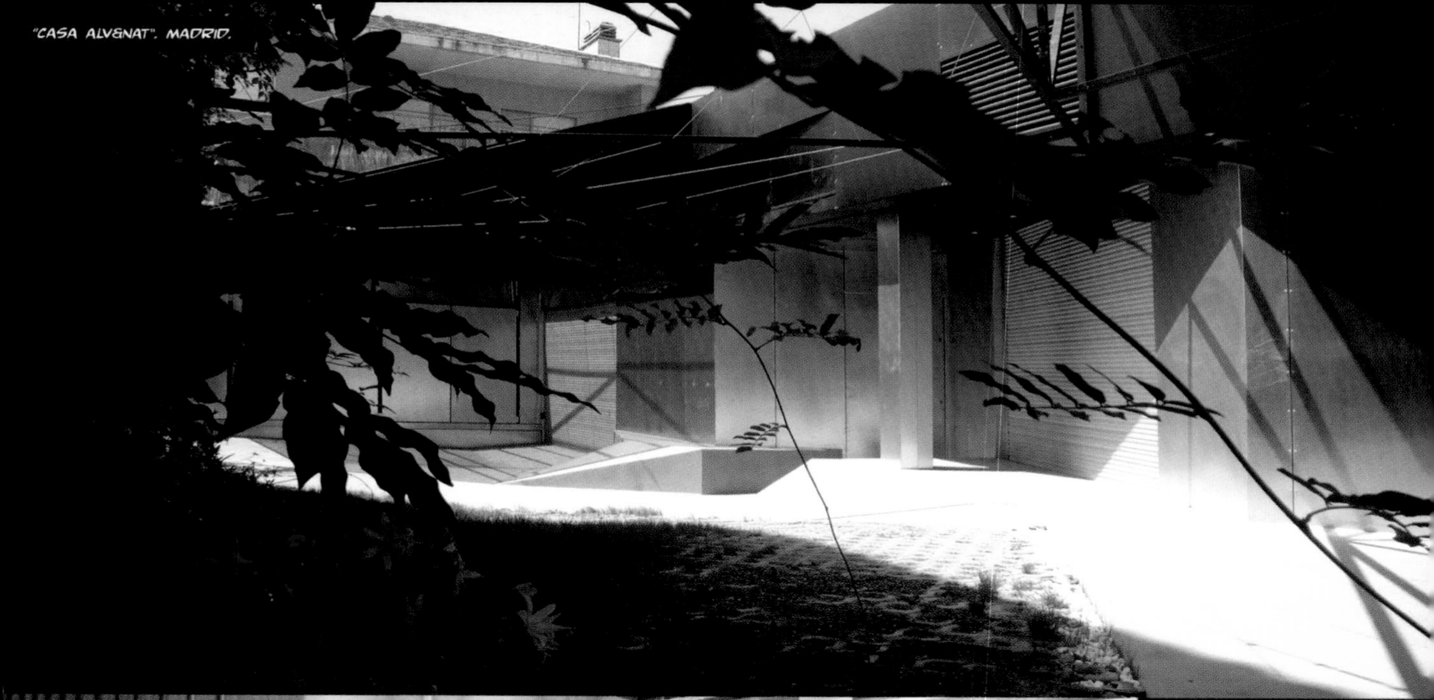

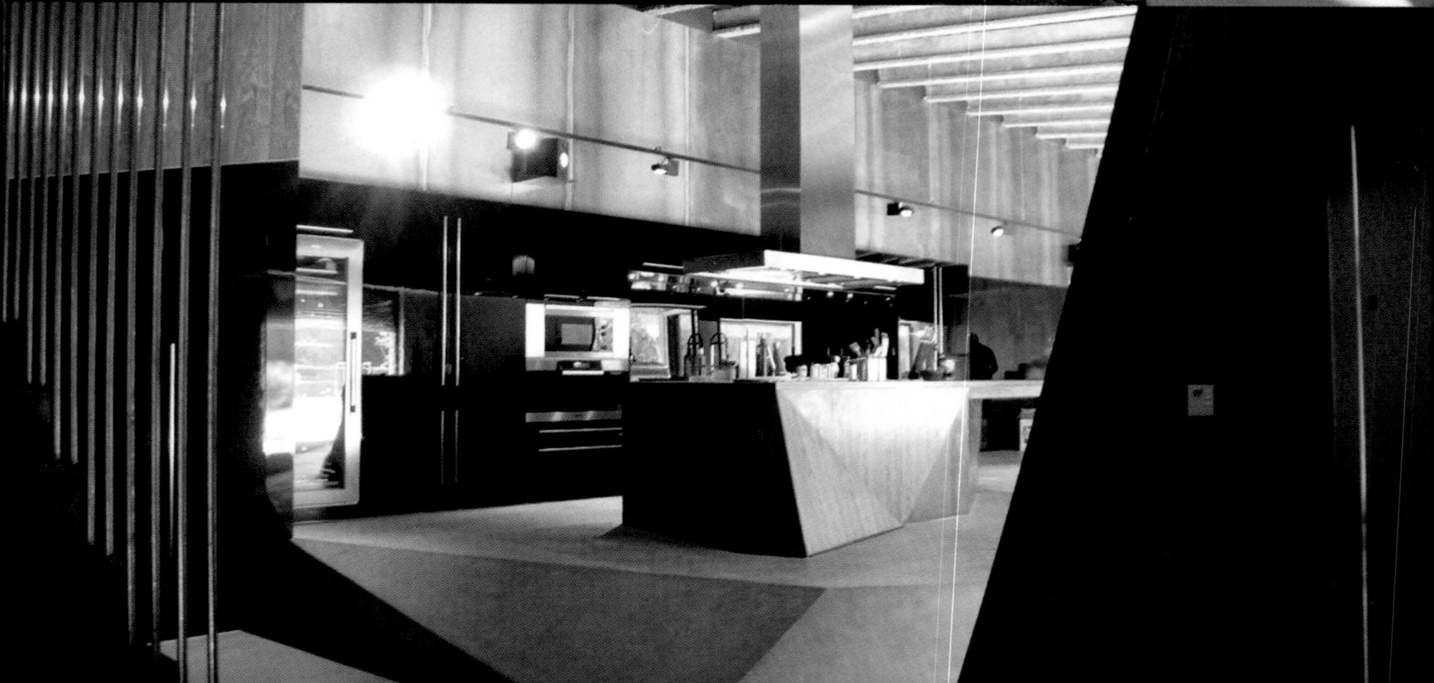

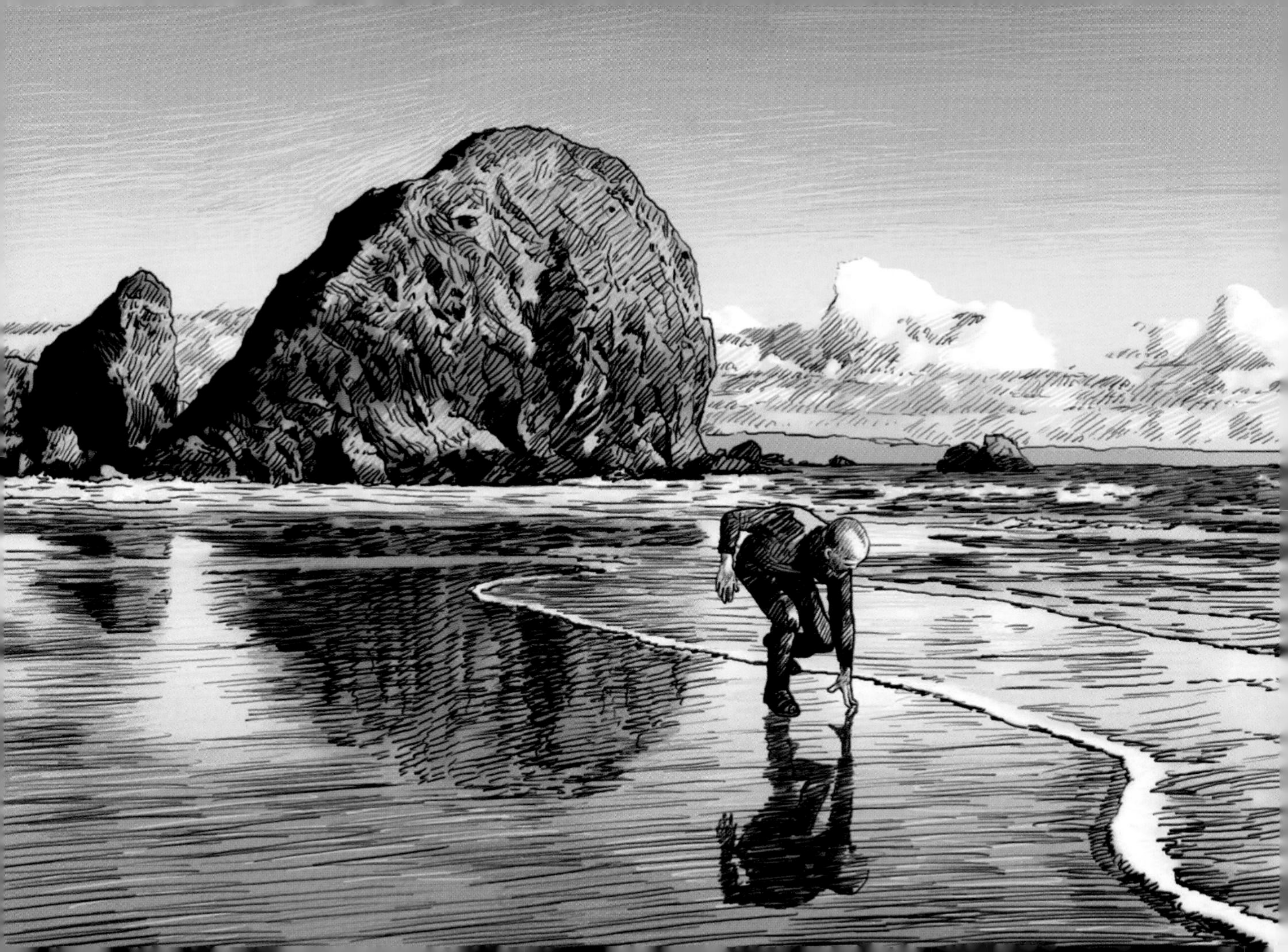

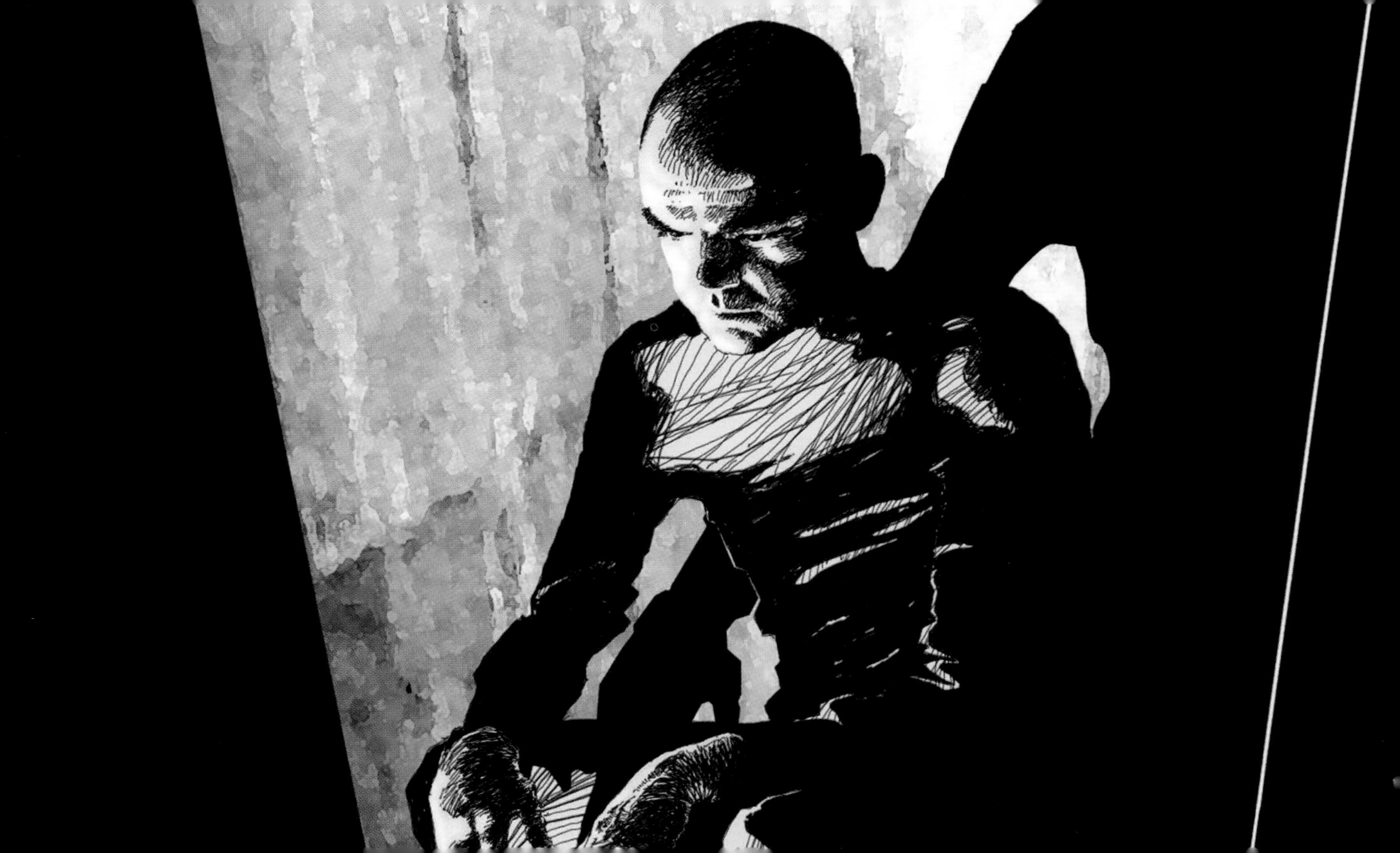

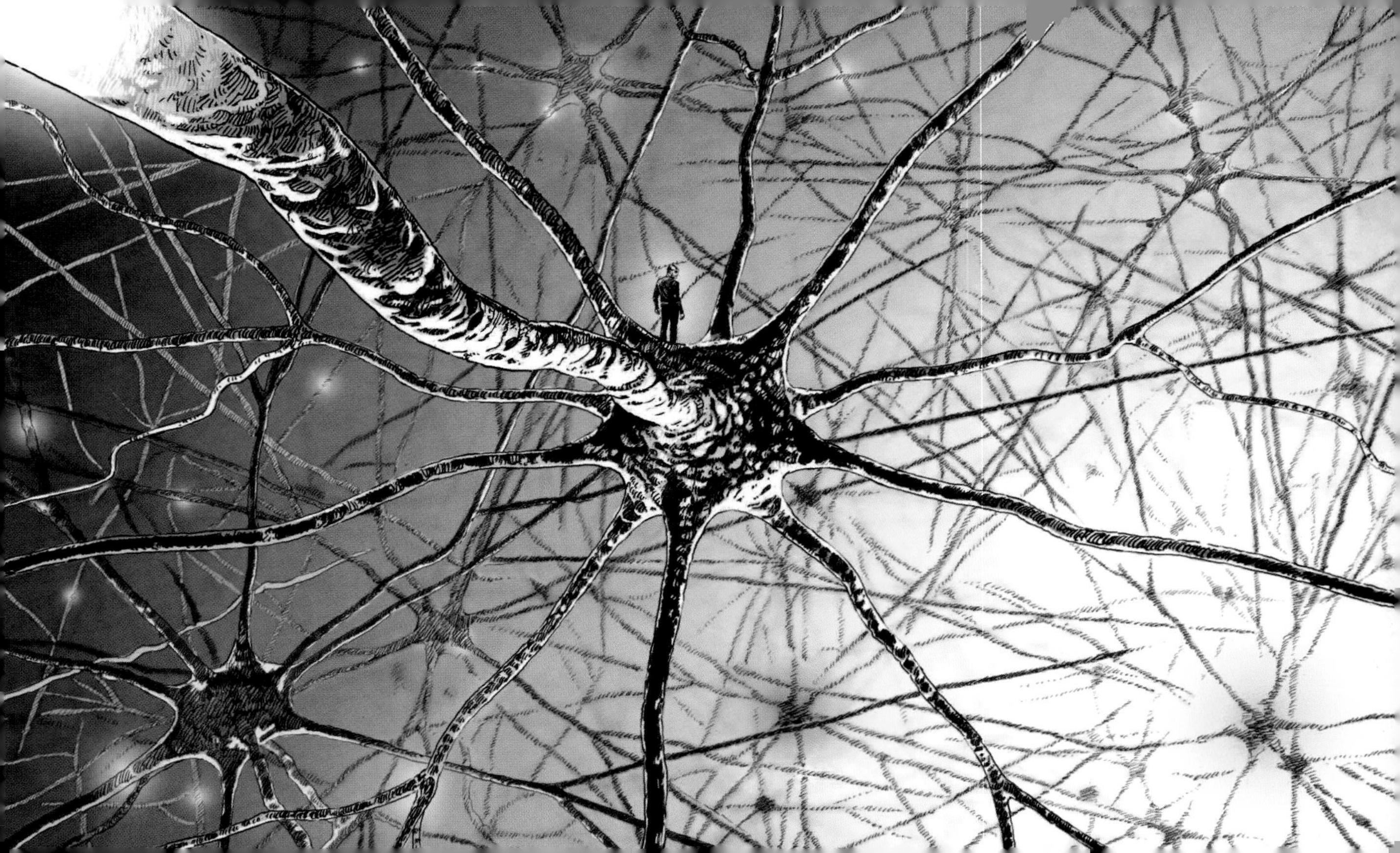

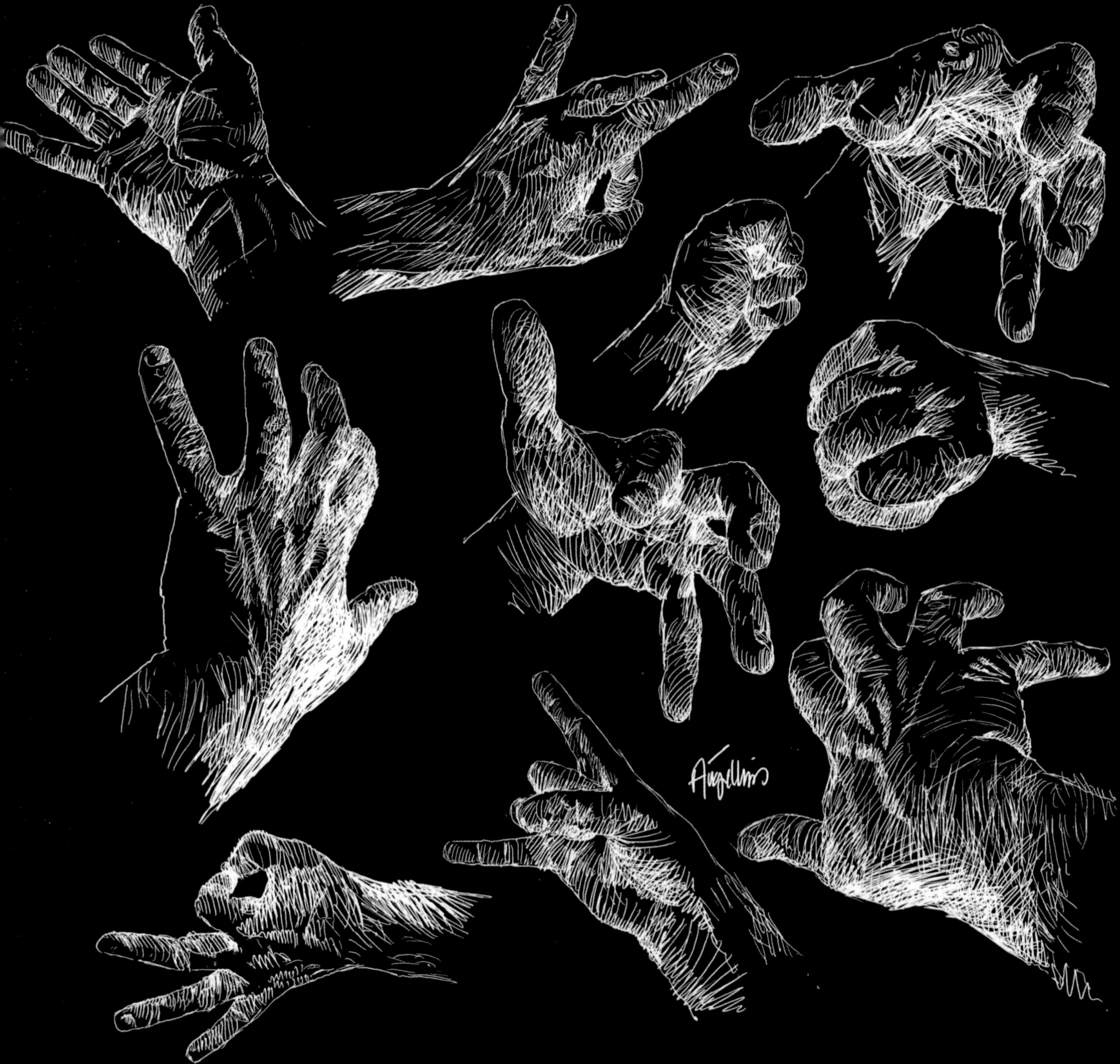

IN THIS DOUBLE PAGE I WANT TO MAKE A SMALL TRIBUTE TO THE AUTHORS OF THIS WORK HAS BEEN POSSIBLE. FANS OF ALT ARCHITECTURE IN FACEBOOK. IN EARLY 2013 WE ARE A COMMUNITY OF ONE MILLION PEOPLE AND EVERY DAY THOUSANDS OF THEM VISIT OUR CONTENT AND PROVID FEEDBACK, TIPS AND QUESTIONS. AND IT'S VERY REWARDING BECAUSE IT MAKES US FEEL THAT OUR WORK IS USEFUL. HERE I LEAVE SOME OF THE REVIEWS OF THE "ALT COMIC" AMONG OUR FOLLOWERS.

WE HAVE RECEIVED HUNDREDS OF REVIEWS SO WE HAVE HAD TO SELECT THEM AT RANDOM, BUT I WANT TO THANK ALL OF YOU WHO TOOK THE TIME TO WRITE.

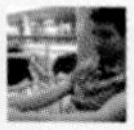
Jairo Fernando Bautista No he parado de observar las imágenes del Cómic Book, es impresionante el detalle de las perspectivas, creo que puedo senti lugar. Bogotá, Colombia.
8 de noviembre de 2012 a la(s) 20:28 · Ya no me gusta · 3

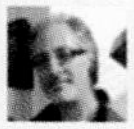
Alejandro Arébalos "A través de estos trazos he viajado, he recorrido lugares de los más diversos, he saltado, he volado, me he asomado al espacio side me he sentido superhéroe, y, lo más importante, he aprendido, y disfrutando, que es la más bella forma de aprender. Gracias por todo ello." Alejandro F. Arébalos. Buenos Aires, Argentina.
8 de noviembre de 2012 a la(s) 20:51 · Ya no me gusta · 6

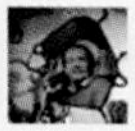
Victor Mejia Rodas Perspectiva, luces , sombras y tiempo ...Todo en un viaje fantástico por los espacios del comic...Los secretos mejor guardados del tr de aventura! (Felicitacione y mucho éxito ALT arquitectura + obra)
8 de noviembre de 2012 a la(s) 21:14 · Ya no me gusta · 1

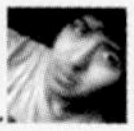
Daniel Martínez Luz, sombra, vano y macizo, ¿qué son estos sin una reflexión de quién los ha creado desde lo más interno de su ser? estos y más eleme nos deben de emocionar, de crecer y de motivar a ser mejores en nuestro quehacer. Un trabajo muy dedicado y motivador para aquellos que se preocup por sacar lo mejor de ellos y hacer un mundo mejor. Daniel Martínez Barranco - D.F., México
8 de noviembre de 2012 a la(s) 21:27 · Ya no me gusta · 1

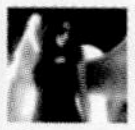
Alex Gonzalez Imprecionante conbinacion de elementos arquitectonicos en diferentes prespectivas creatividad, imaginacion ,espacios,luces,trazos ,tecnologia,etc. En fin no dejo de asombrarme de todo lo que eres posible de crear, gracias por compartirlo, desde Los Angeles Ca.
8 de noviembre de 2012 a la(s) 22:18 · Ya no me gusta · 1

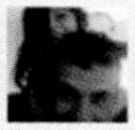
Carlos Saenz Cada espacio va haciendo su propia historia enriqueciendose día a día con las experiencias y vivencias de la gente que en el habita. Esta publicación es parte de esa historia abordando la arquitectura desde una perspectiva distinta y con sentido lúdico. Felicidades por esta nueva propuesta. Carlos Manuel Sáenz Barrera Arquitecto. Cd. Juárez Chih. Mexico.
8 de noviembre de 2012 a la(s) 23:46 · Editado · Ya no me gusta · 1

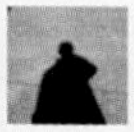
Saaron Prado "... cada trazo en el dibujo, es una huella en el camino... el espacio que representas, es un rincón escondido... tu alma intranquila, no es que la forma obtenida..." Saaron Prado, Torremolinos, España.
8 de noviembre de 2012 a la(s) 23:55 · Ya no me gusta · 1

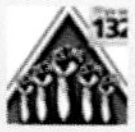
Víctor Hugo Espinosa "una fascinante y sensible visión de la relación entre el espacio, la luz y el ser humano, plasmada con gran talento gráfico" Víctor Hugo Espinosa, Cd. de México, México.
9 de noviembre de 2012 a la(s) 0:18 · Ya no me gusta · 2

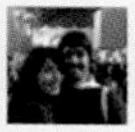
Víctor Felipe Alegría Corona "Una obra donde la narrativa gráfica se despliega para transmitr una especial concepción del espacio, difuminado y diluy los límites dentro de los que típicamente se expresan los arquitectos." Víctor Alegría Corona, Arquitecto e Ilustrador, Santiago, Chile.
9 de noviembre de 2012 a la(s) 0:52 · Ya no me gusta · 3

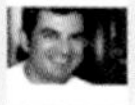
Pedro Vicente Anton Por fin arquitectura y cómic se dan la mano reinventándese gracias a Alt que proyecta toda una lección de expresión gráfica hacéndonos disfrutar hasta cotas de Obra Maestra. Pedro Vicente Antón, Murcia, España.
9 de noviembre de 2012 a la(s) 12:23 · Ya no me gusta · 2

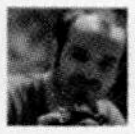
Angel Cozar Peña El comic de Angel nos enseña fantásticamente las relaciones de escala del hombre con entornos muy diversos. Angel Cózar Peña, Má España.
8 de noviembre de 2012 a la(s) 23:00 · Ya no me gusta · 2

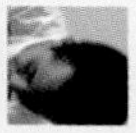
Juan Armendarizz Después de verle proyectando Arquitectura, ahora ALT presenta un volumen lleno de exelsos dibujos y lugares fantásticos, mostrand poder de la linea y el color, así como la relación hombre-entorno. "Eucarionte (Chihuahua, Mex)"
8 de noviembre de 2012 a la(s) 23:24 · Editado · Ya no me gusta · 2

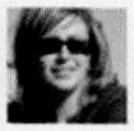
Ana Maria Frances Beneito No tengo grandes conocimientos de arquitectura, pero tengo ojos para ver, y lo que veo me gusta, me transmite mucho realismo, la luz, el color, parecen que los dibujos tengan vida propia. Villena. España
10 de noviembre de 2012 a la(s) 23:37 · Ya no me gusta · 1

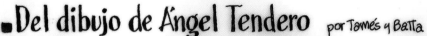

Jonathan Daniel Taipe nunca antes había visto y leído un comic tan bien trabajado y tan real....no...no es que deja poco a la imaginación...hace que tu imaginación vaya más allá de lo que tu propia imaginación hubiera imaginado......
8 de noviembre de 2012 a la(s) 23:03 · Ya no me gusta · 👍 1

Nacho L Carrizo Jamás tuve tantas ganas de leer un cómic, ha sido impresionante descubrir los dibujos poco a poco durante su producción. Madrid.
8 de noviembre de 2012 a la(s) 20:22 · Ya no me gusta · 👍 1

Marcos Bayona Colula la expresion en un comic, imagen del arte dibujado, sensacion de lo que nos rodea, lineas moldeadas por la libertad de la mano, conformando el espacio en un solo plano y solo DIBUJANDO lograste la sensacion de dar vida al espacio. gracias Ángel luis Tendero Martin
8 de noviembre de 2012 a la(s) 20:37 · Ya no me gusta · 👍 1

Montserrath Mijares Arquitectura es un universo completo de formas, volumenes y espacios, que gracias al comic ALT permite analizarlos desde la perspectiva de un arquitecto, un soñador, y artista que permite analizar el espacio desde el espacio mismo Montserrath Mijares Huichapan Hidalgo Mexico
8 de noviembre de 2012 a la(s) 20:48 · Ya no me gusta · 👍 1

Rosa Perez No sólo es el dibujo lo que hace que nos movamos por el imaginario que creas permitiéndonos explorar, de tu mano casi, las dimensiones por las que se agita tu espíritu, es, gracias a tu pasión casi ciega por la obra que vas forjando, por lo que nos sentimos arrastrados a ese lugar donde la aventura del hombre y su vocación se va construyendo. Muchas gracias por habernos dejado estar tan cerca tuyo en el proceso creativo. Rosa Pérez Antón. Barcelona.
8 de noviembre de 2012 a la(s) 21:29 · Ya no me gusta · 👍 1

Samuel Núñez Barrón Simplemente un talento nato con un conocimiento del cuerpo humano y una sensibilidad espacial digna de un Arquitecto. Ademas de un extraordinario dominio de las técnicas para lograr escenarios con texturas, colores, perspectiva y un realismo impresionantes.
Un saludo desde Santa Ana, Sonora, Mexico

Silvia Glass Me he puesto a ver todas las imágenes una por una, nunca vi un trabajo de dibujo tan minucioso para un cómic. Sencillamente genial!!!
14 de diciembre de 2012 a la(s) 22:30 · Ya no me gusta · 👍 1

Isabel Gpuente Alt, desde que te encontré, cada día sigo y espero un nuevo dibujo tuyo que me transporte a nuevos territorios. Como arq paisajista me impresiona el dominio espacial, pero sobre todo me impresiona lo que transmite tu trabajo al contemplar despacio cada trazo. Enhorabuena de verdad y gracias por compartirlo con nosotros!

¡¡¡MUCHAS GRACIAS A TODOS DE CORAZÓN!!!

DE MANERA ESPECIAL QUIERO AGRADECER AL DIRECTOR DE LA FACULTAD DE ARQUITECTURA DE LA UNAM, EN MÉXICO DF, ORGE TAMÉS Y BATTA, EXCELENTE ARQUITECTO Y DIBUJANTE, POR DEDICARME UNA DE SUS CÉLEBRES HISTORIETAS SEMANALES.

MUCHAS GRACIAS AMIGO!

Del dibujo de Ángel Tendero
por Tamés y Batta   28 enero 2013   ®   A todo aquel que dibuja

ÁNGEL TENDERO, ESPAÑOL DE ESPAÑA (¿?), ARQUITECTO ANTES QUE NADA, DIBUJANTE MARAVILLOSO, HACE UNA HISTORIETA SOBRE ARQUITECTURA (ver liga)

¡Cuanta observación! ¡cuanta habilidad!

Y es solo el trazo!

DEMUESTRA QUE LA ARQUITECTURA DIBUJADA EMPAREJA CON LA IMAGINACIÓN Y LA VEMOS A TRAVÉS DE EL PARAFRASEO DEL "HOMBRE ARAÑA", SIENDO ÉL!

¡Ahí está Ángel (sin pelo) observando la ciudad

¡Terminado!

LA LECCIÓN APRENDIDA: TODO ARQUITECTO, DIBUJANTE, TIENE LA HABILIDAD DE OBSERVAR LA ARQUITECTURA DESDE LA REALIDAD Y DESDE LA IMAGINACIÓN: ES ÁNGEL

Te admiramos Ángel desde la UNAM y no necesitas de "hombre araña" para volar y verla arquitectura como la ves!

Tú vuelas en tu interior y eso vale todo!!

Alt

A ÁNGEL TENDERO LIGARLO EN WWW.ALTARQUITECTURA.ES VER TAMBIÉN SU OBRA ARQUITECTÓNICA. AQUÍ, EN LA FACULTAD DE ARQUITECTURA DE LA UNIVERSIDAD NACIONAL AUTÓNOMA DE MÉXICO TE MANDAMOS UN ABRAZO Y FELICITARTE POR LA MANERA QUE NOS ACERCAS A LA OBSERVACIÓN SENSIBLE A LA ARQUITECTURA Y TU MANERA TAN ORIGINAL DE HACERLA. TE PROMOVEMOS DESDE ACÁ Y TE DAREMOS SEGUIMIENTO EN TU PÁGINA: UN ABRAZO ÁNGEL
alt@altarquitectura.es (P.D.) SERÍA INTERESANTE VER TU HABILIDAD PARA EL DIBUJO, EN LOS CROQUIS PREVIOS A TU OBRA, QUE ES TAMBIÉN MUY BUENA!

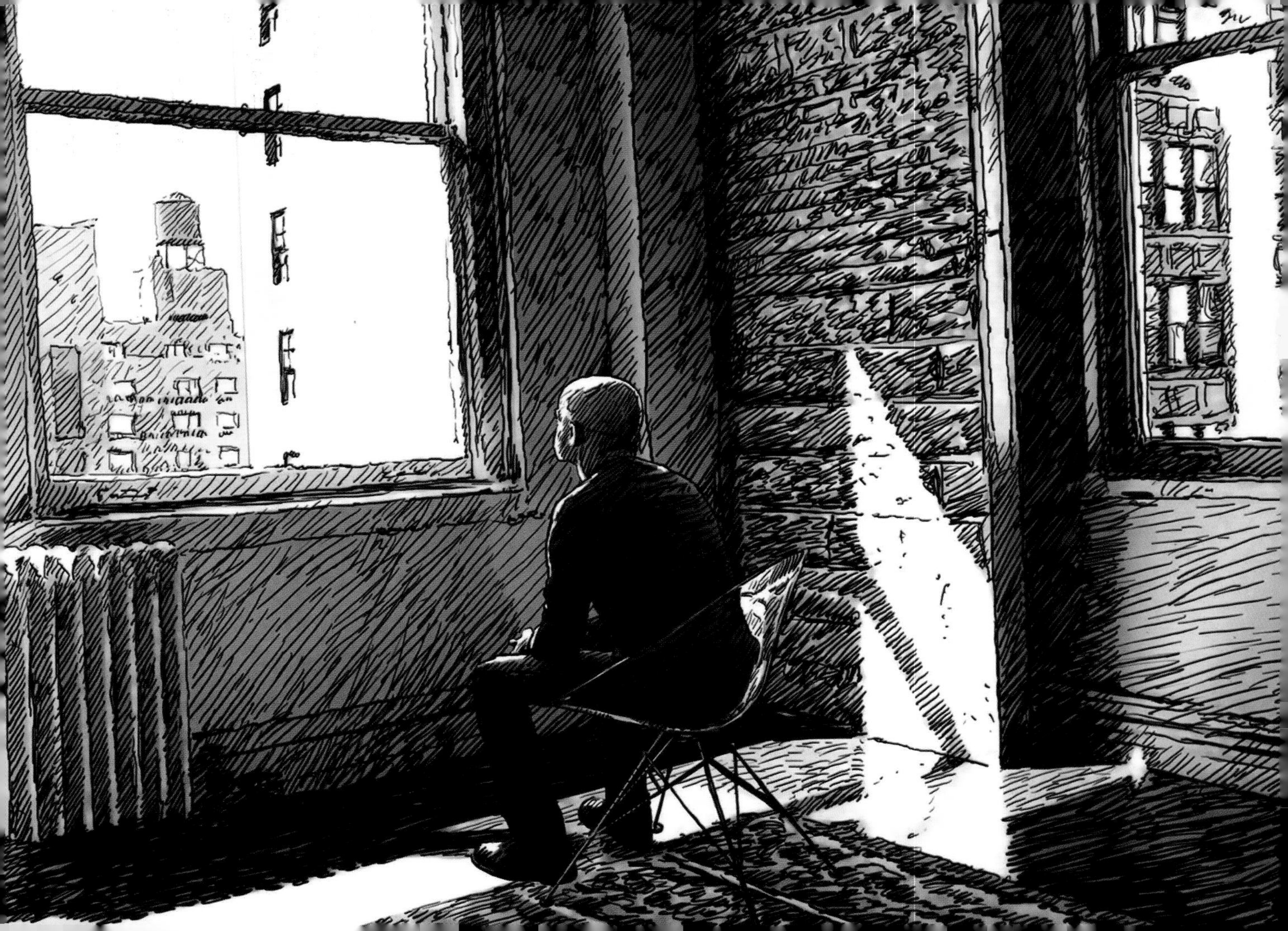

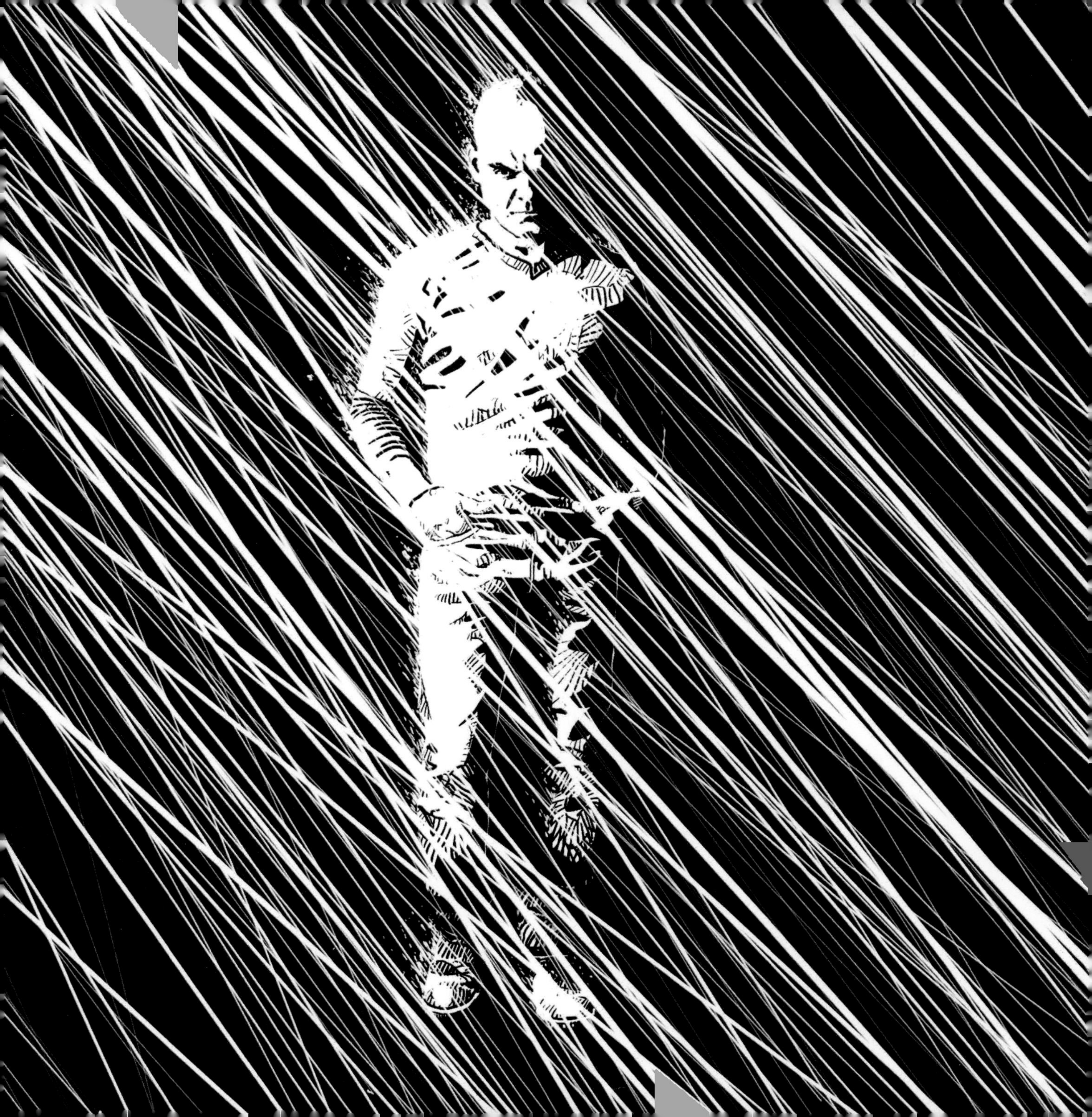

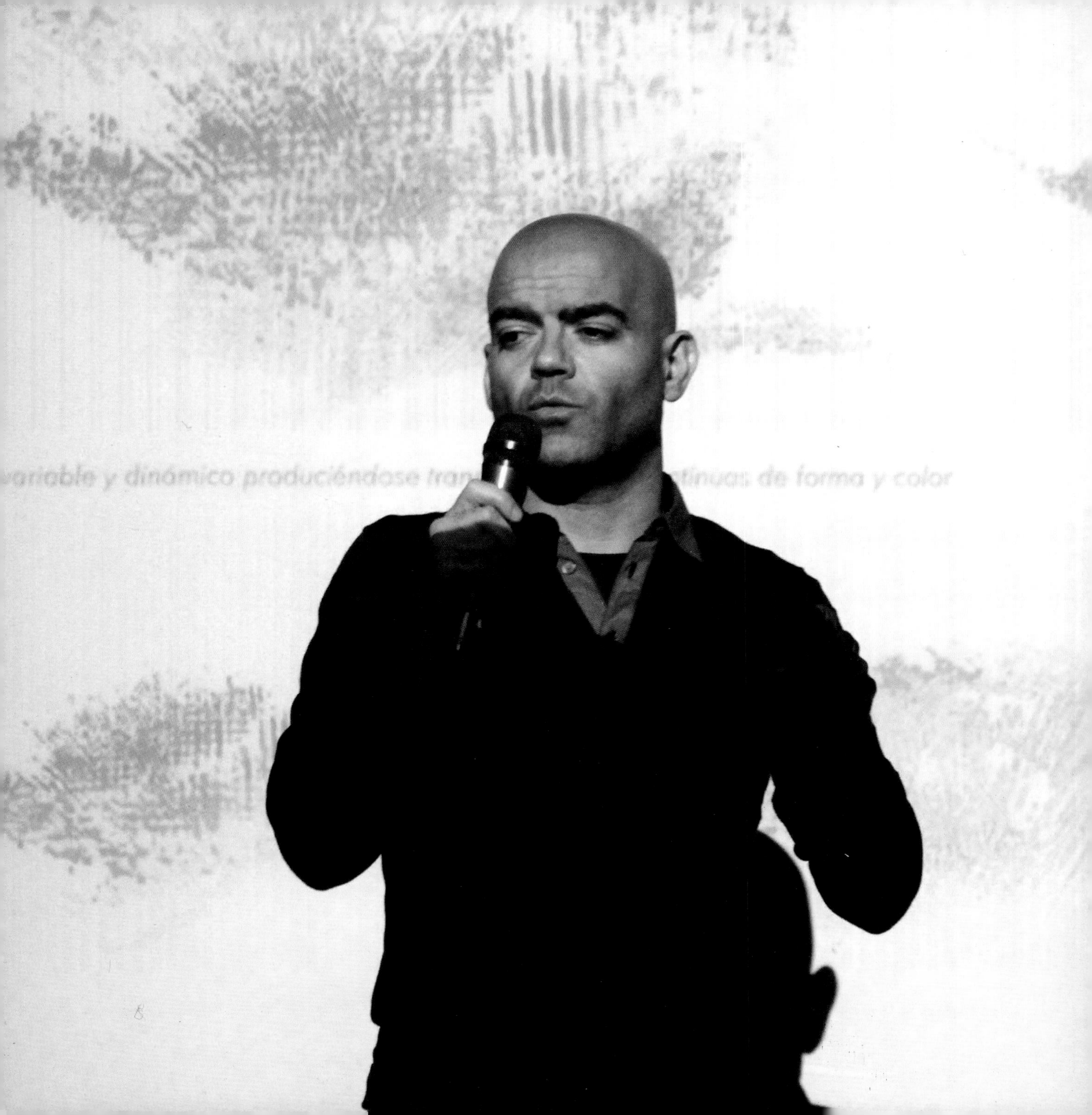
variable y dinámico produciéndose
de forma y color